The Green London Way

To Joel: and to all those who struggled to preserve the open spaces of London for his generation.

The Green London Way

Bob Gilbert

Lawrence and Wishart
London

Lawrence and Wishart Ltd
144a Old South Lambeth Road
London SW8 1XX

First published 1991

Text design by Jan Brown
Photoset in North Wales by
Derek Doyle & Associates, Mold, Clwyd.
Printed and Bound in Great Britain by
Billing and Sons, Worcester.

CONTENTS

ACKNOWLEDGEMENTS

My especial thanks must go to two people, Chris Smith and Graham Scrivener. To Chris for helping me to hatch the idea, carrying out much of the initial route research and then nagging me to get on with the book; to Graham, for all his work on the maps, for meeting impossible deadlines and for being tolerant when I fell asleep during meetings.

I am indebted to the staff of the Local History Libraries and Archives of the London Boroughs for their help in providing information and locating sources, and for running a valuable service which has been hit by round after round of cuts.

I would like to thank Amanda Hopkinson and my parents and all those friends who have helped by walking sections of the route, reading chapters of the text, offering childcare and giving encouragement. And finally, my thanks to Wikcia Zbieranowska, for all her support.

Bob Gilbert

My thanks go to Peter Brawne and Andrew Howard from Poke In The Eye and to Tricia Adams and Pat Treasure, without whose support the maps would never have been completed.

Graham Scrivener

LIST OF MAPS

RIVER, HEATH AND RAILWAY
~17 & 18~

WELSH HARP

16

Harrow
on the
Hill

17

Finsb...
Pa...

START
FINISH

18 Hampstead

THREE HILLS
AND A HARP
~15 & 16~

15

Greenford

ALONG
THE
BRENT
VALLEY

~13 & 14~

14

RIVER
BRENT

Brentford

Kew Bridge

13

SYON
PARK

RICHMOND
AND THE RIVER
~11 & 12~

12

11

RICHMOND
PARK

10

Balham

OF HUSTINGS
AND
HUGUENOTS
~10~

MAPS BY
GRAHAM SCRIVENER

THE GREEN LONDON WAY

VICTORIAN PARKS AND **MEDIEVAL MARSHES**
~1 & 2~

RIVER LEA

②

VICTORIA PARK

③

④

East Ham

FROM THE **LEA** TO THE **LEVELS**
~3 & 4~

⑤

Woolwich

⑦

PIG KEEPERS AND **PALACES**
~6~

ASANTS ATH THE MMONERS LL ~7~

SHOOTERS HILL

⑥ **WOOLWICH** AND THE **WOODLANDS**
~5~

⑧ **COLLEGE, PALACE** AND **COMMONS**
~8 & 9~

ATHAM

Crystal Palace

⑨

N
W — E
S

© SCRIY 1991

SOURCES

The following list covers some of the main London-wide books which have been invaluable sources of information. It does not include the many local texts referred to in individual chapters.

Brooks, J A, *Ghosts of London* (2 volumes), Jarrold 1982

Clark, J, *In Our Grandmother's Footsteps*, Virago 1984

Crowe, A, *Parks and Woodlands of London*, Fourth Estate 1987

Fitter, R S, *London's Natural History*, Collins 1945

Hudson, W H, *Birds in London*, Longmans, Green and Co, 1898

Meller, Hugh, *London's Cemeteries*, Avebury 1983

Ordnance Survey and Taylor, P, *Old Ordnance Survey Maps (The London Sheets)*, Alan Godfrey

Sexby, Lt-Col J, *The Municipal Parks, Gardens and Open Spaces of London; Their History and Associations*, Elliot Stock 1905

Weinreb, B, and Hibbert, C, *The London Encyclopedia*, Papermac 1983

INTRODUCTION

The Green London Way is a long-distance footpath for London. It is a 92 mile circular walking route, not around London but through it. It brings the idea of the long-distance way right into the country's largest city. At the same time it is a route which divides into 18 separate and easily manageable walks, each one with its own distinctive character.

The Green London Way links river and canal, towpath and abandoned railway line, urban footpath and little-known alley, park and common, woodland and heath. It is an introduction to the best and most beautiful of London's open spaces. But it is not intended as an urban equivalent of the rural ramble; it is a mistake to approach even the city's largest and wildest open spaces – Bostall Wood, Wimbledon Common, Horsenden Hill – as a scaled-down version of the countryside. Urban walking is of a different order and requires a different sort of appreciation. Approached without preconceptions this exploration of London offers constant surprises and unexpected rewards, uncovering unsuspected routes and magnificent yet little-known buildings; but more than this it reveals hidden facets of history and a surprising wealth of wildlife. And even in the most squalid of surroundings there is a strange beauty that is completely unconventional. *The Green London Way* provides an overview of London's natural history, of its social history, and of the connections between the two. In particular it illustrates the struggles which have taken place, and which continue to take place, to preserve the city's open spaces.

Geologically London is a conveniently distinct unit. It is generally described as a basin, but in diagramatic form more nearly resembles two soup bowls placed one inside the other. The outer, and higher, rim of these bowls is formed by chalk which outcrops to the north of London as the Chilterns and to the south as the North Downs, both of which lie well outside the reaches of our route. The inner rim is formed by the well-known London clay, blue or orange, and heavy to work. At its highest points the clay is up to 300 feet thick and forms a ridge which constitutes sections of our route. In South London we follow it from Forest Hill to Streatham; in North London, from Haringey to Hampstead, where it is capped with sandy gravels, and then again when it outcrops at Harrow-on-the-Hill. From these high places London slopes down across the clay towards the river. The Thames today is only a fraction of its former size and during its fluctuations over previous millenia it has cut several much wider valleys which survive in the form of terraces to north and south of the existing river route. These terraces are particularly distinct to the south of the river and are capped with sandy and gravelly soils laid down by water action. These poor acidic soils made them less attractive for agriculture; they became common lands and this helped save them to some extent from development. This has given us the long line of heaths and commons which we pick up on our walks at Blackheath and all the way from Plumstead to Lesnes Abbey Woods. It was the modern Thames which fashioned the city of London and which still constitutes its rather neglected heart. Sections of our walks follow the Thames-side paths, and also those of its tributaries and its associated canals.

Though concealed by so much concrete, the geology and the topography of London still have a striking impact upon its natural history. The oak woodlands of Oxleas or Horsenden are on the heavy clay. There are remnants of heathland flora on the sandy gravels of Hampstead, Bostall and even Blackheath. Walthamstow Marshes survives in the low valley of the Lea and the wildlife of East London has an estuarine influence as the Thames valley broadens and flattens on its approach to the sea.

The impact of the human species upon this landscape is obvious and the growth of the city has brought with it development and destruction – an enormous loss of life forms and their habitats. But there is another side to the picture which is less often painted. The story of London's wildlife is an illustration of the tremendous recuperative power of nature. It is demonstrated in almost every street; by the lichen which grows on the pavement, the moss which grows on top of a wall and the wild plants which spring up at the bottom of a lamp-post. If humans built railways, it was foxes which travelled along the embankments. If we built and abandoned a gasworks, then partridge and little owl moved in to nest in the ruins. If old filter beds fell into disuse then in a few years they were colonised by willows, newts and herons. One of the most enduring images of *The Green London Way* is the sight of a skylark singing its heart out above a gas holder.

In addition to this 'recuperation', many developments in London actually brought new species with them. 150 years ago some of our most familiar species, birds and plants which we take for granted, like the black-headed gull or the buddleia, could not have been seen in London. Reservoirs and waste tips brought the gulls, bomb-sites brought the rose-bay willow herb, power stations gave nest sites for the black redstart and tower blocks and school belfries homes for the kestrel. It is significant that the special conditions of London – which might be summarised as its walls and its warmth – facilitated the spread of a whole variety of species from many different parts of the globe. London's flora, like its human population, is international and gives the lie to the conservationists' cliché, that 'native' is good and 'alien' is doubtful.

London has its own selection of rare – or at least unusual – species and many of them are mentioned in these pages: smew at Stoke Newington, danewort along the North London Sewer Way, flixwood on Mill Meads, Essex skipper butterflies at Walthamstow Marshes, tropical grass on the Regents Canal. But the common confusion – that what is most unusual is therefore most interesting – should be avoided. *The Green London Way* should also help to increase our awareness and our appreciation of what is 'common'; of the plants, birds and animals which struggle for survival – and which succeed – all around us.

It is clear that the natural history of London is inextricably linked with its social history. The history of the people who have made, and make up, London is another main theme of *The Green London Way*. For the most part we have avoided the 'famous names' approach; the stories of monarchs and ministers are repeated *ad nauseam* elsewhere. It has to be said, however, that this rule has been broken wherever a story has been too good not to tell or where it has related to an unexpected local connection. The unexceptional Montacute Road near Catford, for example, is cue to the story of the murder of Edward II. The suburban Uxendon Crescent near Preston leads into the story of the Babington plot to spring Mary Stuart from prison. And of course the 'famous names' have always been admitted where they were one side of a struggle over rights of access or the ownership of a common. For the most part, however, we have tried to concentrate on a lost history of the ordinary people of London. Too often our approach to history, particularly as it is practised in guide books, turns ordinary people into the objects, even the victims, of history. Here we have tried to see them as its makers. In Newham, for example, the view of the tower blocks leads to an account of the struggles by their occupants: against local and national opposition, they were able to prove that these buildings were unfit to live in, and to bring about the decision to demolish. Or, on Blackheath, we come across the story of not one but three different peasant uprisings which changed the course of British history. And these stories are not only about struggles but also about a city's ability to celebrate: the great anarchic displays of public exuberance which found expression in the Charlton Horn Fair or in the Garrat mock elections.

There is one particular way in which the lives and efforts of ordinary people have shaped the history of London and which is demonstrated time after time in this book. It is a remarkable fact, and one which cannot be repeated often enough, that almost every park, common, heath and wood of London has had to be fought for at some time in its history. The creation, and the preservation, of London's open spaces is a result of the struggles of the city's people. From Highgate Woods to Norwood Grove, from Wimbledon Common to the Lea Valley, almost every inch of open space has been lobbied over, campaigned about, and demonstrated for – sometimes with a physical battle. The stories of these struggles are some of the most exciting and inspiring of our journey. In Plumstead and in Forest Hill people marched in their thousands to save their commons. In Richmond it was a lone local brewer who took on the courts and the monarchy to re-establish the right of access to the park. In Hampstead fifteen different parliamentary bills had to be defeated in the struggle to preserve the heath. In Streatham local people turned out in secret to tear down gates and fences on the common as fast as the Lord of the Manor could put them up. And in scores of less dramatic cases, local residents set up committees, raised funds, pressurised Councils, challenged developers or contested Enquiries. The open spaces of London today are a monument to their efforts.

This tradition of struggle has been a long one. The earliest account along *The Green London Way* concerns the people of Norwood and Forest Hill who, in the 17th century, marched behind the Reverend Colfe into the City to petition the king for the saving of West Wood. From then on, one account follows another, reaching an apogee in the 19th century, the period of London's most rapid expansion. Those who call for a return to 'Victorian values' should be aware that the Victorians were passionate defenders of London's open spaces; it was Victorians who were prepared to break the law and to go to prison in defence of Plumstead Common and One Tree Hill. The Victorians too produced writers with a caustic wit which was frequently brought to bear in books and articles on the subject, and they are often quoted within these pages.

The struggle for London's open spaces is as intense today as it ever was. If, in 1990, the Department of Transport had accepted the recommendations of its own consultants, it would have ushered in the destruction of open spaces on such a scale as to make the Green London Way impossible. Walthamstow and Hackney Marshes, the 3 mile Parkland Walk, Horniman Gardens, Dulwich Park, most of the South London commons and even the leafy suburbs of Kew would all have been covered in tarmac or sliced through the middle for major new road schemes. It was the vociferous, passionate and often imaginative campaigning of dozens of groups, both local and London-wide, that led to the defeat of these proposals. Yet at the time of writing very little now stands in the way of another Department of Transport scheme that will run a six-lane highway through Woodlands Farm and the beautiful Oxleas Wood, London's largest remnant of ancient forest lands. It is as a contribution to this and all the other struggles to preserve London as a place fit to live in, that this book has been written.

CYCLING THE GREEN LONDON WAY
Although *The Green London Way* was written with walkers in mind, much of the initial route research was done by bike. It is possible to follow the whole of the route by bike, provided the rider is prepared to dismount in public parks and to negotiate rough ground and the occasional obstacles such as flights of steps. In one or two places the route instructions indicate alternatives which avoid stiles etc.

USING THIS BOOK
The Green London Way has been written for armchair as well as for active walkers. For this reason, and to maintain a narrative flow, it has been divided into chapters each dealing with a different part of London. The chapters describe one or two walks which are numbered in clockwise order around London, beginning and ending at Finsbury Park in North London. Each walk is accompanied by a map which is intended as an overview and aid to navigation. For full details the walker will need to refer to the written route instructions. It could also be helpful to take a copy of one of the London street guides on walks. As well as being of assistance should any route-finding problems arise, it also allows for the fact that London is a living and therefore an ever-changing city. The street guide would help a walker negotiate a way around any changes which might have have occured since the time of publication.

Details of bus, train and underground routes are shown on the maps at the beginning and end of walks. The text for each walk begins with a section entitled 'Getting Started'. This shows how to begin the walk from the nearest public transport facilities and how the walk connects with the previous walk in the circuit. The walk is then described in several stretches, the text being preceded by an information section including 'Route', 'Facilities' and 'Looking at Wildlife'. The

'Facilities' entry covers cafés, pubs, toilets and places to visit along the way. The 'Looking at Wildlife' entry aims to summarise the main natural history features of that section of the walk and points out particular species of trees, wild flowers, animals, birds or insects to look out for. There will generally be further detail on this in the text. There has been no attempt in this book to help with the identification of animals and plants. This would have been an impossible task and the reader is referred to the many excellent field guides available for this purpose.

With the help of these instructions, and with the text that accompanies each section of *The Green London Way*, the walker and the reader will find themselves exploring new aspects of London and of its life. Savour it. And help to save it.

ABOUT THE WALKS

The Green London Way describes a circular route of approximately 92 miles. For those hardy souls wishing to attempt the whole thing in one go, we have included details of two camp-sites along the route; one on Hackney Marshes and the other in Co-operative Woods near Plumstead. We have not however included any other details of possible accommodation.

Most users of this book will want to take shorter walks and for this reason the route has been divided into 18 separate walks, from 3 to 6½ miles in length, beginning and ending at points well served by public transport. The one exception to this rule is the Woolwich and the Woodlands walk described in Chapter 3. At 10 or 12 miles, depending on which alternative you use, it is far longer than most and is the only circular walk in the book.

It is easy to combine different walks together to make longer routes and instructions are always given to link a walk to the ones before and after it. It should be remembered however that urban walking can be more tiring, though in a different way, than country walking and that longer routes would remove the element of exploration which has been seen as an important part of this book. Although urban walking requires no special equipment, good footwear is important. Most routes cover rough ground and some can be muddy, especially in winter. Stretches of road, or even of tarmac path, can also be very demanding on the feet.

The walks in this book can be undertaken at any time of year. In researching them we have walked them at almost every time of day and throughout the seasons; in conditions varying from summer drought to deep snow. Like the countryside, London has different atmospheres in different weathers and there are even stretches which we have enjoyed most in the rain. The walks can be – and have been – easily adapted to suit children and to help with this we have included details of some additional attractions to keep them interested along the way.

For help in making a choice of routes, the 18 walks are summarised below.

WALK 1: FINSBURY PARK TO CLAPTON   6·miles
Finsbury Park, Stoke Newington Reservoirs, Clissold Park, Church Street and the 'village' area of Stoke Newington, Abney Park Cemetery (nature reserve), Walthamstow Marshes (nature reserve) and the River Lea.
Some stretches of road walking, but of significant interest in themselves.

A very varied walk including bird-rich reservoirs, an overgrown cemetery and the Walthamstow Marshes; a unique site in Central London and the only extensive marshland on the Green London Way.

WALK 2: CLAPTON TO VICTORIA PARK   4½ miles

Millfields, Middlesex Filter Beds Nature Reserve, the 'Old Lea' and Hackney Marshes, Victoria Park, Regents Canal.
Little road walking.

An easy walk which includes a new nature reserve, a very attractive riverside stretch and East London's largest park, now being restored to something resembling its grand Victorian original.

WALK 3: VICTORIA PARK TO WEST HAM   4 miles

Regents Canal and Hertford Union Canal, North London Sewer Way, Bow Back Rivers, Three Mills and Mill Meads.
Very little road walking.

One of the most fascinating walks in the book with a very special atmosphere of its own. It cuts through the East End along waterways and sewer embankmants passing old mills, abandoned meadows and ending near the Abbey Mills sewage pumping station; one of the most beautiful buildings in London.

WALK 4: WEST HAM TO NORTH WOOLWICH   5 miles

North London Sewer Way, St Mary's and the East Ham Nature Reserve, Beckton Alps, Gallions Reach and the Royal Docks, Thames-side path ending at the Woolwich Ferry and foot tunnel.
Two stretches on road.

Another unusual walk leading along the Sewer Way and then down through the abandoned docks site to the riverside. It includes such curious features as the Beckton Alps – an artificial hill built on gas works slag – and a footpath which runs across two sets of dock gates.

Development work may lead to changes in the route.

WALK 5: WOOLWICH FERRY TO WOOLWICH COMMON   9½ or 10½ miles

Woolwich riverside, Woolwich Arsenal and Beresford Square market, Plumstead and Winn's Commons, Bostall Heath and Woods, Lesnes Abbey and Woods, Woodlands Farm, Oxleas Wood, Castle Woods and Severndroog Castle, Eltham and Woolwich Commons.
Very little road walking.

A long circular walk – though it can be shortened at several points. After the initial climb up from the riverside it is almost entirely 'rural' and links commons, heaths, a ruined abbey, the nearest working farm to Central London and the ancient Oxleas Wood.

Sections of this route are under threat.

WALK 6: WOOLWICH TO GREENWICH   6 miles
Woolwich Common, Charlton Park and Charlton Village, Maryon and Maryon Wilson Parks, the Thames Barrier and the Thames-side path leading into Greenwich.
Minimal road walking.

A walk which is particularly rich in history and with two very attractive parks as well as an interesting riverside stretch. It includes the fascinating but little-known Charlton House, one of best Jacobean houses in Britain, as well as the Cutty Sark and the more famous buildings of Greenwich.

WALK 7: GREENWICH TO FOREST HILL   6½ miles
Greenwich and Greenwich Park, Blackheath and The Point, Brookmill Park and Brookmill Nature Reserve, Hilly Fields, Ladywell Fields, Blythe Hill Fields, One Tree Hill, Horniman Gardens.
Some stretches of road walking.

A varied walk leading from the riverside down into South London with a number of excellent viewpoints. Its open spaces vary from the formality of Brookmill Gardens to the wildness of One Tree Hill and the route ends beside the Horniman Museum, well worth a visit in itself.

WALK 8: FOREST HILL TO CRYSTAL PALACE   3½ miles
Dulwich Wood and Sydenham Hill Wood (nature reserve), Sydenham Wells Park, Crystal Palace Park.
Minimal road walking.

A short walk which includes the beautiful woodlands at Dulwich and the large park built for the old Crystal Place, best known for its 'prehistoric monsters'.

WALK 9: CRYSTAL PALACE TO BALHAM   5 miles
Dulwich Upper Wood, Norwood Park, Norwood Grove, Streatham Common and The Rookery, Russell's Path and Tooting Common.
Several stretches of road walking.

The high point of the walk is the complex of commons and public gardens around Streatham, including the very attractive Rookery. From here, Russell's Path, a surprisingly long stretch of urban footpath, leads on towards the wooded sections of Tooting Common.

WALK 10: BALHAM TO TIBBET'S CORNER   4½ miles
Wandsworth Common and The Scope, Wandsworth Cemetery, Wimbledon Park, Wimbledon Common.
Mostly road walking.

A linking section of the Green London Way across a difficult part of central South London. Good beginning and ending stretches at The Scope and at Wimbledon Common, and some rich historical connections, especially the story of the Garrat elections. Nonetheless, the least satisfactory walk along the Way.

WALK 11: TIBBET'S CORNER TO RICHMOND   5 miles
Wimbledon Common, Richmond Park, Petersham Common, Richmond riverside.
No road walking.

A route which proves that it is possible to go for miles in some parts of London without ever reverting to a road. Includes some of the most attractive walking in London.

WALK 12: RICHMOND TO KEW BRIDGE   3 miles
Richmond and the riverside, Old Deer Park and Kew Gardens.
No road walking.

The whole walk is along the riverside, with views of Syon House and Isleworth on the opposite bank and of some of the Thames islands.

WALK 13: KEW BRIDGE TO HANWELL   4½ miles
Waterside Park, Brentford and The Butts, River Brent and the Grand Union Canal.
Little road walking.

A very good walk which begins on the north bank of the Thames and then runs through the old part of Brentford. It then follows the River Brent and the Grand Union Canal up as far as the famous Hanwell flight of locks.

WALK 14: HANWELL TO GREENFORD   3½ miles
Church Fields and Wharncliffe Viaduct, Brent Lodge Park (and zoo), Bole's Meadows, Perivale Park.
Minimal road walking.

A short walk which continues to follow the River Brent through a string of riverside parks and meadows.

WALK 15: GREENFORD TO SOUTH KENTON   5 miles
Grand Union Canal, Horsenden Hill and Woods, Harrow-on-the-Hill and Northwick Park.
One central section on roads.

A very attractive walk with some excellent views. Horsenden Hill ranks high amongst London's open spaces and Harrow-on-the-Hill, whatever you make of it, is unique.

WALK 16: SOUTH KENTON TO BRENT CROSS   5 miles
Barn Hill and the Fryent Way Country Park, West Hendon Playing Fields and the Welsh Harp Reservoir.
Some stretches of road walking.

The walk includes two more of the most valuable open spaces in London; the Fryent Way site has the most extensive areas of ancient meadows along the route, while the Welsh Harp Reservoir and its wooded edges are rich in bird life.

WALK 17: BRENT CROSS TO HAMPSTEAD **5½ miles**

Hendon Park, Brent Park, Brookside Walk, Hampstead Garden Suburb, Big Wood and Little Wood, Hampstead Heath and Hampstead.

An interesting and varied walk that begins at the hideous Brent Cross but soon follows the upper reaches of the River Brent and its tributary, the Mutton Brook, to reach Hampstead Garden Suburb, a fascinating experiment in social engineering. The final section crosses a corner of the heath to reach Hampstead and includes The Hill, one of the best public gardens in London.

WALK 18: HAMPSTEAD TO FINSBURY PARK **6½ miles**

Hampstead Village, Hampstead Heath and Kenwood, Highgate, Highgate Wood and Queens Wood, Parkland Walk.

A small amount on roads but always interesting.

One of the best walks in the book with urban 'villages', excellent open spaces and a final three mile stretch along an abandoned railway line.

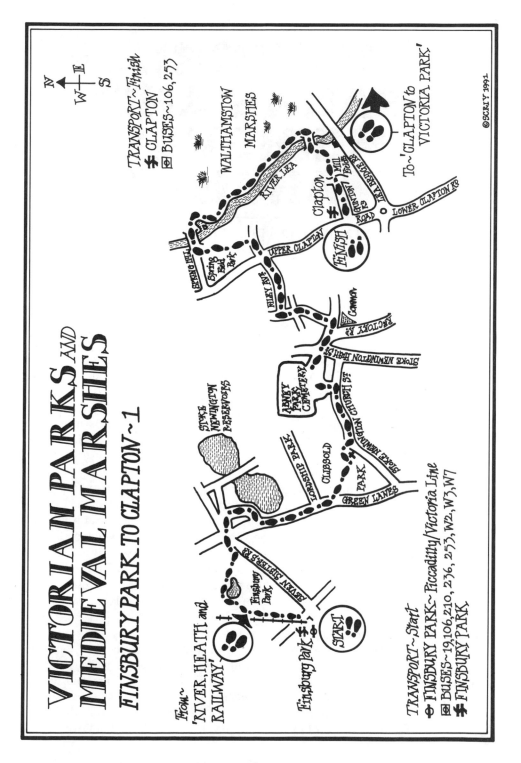

VICTORIAN PARKS AND MEDIEVAL MARSHES

FINSBURY PARK TO CLAPTON ~ 1

From~ 'RIVER, HEATH and RAILWAY'

N / E / W / S

TRANSPORT ~ Finish
≠ CLAPTON
🚌 BUSES ~ 106, 253

WALTHAMSTOW MARSHES

RIVER LEA

Clapton ≠

MILL

QUINTON RD

ROAD LOWER CLAPTON RD

To ~ 'CLAPTON to VICTORIA PARK'

© SCRIV 1991

SPRING HILL

Spring Field Park

UPPER CLAPTON

FINISH

RILEY AVE

RECTORY RD

Common

Stoke Newington HIGH ST

STOKE NEWINGTON RESERVOIRS

ABNEY PARK CEMETERY

Stoke Newington CHURCH ST

LORDSHIP PARK

CLISSOLD PARK

GREEN LANES

SEVERN SISTERS RD

Finsbury Park

Finsbury Park ≠ 🚇

START

TRANSPORT ~ Start
🚇 FINSBURY PARK ~ Piccadilly/Victoria Line
🚌 BUSES ~ 19, 106, 210, 236, 253, W2, W3, W7
≠ FINSBURY PARK

-1-

1. VICTORIAN PARKS AND MEDIEVAL MARSHES

FROM FINSBURY PARK TO VICTORIA PARK

Everything meets at Finsbury Park. The boundaries of Hackney, Haringey and Islington coagulate somewhere around that down-at-heel traffic interchange where trunk roads, bus routes, tube and rail lines all come together. Only the meeting of many cultures, of Asian stores, Chinese supermarkets and West Indian restaurants, gives these fume-laden streets their colour. Cultures meet here, too, in another way, making this a transition along the long circular route of the Green London Way: it is at Finsbury Park that the leafier outer suburbs meet Inner London; at Finsbury Park we quit Hampstead for Hackney, and with Hackney we enter the East End.

While Hampstead and Highgate, Muswell Hill and Alexandra Palace occupy the healthier heights along the clay ridge that curves around North London, the poorer communities were concentrated down in the damp and marshy valley of the Lea, and further east along the banks of the estuarine Thames. This section of our route takes us from one corner of Hackney to the other, from Stoke Newington down to Cambridge Heath and the edges of Globe Town and Bow, across the Borough which was listed in the 1980s as being the poorest in Great Britain. Yet this is a route which is rich in both variety of feature and in open spaces; it takes in bird-rich reservoirs, an 'abandoned' cemetery, the main street of one of London's villages, two nature reserves, a mediaeval marsh and a canal. And it owes its wealth of open space to two other features – the Victorian parks and the River Lea.

The Lea provides the backbone of these two walks. It was the Lea too which shaped the marshes, though it was the struggles of local people which preserved them. The Walthamstow Marsh is today one of the most significant and unusual natural history sites in London. It has a strange and brooding beauty, a beauty which is unconventional, particularly in winter, with its flat, brown and wind-blown reed-lands set in a landscape of pylons, railways, tower blocks and industry. This is typical of much of *The Green London Way*; it should never be approached as an urban substitute for the countryside but with an openness towards its own strange and singular character.

A long string of Victorian parks also shapes this section – Finsbury Park, Clissold Park, Springfield Park and Victoria Park. Few people today recognise the significance of these parks in the social history of London in general, and of the East End in particular. They arose from a concern for the well-being of working people at a time when almost intolerable living conditions were combined with a rapid loss of existing open spaces as London spilt outwards. Their existence is a tribute to vigorous public campaigning by wealthy philanthropists, social reformers, the new middle classes and the London poor. These 19th century campaigns have been echoed in the struggles of recent years to retain the remaining open spaces of Hackney – Abney Park, the New River and Stoke Newington Reservoirs, and the Walthamstow Marshes have all been threatened and defended and most recently there has been a battle against road proposals which would have despoiled the whole southern reach of the Lea valley. In our route across this area, and sometimes in the most striking surrounds, we find both social history and natural history combined.

This chapter covers 9½ miles from Finsbury Park to Cambridge Heath Road in Hackney. It can be treated as two separate walks:

WALK 1: From Finsbury Park to Clapton (6 miles).

WALK 2: From Clapton to Victoria Park and Cambridge Heath (4½ miles).

WALK 1: Finsbury Park to Clapton

Getting Started

From Finsbury Park Station (BR and tube) and buses:
> From the main station forecourt on Station Place turn left to cross the road in front of the bridges and take the gap in the wall leading onto the Parkland Walk. Follow the walk until it arrives at a T junction (with a footbridge over the railway to your left). Turn right to enter Finsbury Park.

From Walk 18:
> After crossing the footbridge at the end of the Parkland Walk, keep straight ahead into Finsbury Park.

Finsbury Park and Woodberry Down

ROUTE:
● On entering the park keep straight ahead to cross the road and pass the café, then bear left to reach the lake.

- Follow the lake around to the left and after passing between the lake and the athletic track, follow the track perimeter round to the left.
- On reaching a wooden shelter turn right. Keep ahead to leave the park through the large Manor House gates. Cross to the diametrically opposite corner of the road junction or take the subway, leaving by the exit marked Seven Sisters Road East (South side).
- Follow Woodberry Down, the small road beginning beside St Olave's church.
- TO VISIT STOKE NEWINGTON RESERVOIRS: Continue to end of Woodberry Down then turn right to reach the bridge between the two reservoirs.
- TO FOLLOW MAIN ROUTE: Take the first turning on the right off Woodberry Down, alongside the white bulk of Nicholl House. At the bottom follow round to the right to reach the main road (Green Lanes).
- Turn left along Green Lanes, passing the pumping station to reach the first gate into Clissold Park on the left.

FACILITIES: Café (March to October) and toilets in Finsbury Park. Cafés, pub and toilets at Manor House.

LOOKING AT WILDLIFE: Finsbury Park has a variety of tree species and there is often a heron on the lake. Stoke Newington Reservoir is an important site for wildfowl, especially in winter. Grebe, heron and cormorant are present most of the year.

Hornsey Wood, set on the south-facing slopes above London, was once the most southerly outpost of the great Forest of Middlesex. Its swathe of tangled woodlands and sunnier clearings provided a convenient site for Londoners with a score to settle, and became the frequent haunt of duellists. It is this tradition which is commemorated today in the mosaic design of crossed pistols on the platforms of the Finsbury Park Underground Station. At the highest point of the road that cut through these woods there stood the Hornsey Wood Tavern, a little roadside inn fronted by three widespread oaks. For many years, according to Hone's 1826 *Everyday Book*, it was run by Mrs Lloyd and Mrs Collins, two 'ancient women and large in size', who would sit on a bench slung between two of the oaks, drinking beer and chatting with the customers. Having lived and worked and drunk together, they died within a few months of each other.

When the craze for tea-drinking arrived the oak trees were cut down, the tavern enlarged into a tea-house and an ornamental lake dug alongside it. Hornsey Wood became one of the most popular venues in London for angling and pigeon shooting, and for taking tea and promenading in the gardens. But by the early 19th century the tea craze was past, the gardens were in disrepair and most of the old woodland had been felled. It was this despoiled site that was chosen for the new Finsbury Park.

The 19th century saw London's expansion from a comprehensible city into an illimitable urban sprawl. As the population exploded the City's surrounding villages were swallowed up in its uncontrollable growth. During this period the population of the inner London Borough of Finsbury reached half a million and the Borough's fields and gathering grounds disappeared under a sea of housing. Finsbury people became so concerned that in 1850 they convened a meeting to press for the creation of a new public open space on the City outskirts. The campaign thus launched led in 1857 to the Finsbury Park Act, the very first legislation enabling the creation of a public park in London, although it was not until 1869 that the park was opened.

The park is not rich in wildlife but there is at least one bird for which it has provided a significant sanctuary: writing in 1898 W.H. Hudson, that best of writers on London's wildlife, describes the song thrush as common here even though it was rare in the rest of London:

> Even in December and January, on a dull, cold afternoon with a grey smoky mist obscuring everything, a concert of thrushes may be heard in this park with more voices in it than could be heard anywhere in the country ... What makes this all the more remarkable is the noisiness of the neighbourhood ... Here, more than anywhere in London, you are reminded of Milton's description of the jarring and discordant grating sounds at the opening of hell's gates: and one would imagine that in such an atmosphere the birds would become crazed.

Leaving the park at Manor House and going straight onto the busy junction of Seven Sisters Road and Green Lanes, this description seems particularly apt.

On the far side of the junction we enter Woodberry Down, once the 'posh' end of the Borough of Stoke Newington, now the site of a large and, in its time, pioneering estate. In 1934 a new Labour administration came to power in the London County Council, pledged to the radical reform of the capital's housing, and to relocating London's huge and overcrowded 'slum' population. Woodberry Down, an area of large and ageing Victorian villas, was chosen for one of the first new rehousing schemes. The LCC set about the task of clearing 64 acres of land for the new homes by taking out Compulsory Purchase Orders on the existing properties, many of which were old, dilapidated and in multi-occupation. The scheme was opposed by many existing owners and lease-holders, and by the Conservative controlled local council and the local press. '£1,000,000 Slum Dwellers' Paradise', the *North London Recorder* tagged the proposed development. Plans for the estate were delayed by a public enquiry, a High Court challenge, and finally by the outbreak of World War Two. By the end of the war 90 per cent of all Stoke Newington's housing had suffered damage while the Borough's population was growing by 150 a month. The 1945 elections saw Labour win every seat in the Borough and elect its first ever Mayor. It was in this new climate that the development began.

It was to be a showpiece estate, with 6,500 people living in nearly 1800 homes. There was to be 24 acres of open space, a community centre, a library, shops and an old people's home. The plans included the first purpose-built Health Centre in the country and the first purpose-built Comprehensive School in London. Architecturally new ground was broken in the designs of two of the largest blocks, Nicholl and Needwood Houses. They are still striking today, massive, white and determinedly modern buildings with an imposing cornice and a severe facade, relieved only by a juxtaposition of vertical and horizontal lines. The first tenants, from Bermondsey, Stepney, Clerkenwell and Aldgate, moved in in 1948. 'We felt like King and Queen', said Olga Adams, who had previously shared one room in Finsbury with her husband and two children.

It was a brave attempt, but it is not the Woodberry Downs of today. Forty years on the school has gone, the older flats are damaged by the rumblings of the Victoria Line underneath, and two of the newer blocks – part of the 1960s wave of system building – have already had to be demolished. Whatever the intentions, social engineering on this scale has been shown to throw up at least as many problems as it was designed to solve.

From Woodberry Down the detour as far as the Stoke Newington Reservoirs is well worthwhile, and especially in winter. From the low bridge on Lordship Road it is possible to see some of the wildfowl that gather here; shovellor, wigeon, great-crested and little grebe, visiting rarities like the Slavonian grebe, and an increasing number of ruddy duck. For many years this was a regular wintering ground for one of our most beautiful ducks, the smew, but sadly they have not appeared here in recent years. With the privatisation of Thames Water and the completion of London's new ring main, the future of the reservoirs is in doubt. The New River Society and the Save the Reservoirs Campaign have fought a vigorous campaign to retain them and the likely outcome at the time of writing is that one reservoir will be built over and the other retained as a water sports area and nature reserve.

Following our main route along Green Lanes we come across another feature connected with the reservoirs: the wonderfully eccentric pile of the Stoke Newington Pumping Station. The New River, which we cross just before the Pumping Station, is neither new nor a river, but an artificial water course dug in 1613 to bring a supply of fresh water from Hertfordshire into London. By the 19th century this supply was no longer adequate and in 1833 the New River Company built the two reservoirs, now the oldest of their kind in the world. One of the recurring features of London life at this time was the cholera epidemics which swept the capital every few years; by the mid-century the link had been established beween cholera and the state of the water supply and the Metropolitan Water Act made the filtration of water compulsory. The response of the New River Company was to build the filter beds on the opposite side of Green Lanes and this huge new pumping station to drive the water through them. Completed in 1856, it was designed by William Chadwell Mylne. To meet local objections, and disguise the station's real functions, he adopted the style of a mediaeval Scottish castle. The 'keep' housed 6 steam engines and their 18 boilers, the main tower contained the chimney and the buttresses concealed the fly wheels. It remained in operation until 1946 and, though now a Grade II listed building, its future, too, is uncertain.

Clissold Park and Church Street

ROUTE:
- On entering the park follow the main drive ahead towards Clissold House and the church spire.
- Take the path on the left immediately after Clissold House, following it round the back of the house and then to the right and along the back of Old St Mary's.
- Take the gate on the right leading to a footpath through the churchyard and onto the main road (Stoke Newington Church Street).
- Turn left to follow the main road for about ¼ mile through Stoke Newington until you reach a gate into Abney Park Cemetery on your left.

FACILITIES: Toilets and café in Clissold Park. Toilets in Stoke Newington Church Street and a wide choice of cafés, pubs and wine bars.

LOOKING AT WILDLIFE: Clissold Park has a wildfowl collection, a herd of fallow deer and an aviary. There is also an interesting collection of exotic tree species including dawn redwood, ginkgo, holm oak, manna ash, Judas tree, mulberry, black walnut and a yellow-leaved ash. Wild duck sometimes visit the lower lakes in winter.

At the end of the 18th century Stoke Newington, on its higher seat above the City and the Lea, was developing as a country retreat for wealthy Londoners. It proved particularly attractive to merchant bankers and among those who moved here was Jonathon Hoare, building himself 'Paradise House', a large yellow-brick home with a six-pillared portico. By 1811 the leasehold on the house had passed into the hands of another banker, William Crawshay, who paid a yearly rental for it of '£109 and a fat turkey'. Mr Crawshay and his family attended the nearby parish church of St Mary's and it was there that his daughter Elizabeth fell in love with a young curate, Augustus Clissold. The two began a discreet romance, which infuriated old Mr Crawshay. He took drastic measures to keep the young couple apart: after forbidding their meetings he raised the height of all the walls around his 54 acre estate and, when that seemed to have failed, he threatened to shoot anyone caught delivering messages between them. Despite, or perhaps because of, all the obstacles, Elizabeth and Augustus remained constant and were finally able to marry after Crawshay's death. They also inherited the family home and Clissold House is now named after them. In 1886 the house and its grounds went on the market, due to be sold off as building plots. After a public outcry a newly formed Preservation Society began a campaign to save the site, and after raising much of the money itself, the Society persuaded the LCC and the local vestries to buy the estate. It was opened to the public as Clissold Park in 1899.

It must have been a fascinating place in those days, for two quite separate 'rivers' ran through it, one natural, the other artificial. Traces of them both can still be seen. The Hackney Brook rises in Islington and runs into the River Lea at Hackney Wick, but it has become one of the 'lost' rivers of London, now running in concrete casing underground. The two ponds in the slight depression where we enter Clissold Park are one of its few remaining traces and were dug out from the river to provide bricks during the building of Paradise House. At the top of the hill, the long curving pond in the deer enclosure is a remnant of the New River, which now terminates at the Stoke Newington Reservoirs, but before the Second World War continued from here down through Islington to the New River Head near The Angel. Apart from the ponds and one or two other remnants, these last few miles of its course were then filled in.

The path which leads us through the graveyard of Old St Mary Church is short but has a real rural quality. The low red church has ancient origins but underwent a restoration in 1583, a date which can be seen carved above the south doorway. As Stoke Newington rose in both size and status it was decided to build a new and larger Parish church, and this alone has saved Old St Mary's from the excesses of a further, Victorian, renovation. The new St Mary's was built in 1858 and the two now face each other across Church Street, symbolic of the transition of Stoke Newington from rural village to middle-class suburb. The new church is grey and stark and less appealing. Its architect was George Gilbert Scott, several of whose buildings are along the route of *The Green London Way*. In the new church the worldly wealth, rather than spiritual yearnings, of his clients is reflected in the 254 foot spire, in its day the highest church steeple in London.

Stoke Newington Church Street leads us through the heart of the old village. It is a jumble of a street where fine old houses rub shoulders with ugly post-war development. Following years of dilapidation Stoke Newington has become one of the centres of inner city gentrification, as the professional classes recolonise and new wine bars are opened to serve them. Sisters Place, a Queen Anne house immediately opposite the public library, is one of the oldest and finest buildings, built in 1714 for the four Bridge sisters. Further along on the same side is Defoe Road and it was in a house near here that Daniel Defoe wrote *Robinson Crusoe* in 1719. His is not the only famous name connected with Stoke Newington. Edgar Allen Poe was educated here while Leigh Hunt, the poet, John Howard, the prison reformer, and Isaac Watts, the hymn writer, all lived here. There are many who took up a far more permanent residence after death for not far along on the left hand side is the gate into Abney Park, one of London's great Victorian cemeteries.

Abney Park and Stoke Newington Common

ROUTE:

● Enter the cemetery and on reaching the main path turn left. Follow this broad route ahead until you come to a major crossing of paths with the chapel buildings visible to your right. Turn right passing the chapel and continue to the main gates.

● From the gates cross the main road to follow Northwold Road opposite and slightly to the right.

● From Northwold Road take the second main turning on the left into Kyverdale Road. Cross Cazenove Road ahead then turn right into Filey Avenue.

- At the end of Filey Avenue cross the main road (Upper Clapton Road) and take Springfield almost opposite and to the left. A short distance down Springfield take the gate into Springfield Park on the left.

FACILITIES: Toilets on Stoke Newington High Street at the cemetery entrance.

LOOKING AT WILDLIFE: Abney Park Cemetery has secondary woodland with exotic species surviving from the original planting. These include Bhutan pine, hybrid oaks, service tree of Fontainbleu, Monterey cypress and stone pine. There are around 30 species of breeding bird with many more, including goldcrest, which occur as visitors. There is a good selection of butterflies with speckled wood a speciality.

Among the great villas erected in Stoke Newington, two were particularly imposing. One of these was Abney House built by Thomas Gunton in 1714 and subsequently occupied by Sir Thomas and Lady Abney. Thomas Abney was another banker, later to become a founder of the Bank of England and a Lord Mayor of London. The Abneys were host to many house guests, and among them was Isaac Watts, who arrived in 1714 for a 'few weeks' recuperation after a nervous breakdown. He stayed for 35 years. He composed many of his best-known hymns here, including 'O God our help in ages past', and is commemorated by a statue in the cemetery.

There is a mound in the north east corner of the present park, now marked with a plaque, where Watts is supposed to have sat whilst composing. This mound has another famous association: according to local tradition Oliver Cromwell was buried beneath it. At the time of his official funeral at Westminster Abbey it was already feared that Cromwell's tomb might be subject to future violation, and a substitute body was therefore interred at the Abbey while the genuine item was brought here for safe-keeping. But why to Stoke Newington? The connection is with the other great house in Church Street.

While Abney House occupied the site now marked by the entrance to the cemetery, immediately next to it, on the site of the present Fire Station, was Fleetwood House. This was built in 1662 for Charles Fleetwood, previously Commander-in-Chief of the Commonwealth armies. His wife, Bridget, was Oliver Cromwell's eldest daughter. This gave rise not only to the story about the burial but also to a long running connection between Stoke Newington and religious dissenters. Two centuries later, when the estates of Fleetwood House and Abney House were amalgamated to form the Abney Park Cemetery, it was specifically planned as a burial ground for nonconformists. Among the most famous of these was William Booth, founder of the Salvation Army, whose grave, together with those of a number of other early Salvationists, can be seen shortly after we enter the cemetery grounds.

Abney Park Cemetery was designed by William Hosking, Professor of Architecture at Kings College, London. The centrepiece was to be the neo-Gothic chapel and to satisfy the needs of a variety of nonconformists the usual cruciform shape was eschewed for the Greek cross – a cross with four equal arms. This effect however was rather undone by the subsequent addition of a large carriage porch at the southern end. The park opened in May 1840 and within fifteen years 14,000 burials had taken place here. To the Victorians a cemetery was not just a reminder of human mortality, it was a place for a pleasant promenade, a picnic or a family outing, and Abney Park was certainly laid out with this in mind. It was landscaped by Loddiges and described as 'one of the most complete arboretums in the neighbourhood of London'. Over 2,500 trees were added to those preserved from the original estates and 1,029 roses were planted. But this proud place was soon to fall into decay. The early popularity of the cemetery ensured that it was soon full and the proprietors, in an attempt to maintain their revenue, went on packing the bodies into whatever space they could find for them – taking up paths, reducing the verges and filling the gaps between graves. By the 20th century little maintenance was being done and the park was running wild. Death had ceased to be profitable, and by the 1970s the cemetery company was bankrupt. It was then that the Save Abney Park Cemetery Committee was formed to preserve the site, and at the instigation of this group it was eventually purchased by Hackney Council for the nominal sum of £1.

The delightfully overgrown Abney Park of today is an island of secondary woodland in an intensely urban area. Thick growths of sycamore, birch and ash cover much of the ground, concealing here and there the more mature trees of the original planting. Horsetail is abundant and woundwort and red campion flower along the woodland edges and Canterbury bells, asparagus and asters spread out from the graves on which they were planted. A breeding birds survey has listed 29 species here, including stock dove, kestrel, tawny owl, blackcap, spotted flycatcher, coal tit and bullfinch. More surprising than any of these perhaps is the mallard. Twenty pairs bred here in 1983 and on fledging the young ducklings have to be walked the half mile or so to the nearest park lake. Some at least must survive the many hazards en route, for the number of breeding pairs has been increasing. In summer visiting whitethroat and great spotted woodpecker increase the variety of birds, while in winter linnet, redpoll and goldcrest might all be seen feeding here. In 1883 James Braithwaite French wrote a book entitled *Walks in Abney Park*. 'Death', he mused, 'is but a contrivance for gaining more life.' That statement must be even more true for the Cemetery today.

The main gates to Abney Park are formed by four solemn white Egyptian pylons decorated with lotus flowers, leaf motifs and the winged orbs emblematic of eternal life. On either side are flanking temples – once stonemasons workshops – bearing hieroglyphic legends which translate as 'The gates of the abode of the mortal part of man'. From these gates our route crosses the Stamford Hill road – its name derived from a stoney ford over the Hackney Brook – and continues alongside Stoke Newington Common. This genuine remnant of ancient commoners rights is today a drab and uninviting affair, gouged by the railway and enlivened only by the lines of mature plane trees. Once nightingales sung here, today they would hardly be heard above the traffic.

The main housing development around the Common took place in the late 1870s. It was during this time that Mr Worthington-Smith, a 'local antiquarian', noted in the sides of foundation trenches a thin band containing numerous sharp flint fragments. His discovery turned out to be one of the most important early Palaeolithic sites in the country, a buried land surface where 200,000 years ago men and women had lived and worked at what must have been a regular hand axe industry. Two to three hundred of these small flint tools were discovered here, as well as innumerable flint flakes from the workings. The surface extended from the cemetery in the west, across the common and as far as Upper Clapton Road in the east. Our route along Kyverdale Road and Filey Avenue runs across the very centre of it. It brings us to the gate of Springfield Park, and from here, to the marshes.

Walthamstow Marshes

ROUTE:
- On entering the park follow the main path between the White House and the lake. At the branching of paths, do not take the path which follows the lake perimeter but the one immediately to the left of it which curves away left to two large beech trees.
- At the crosspaths beside the two trees, turn left and follow this path all the way along the side of the hill and eventually down to the gate onto the road (Spring Hill).
- Turn right onto Spring Hill and at the bottom continue across the footbridge over the river.
- EITHER: Follow the perimeter fence of the marina round to the right to eventually regain the riverside. OR:
Take the wooden stile opposite the marina fence to enter Horseshoe Thicket. Keep to the right on the paths to pass a pond and emerge close to the riverside. Turn left along the river.
- Follow the riverside passing under the railway and continue over the next stretch of marsh to recross the river at the next footbridge.

FACILITIES: Toilets and café in the White House. Café beside the river at the bottom of Springfield Hill.

LOOKING AT WILDLIFE: Walthamstow Marsh has reed and sedge beds and a great variety of marshland plants. There is a breeding colony of Essex skipper butterflies and five species of dragonfly. Together with the neighbouring reservoirs this is one of the most important area for birds in Inner London. Herons and cormorant are frequent. Terns appear around Horseshoe Point in summer and reed buntings,sedge and reed warblers can all be seen or heard in the reed beds.

'Fresh air,' said Mr Cornwall when he performed the opening of Springfield Park in 1905, 'will help to change the habits of the people and to keep them out of the public houses'. This worthy aim was not entirely realised. It was however typical of the intentions of many of the Victorian reformers for whom public parks were as important for the moral as for the physical well-being of the labouring classes. Certainly Springfield Park was built on an 'uplifting' site, with its panoramic view of the Lea Valley and the marshes; but it is a view more fascinating than beautiful: wide expanses of tall grasses and reed-beds alongside the waterways, yet dominated by railways, electricity pylons and the tower blocks of Leyton. The top of the slope with its extensive view and little spring must have made it an attractive site for a settlement. The Romans thought so, and two of their stone coffins were unearthed here in the 19th century. The existing house is Georgian and was part of a 32 acre estate stretching down to the river at Horseshoe Point. This estate, together with its 'White House', was put up for sale in 1902 and purchased at a cost of £40,000 by the LCC and the local Boroughs. There is Jack-by-the-hedge and campion amongst the uncut grasses of the steeper slopes and many birds use it as an extension of the habitats provided by the neighbouring marshes. It is to these that we make our way via the footbridge at the bottom of Spring Hill.

That Walthamstow Marsh has survived at all is something of a marvel. Once the wetlands and the watermeadows would have extended for miles along the bottom of the broad valley of the Lea, but Tottenham Marsh, Leyton Marsh, Hackney Marsh, and many more, have disappeared beneath infilling and football pitches, reservoirs, housing and the formal leisure 'complex'. But here, at the heart of it all, is 88 acres of ancient lammas land which has enjoyed an uninterrupted continuity since the middle ages. The antiquity of the marshes is demonstrated by the plants themselves. One of the commonest sedges here is the hybrid *Carex x subgracilis*. This hybrid is infertile which means that the large stands on the marsh must have spread themselves vegetatively over hundreds of years from a single accidental clone. This site is therefore unique – yet it would not have survived without the efforts of the Save The Marshes Campaign.

In 1979 the Lea Valley Regional Park Authority declared its intention to extract gravel from the marsh and turn it into a marina for motorized water sports. The Save the Marshes Campaign led and won the fight against this proposal. Again in 1982 when British Rail proposed to tip 8,000 tons of ballast onto part of the marsh it was the Campaign which led the protest. It is only in recent years that the various statutory authorities have caught up with local people and come to regard an ancient marsh as something worth preserving. In 1984 formal notification of the marsh as a Site of Special Scientific Interest was commenced and by 1985 the Lea Valley Regional Park Authority was proposing to manage the area as a nature reserve. The Save the Marshes Campaign was able to transform itself from an ad hoc campaign into a permanent 'Walthamstow Marsh Society'.

The marsh consists of a succession of habitats from open water to dry grassland. Much of the area is covered with reed, sedge and marshland grasses. In spring and summer there are great swathes of colour from the purple-blue Russian comfrey, the white and frothy meadow sweet, the upright poles of yellow flag iris and the delicately drooping pink and cream blooms of great willow herb. In autumn they are supplanted by the rich brown seed-heads of the docks and the dark blue ranks of Michaelmas daisy. These are the dominant plants, but there are many more to be found among them; water figwort, ragged robin, soapwort, orange balsam, purple loosestrife, wild angelica, even the little adder's tongue fern, another indicator of antiquity. It is the docks which have most excited the specialists, for among the many species to be found here there have arisen some very unusual hybrids. One of these, a cross between Greek dock and broad-leaved dock, has been named *Rumex x lousleyi* in honour of the botanist Ted Lousley, a leading light of the London Natural History Society who died in 1975. The plant on the marsh is one of only two specimens known anywhere in the world. It is an example of evolution proceeding in our own time.

A diversity of plant life gives rise to a diversity of insect life. Harry Britain of the Save the Marshes Campaign has identified 800 species so far, though there must be many more. He calculates that the total population of bees and wasps alone outnumbers the human inhabitants of Hackney by three to one. There are five species of dragonfly to be looked for and nineteen species of butterfly – seventeen of them breeding here. The Essex skipper is a butterfly that was only discovered in this country in 1888. It is on the extreme northern edge of its world range here and differs from the small skipper only in having a small dot on the underside of its antennae. The marsh is one of its outposts, with a good breeding population, constituting probably the closest colony to Central London.

There are specialities among the birds as well. The reservoirs to the north of the marsh have one of the largest heronries in the country and at almost any time of day, but particularly at dawn and dusk, these birds can be seen flying overhead like lumbering pterodactyls. The reservoir and the marsh combined have produced a species list of over 180 birds and 27 of them are known to breed here. They include little grebe, cuckoo, skylark, sand martin, stonechat, reed warbler, sedge warbler, whitethroat, spotted flycatcher, yellow wagtail, reed bunting and linnet. It is a unique experience to stand in a reed-bed under the shadow of a railway embankment and hear, on a spring day, the busy chirruping of a hidden sedge warbler while overhead a skylark, framed by pylons, looses its unending stream of notes as though in the heart of the country.

Our route over the marsh takes us from Coppermill Bridge around the back of the Springfield Marina where, at dusk, pipistrelle bats come out to feed. The marina was created in the early 1970s by enlarging the old bend in the river at Horseshoe Point. The extracted silt was dumped on the adjacent marsh and has given rise to Horse Shoe Thicket, a dense growth of sallow supporting a large population of finches, tits and warblers. The section of the marsh down to the railway is known as Inner Marsh. On the far side of the arches a plaque explains that A.V. Roe built a little triplane here in 1909 and made history by staging the first all-British powered flight. His plane can still be seen in the Science Museum at South Kensington. From here the route continues across Outer Marsh until we reach a sudden rise marked by a line of tall trees. This rise marks the old boundary between Walthamstow and Leyton; and also between their contrasting treatment of the marshlands. Behind us is a scene of rich and ever-changing natural complexity. Ahead of us is Leyton Marsh, a marsh in name only, infilled with rubble after the blitz and turned into playing fields. Its drab expanse attracts nothing but Sunday footballers and seagulls.

To Complete Walk 1
● From the footbridge continue ahead along the riverside for a short distance and after

the warehouses turn right on the path onto Millfields. Follow the path which runs between the blocks of flats and the open fields until reaching the road.
- Turn left then immediately right up Gunton Road to reach Upper Clapton Road for buses and BR station.

WALK 2: Clapton to Victoria Park

Getting Started

From Walk 1:

After crossing the footbridge continue along the riverside path.

To start walk here:

Turn left from Clapton BR Station then immediately left into Gunton Road.
At the bottom of Gunton Road follow the path ahead and to the left which runs along the edge of the fields to reach the riverside.
Turn right along the riverside path.

Hackney Marsh and the Millfields

ROUTE:
- Follow the path under Lea Bridge Road. Shortly beyond this it crosses a footbridge onto the opposite bank and runs alongside the Middlesex Filter Beds Nature Reserve.
- At the end of the Filter Beds turn left and cut directly across the grass to reach the banks of the Old Lea. Turn right to follow the riverside path for about ½ mile.
- Shortly before the main road bridge leave the riverside to the right and follow the perimeter of the depot buildings through a car park and onto the main road.

FACILITIES: Prince of Wales pub on Lea Bridge Road. Camp-site on Hackney Marshes (summer only).

LOOKING AT WILDLIFE: The Middlesex Filter Beds contain ponds, reed-beds and willow scrub with a variety of water and waterside plants. Both the Filter Beds and the Old Lea are good for birds; look out for heron, kingfisher, little grebe and a variety of wintering wildfowl, with gadwall a speciality. Giant hogweed grows all along the Old Lea and arrowhead is abundant in the Lea Navigation. The Middlesex Filter Beds Nature Reserve is currently open Saturdays, Sundays and Bank Holidays from 10 to 4.

In the year 527 the Saxon leader Erchewin rebelled against Octa, his king, and went off to form a kingdom of his own with its capital at London. Determined to suppress this rebellion Octa sailed here from Rochester with a force of 15,000 men. He planned to leave his boats on the Lea and march south on London.

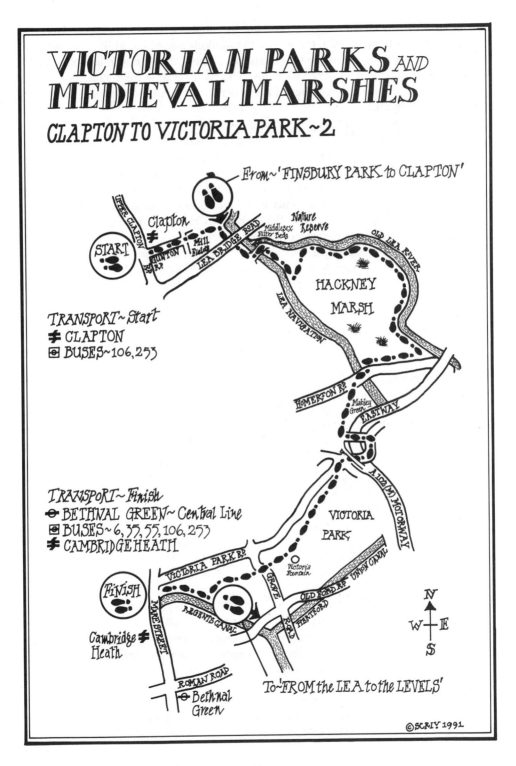

VICTORIAN PARKS *and* MEDIEVAL MARSHES

CLAPTON TO VICTORIA PARK ~ 2

From ~ 'FINSBURY PARK to CLAPTON'

Clapton

Nature Reserve

Middlesex Filter Beds

OLD LEA RIVER

UPPER CLAPTON ROAD

START

GUNTON RD

MILL Fields

LEA BRIDGE ROAD

LEA NAVIGATION

HACKNEY MARSH

TRANSPORT ~ Start
- CLAPTON
- BUSES ~ 106, 253

HOMERTON RD

Mabley Green

EASTWAY

A 102 (M) MOTORWAY

TRANSPORT ~ Finish
- BETHNAL GREEN ~ Central Line
- BUSES ~ 6, 35, 55, 106, 253
- CAMBRIDGE HEATH

VICTORIA PARK

VICTORIA PARK RD

Victoria Fountain

GROVE ROAD

OLD FORD RD

HERTFORD UNION CANAL

FINISH

MARE STREET

REGENTS CANAL

Cambridge Heath

ROMAN ROAD

Bethnal Green

To ~ 'FROM the LEA to the LEVELS'

N
W   E
S

© SCRIY 1991

Erchewin forestalled him and arrived here to cut short the advance. The Battle of Hackney was fought beside the river, on the unlikely site of the Millfields. Octa was seriously wounded in a struggle which cost the lives of thousands of his followers. It was the 'Londoners' who were victorious. The river became the boundary between the two saxon kingdoms, and later of the two English counties derived from them – Essex and Middlesex.

The Millfields owe their name to a later, more peaceful time. In the 18th century there were huge mills here grinding out 300 quarters of corn a week. The story of the cornmills also ends in calamity however for in 1791 an immense fire consumed the whole mills, including 30,000 quarters of wheat and flour, in less than two hours. The fields were also the site of extensive diggings, for they yielded the valuable brick-earth, a soil deposit frequent across East London, formed by a combination of glacial and river action. Until the 1830s this was mixed with road sweepings and other refuse to make the characteristic London brick.

Beyond the Lea Bridge Road we cross the river to reach one of the most attractive sites along the whole Lea Valley, the abandoned Middlesex Filter Beds. Twenty years ago, when last in use, this succession of concrete tanks must have presented a somewhat bleak prospect, but today as the old tanks fill with silt and are colonised by plants they provide an almost textbook illustration of fen evolution. Just about every stage in the progression from pond through reed-bed and willow scrub to eventual woodland is evident here. Many of the plants – water plantain, water crowfoot, almond-leaved willow – must have come in on the feet of visiting wildfowl. Increasing numbers of duck visit in winter and in early summer there is a frantic chattering chorus from the warblers in the reed beds. This is a closer, more private site than the open marshes, and has a real sense of seclusion despite the factories and tower blocks a few hundred yards away across the river. The filter beds have now been turned into a Nature Reserve by the Lea Valley Regional Park Authority, a move which has guaranteed their future survival. It is hard however to suppress a little regret that this beautiful site, once unofficially explored and enjoyed by the locals who knew of it, is now subject to the restricted opening and more precious regime of 'official' conservation.

Over this part of the marshes the channel of the Lea has split into two. The direct route ahead follows the canalised channel of the Hackney Cut, dug in 1776 to provide flood relief and shorten the Lea Navigation. The River Lea has been in regular commercial navigation since at least 1220. Even before this, in the ninth century, channels were dug by King Alfred, as a defensive measure. In 895 the Danes had sailed up here to attack the town of Ware in Hertfordshire. The citizens of London turned out to oppose them en route but were driven off with heavy losses. King Alfred then ordered the digging of drainage channels at various places along the river, including here at Hackney, which reduced the water level in the Lea. This stranded the Danes up-river, where, without their precious boats, they were attacked and defeated.

The drainage channels would have had the additional effect of lowering the water table on the marshes, thus rendering them usable as hay meadows. The Hackney Marsh, like much of the rest of the area, became lammas lands. From the lammas festival in August, through to the next April, the landowner had exclusive right to the hay harvest, but for the rest of the year the marsh was open to common grazing. These various rights were supervised and protected by 'marsh drivers' who were elected annually by the court of the manor. But gradually the area became more and more popular as a playground for the East End, one bull-baiting contest in 1791 being watched by as many as 3,000 people. And by the end of the 19th century the marsh drivers were coming into conflict with participants in a newer sport – football. Largely as a result of pressure from mission halls and other places which organised teams, the London County Council bought the 350 acres of Hackney Marsh in 1893, the site eventually providing over 120 football and cricket pitches.

The view out across the 120 pitches is one of unrelieved tedium; it is all the more surprising, therefore, to find on the far side of this flat plateau of playing fields a riverside walk of considerable attraction. Unlike the straight and stiff-banked channel of the navigation, the Old Lea meanders under overhanging trees, its earth banks the home of waterside plants, moorhens and even a kingfisher or two. In winter the duck fly in, in numbers which increase with the harshness of conditions, common sandpiper fly low over the water and small parties of little grebe circle and dive, seeming to spend as much time under the river as on top of it. In summer it is the giant hogweed which dominates the scene. This monster of a plant can reach up to twelve foot high, with flat white flower heads up to three foot across. It advances up the river valley like an invading army, which perhaps is what it is. Having arrived here from the Caucasus, the plant is rapidly spreading across southern and eastern England.

Victoria Park

ROUTE:
- Turn right along the main road, crossing the Hackney Cut, to reach Mabley Green, another area of pitches, on your left.
- Head across Mabley Green making for the diametrically opposite corner. From here take the footbridge over the main road and onto Red Path.
- At the end of the path turn right. Follow the road (Eastway), round to the right under railway and motorway bridges to reach the pedestrian crossing which leads across the road to the gate of Victoria Park.
- Walk ahead and turn right in front of the lodge to follow the large drive through the park to Royal Gate.
- Go straight across the road and into the next section of the park. Follow the drive ahead and then turn left in front of the deer enclosure.
- At the circular wooden shelter take the central path ahead. Follow it to the tip of the lake and then double back to the left along the bottom of the lake to find the gate onto the canal towpath to your right.
- EITHER turn left on towpath to join Walk 3
OR turn right and follow the towpath under Bonner Hall Bridge and on to the next road bridge.
- Leave canal here and turn left for buses and stations.

FACILITIES: Café and pub on Grove Road between the two sections of park. Cafés, restaurant and toilets in Victoria Park.

LOOKING AT WILDLIFE: Deadly nightshade on Red Path. Victoria Park has several lakes, a collection of wildfowl and and a paddock with fallow deer, cranes and guinea fowl. There is a variety of native and introduced trees including hornbeam, cockspur thorn, turkey oak, Indian bean tree, ginkgo, strawberry tree and mulberry.

From Mabley Green the Red Path runs alongside the Hackney Wick Coal and Goods Depot. The most interesting feature here is the clump of deadly nightshade growing on the right-hand side of the path. This is usually a plant of chalk woodland and its occurrence here is something of a puzzle. Deadly nightshade is also known as belladonna, literally 'beautiful woman'. The nightshade contains atropine which when dropped into the eye has the effect of dilating the pupil. It is used by opticians today to assist in eye examinations but was once used by Roman women to make their eyes look larger and, it was held, more alluring.

Victoria Park was built as a direct response to the squalid, overcrowded conditions of Bethnal Green and the East End. In 1839 a 'sanitary reformer' by the name of William Farr pointed out that fresh air and exercise provided by a park would 'probably diminish deaths by several thousand and add years to the lives of the entire population.' He further noted that 'epidemics which arise in the East End do not stay there, they travel to the West End and prove fatal in the wide streets and squares.' This was no doubt the clinching argument. In the following year a committee was set up under the local MP, and began to organise a petition which eventually attracted 30,000 signatures. It was presented to Queen Victoria and it was her interest in the project which ensured its original designation as a royal park. It was laid out by James Pennethorne in the Romantic style and planted with over 10,000 trees and shrubs.

The site used for the park was Bonners Fields, named after an infamous Bishop of London noted for burning protestant heretics during the reign of Mary I. These fields had long been a gathering ground for workers' rallies and radical demonstrations and this tradition was carried over into the new park. In 1848 the last great Chartist rally was scheduled to gather nearby and the park was turned by the authorities into an armed encampment for the occasion. Stationed within the gates were 1600 foot police – 500 of them armed with cutlasses – 100 mounted police and 500 recalled police reservists. Just to make up the numbers a cavalry detachment from the 1st Life Guards was stationed on the opposite bank of the canal.

In subsequent years the radicals regained the park for themselves. The militant suffragettes gathered here, as did striking dockers, and, in the late 1970s, the Anti-Nazi League. One group which didn't make it was Oswald Mosley's Blackshirts, who tried to march to the Park but were halted by barricades along the way. The area known as The Forum – or locally as The Forem and Agin 'em – became a second speakers corner. Speakers here included Bernard Shaw, William Morris, Tom Mann and Ben Tillett. The Forum, sadly, ran out of steam round about 1939.

The lake was added to the park in 1846, the work being carried out free by the East London Waterworks Company using old brick-earth pits. The completed lake was stocked with wildfowl by the Ornithological Society on condition that a Victoria Park branch was set up. The branch recruited local members, charged dues and organised lectures and 'bird observations', generally surprising respectable folk that the working classes were capable of such pursuits. W.H. Hudson complains that the park was too heavily used – 20,000 visitors on Good Friday 1845 for example – to admit of much interesting bird life, but these lakes have been the scene of at least one milestone in ornithological history. The tufted duck, such a common sight now on our park ponds and urban canals, has reached high numbers only in the course of this century. When a pair raised a brood here in 1912 it was one of the very first breeding records for the whole of London.

The most striking architectural feature in the Park is the Victoria Fountain. In 1862 the Baroness Angela Georgina Burdett-Coutts, the richest woman in England, took it upon herself to remedy the shortage of drinking water for the masses who thronged the park. The Baroness was a philanthropist and friend of Dickens, a woman with a very independent turn of mind and a special interest in the East End; her acts of charity could be fulsome and sometimes even foolhardy. The Victoria Fountain is on her usual grand scale. Over fifty feet high, it is built of red Aberdeen granite, in what Pevsner calls a 'Gothic-cum-Moorish' style. The drinking cups were originally of bronze, silver-plated on the inside and bearing outside the motto 'Temperance is a bridle of gold'. The whole thing cost her nearly £7,000 and makes an extravagant memorial to an extravagant but generous woman.

FROM THE LEA TO THE LEVELS

VICTORIA PARK TO WEST HAM ~3

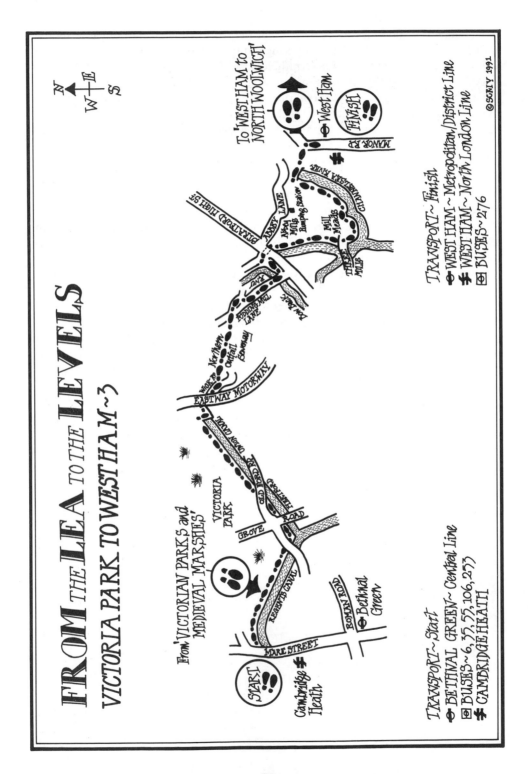

©SCRLY 1991

From 'VICTORIAN PARKS and MEDIEVAL MARSHES'

To 'WEST HAM to NORTH WOOLWICH'

TRANSPORT~ Start
- ⊖ BETHNAL GREEN~ Central Line
- ⊞ BUSES~ 6, 35, 55, 106, 253
- ⚑ CAMBRIDGE HEATH

TRANSPORT~ Finish
- ⊖ WEST HAM ~ Metropolitan/District Line
- ⚑ WEST HAM~ North London Line
- ⊞ BUSES~ 276

2. FROM THE LEA TO THE LEVELS

FROM HACKNEY TO NORTH WOOLWICH

The few villages of the Saxon manor of Hamme stood on a gravelly terrace stretching from the River Roding to the River Lea. Around them was a remarkably inhospitable area; the huge forest of Middlesex to the north, and to the south a great area of marshes or 'levels' running down to the Thames. The peculiar geography of the area left it unchanged in a wind-swept isolation for hundreds of years; but from the 19th century it helped to shape its particularly rapid and difficult development. From the industrial revolution onwards the two Hams, East and West, became an area of concentrated disadvantage.

When the City of London passed an ordinance outlawing 'noxious industries', they came here instead: the chemical works, the 'oil boilers, gut spinners, varnish makers and printers' ink makers'. The availability of cheap, level and low-lying land, alongside the river and free of all legal restrictions, brought these, the docks, the iron-works and the ship-builders. With them came the mass of impoverished labourers, forced to build their shanty-towns upon the water-logged marshland. Living in a community without paved roads, drains or sewers, and afflicted with smallpox, cholera and typhoid, they did the work that kept the City wealthy.

The intervening years have not been much kinder. The Royal Docks brought a casual and precarious employment, and then took it away again. The largest gas works in the world have come and gone. The area lost two thirds of its housing and several thousand lives in the massive World War Two bombardment. And then the tower blocks were put up – and some of them fell down again. Today we see a fascinating and disturbing example of history repeating itself. This area, which owed its original development to the fact that it was free of legal restrictions, is now a 'free enterprise zone', a massive development area administered by the London Docklands Development Corporation, where the normal planning constraints and controls – and protections – have been swept aside in the interests of rapid and unrestrained 'growth'.

The face of this corner of Newham remains an uneasy mix of development and dereliction. Neither of these however provides the theme for this chapter. It is instead, one of survival: the survival of a people who have built strong and lasting communities and whose character has become a part of popular mythology. And survival too of wildlife in amazing abundance: angelica on an old lock-gate, pheasant on abandoned allotments, danewort colonising the sewer banks, black redstart in the ruins of the gasworks, dabchick and shelduck in the empty docks and teal and foxes on the muddy banks of the Thames.

The chapter covers 9 miles from Hackney to North Woolwich. It can also be taken as two separate walks:

WALK 3: Cambridge Heath Road to West Ham Station (4 miles).
Sections of this walk can be muddy or overgrown.

WALK 4: West Ham Station to North Woolwich (5 miles).

The final section of this walk, through the docklands area, is undergoing very rapid and comprehensive redevelopment and the walker may experience difficulty from route changes. The redevelopment should finally result in a greater choice of footpaths.

WALK 3: Victoria Park to West Ham

Getting Started

From Cambridge Heath Station (BR) and buses:
   From entrance to station turn left to cross Hackney Road and continue in same direction up Cambridge Heath Road to join the canal on the right hand side, just after Vyner Street.
From Bethnal Green Station (tube):
   Take exit signposted for Cambridge Heath Road (East side) and continue up the road, passing the Museum of Childhood. Join the canal on the right hand side after Vyner Street.
From Walk 2:
   Where Walk 2 leaves Victoria Park onto the Regents Canal towpath, turn left to join Walk 3.

The Regents Canal and the Hertford Union

ROUTE:
• Follow the tow-path to a junction of canals by a hump-back bridge. Take the left branch (Hertford Union) and follow it as far as the second lock.
• Cross over the top of the lock gates and follow the path which leads between fences onto Jodrell Road. *If you cannot face crossing the lock gates go back to previous footbridge and cross it to join Jodrell Road.*
• Turn left and at the end of Jodrell Road turn right into Wick Lane. Follow it under the motorway, crossing the road at the zebra.

- Continue to where two footpaths begin on the left. Take the second of these paths, beside the gates, onto the sewer embankment.

FACILITIES: Pubs and cafés on Cambridge Heath Road.

LOOKING AT WILDLIFE: There is a rich flora along the tow-paths including several rare aliens. Interesting wild flowers along this section of the sewer embankment include danewort and several naturalised species of rose.

The Regents Canal was the work of John 'Beau' Nash; Victoria Park, which it runs alongside, that of his protegé and adoptive son, James Pennethorne. Since Nash was rumoured to be 'medically unfit for marriage', it caused some surprise among the court circles of which he was a habitué, when he announced his intention of marrying Mary Anne, a coal merchant's daughter. Their marriage was punctuated by six strange interludes during which Mary disappeared from society for a while. Each time she reappeared with a child which, she said, had been 'given' to her by a poor 'Mrs Pennethorne'. This steady growth in the Nash family was matched by only one thing; John's wealth and status within the court of his friend and patron, the Prince Regent. The Prince was notorious for his immorality and had a house close to the Nash's country retreat on the Isle of Wight. This naturally led to a certain amount of unpatriotic speculation about the real origins of the Pennethorne children. A grateful Nash went on to name not only his canal but also Regents Street and Regents Park in honour of his patron and here, where Nash's Regents Canal passes Pennethorne's Victoria Park, all the characters in this little drama are brought together again.

The hump-backed bridge along the towpath marks a junction. The main canal heads on south through Mile End and Stepney to connect with the Thames at the Limehouse Basin. Our route lies behind the bridge and off along the branch to the east, the 'Hertford Union', a slightly later addition to the canal network. The early years of the Regents were so successful that in 1830 Sir George Duckett had the idea of launching a private venture that would link the traffic on the Regents Canal to that on the River Lea. His expectations of quick profits however were to be disappointed and within a few years he was forced to ask the Regents Canal Company to take the canal off his hands. The Hertford Union – or Ducketts Cut as it is commonly known – joins the two waterways at their closest point, running in a straight line for over a mile between Victoria Park and the rows of warehouses which once supplied timber to East End craftsmen.

There has been an increasing awareness in recent years of the wildlife value of this East London canal network. Despite its murky appearance there are fresh-water sponges on the wooden piles of the locks, swan mussels in the muddy bottoms of the cuts, and wandering snails and fresh-water winkles clinging to the concrete piles of the towpath. These provide food for tufted duck and pochard, and in winter grey wagtail are regular visitors all along the waterways. But it is for their flora that the canals have become best known. The Regents, the Lea and the Hertford Union provide an urban habitat for the sorts of plants which one would much more readily associate with a quiet pastoral stream: gypsywort, soapwort, hemlock water dropwort, angelica, skullcap and comfrey.

In addition there are national rarities and a number of colonising, invading 'aliens'. One of these, is a tropical grass *Paspalum paspalodes*, which is found in only one other place in Britain. Another is an American bur-marigold, *Bidens connata* which while rare elsewhere has spread all the way along the canal-side from Southall to Bow. The water-borne seeds are clearly washed along until they lodge and take root in crevices in the concrete bank; a practical demonstration of the way in which the canal system provides arteries for the spread of wildlife.

At Jodrell Road and Wick Lane we make a temporary departure from the waterways in order to join the first section of the North London Outfall Sewer. This is the great cross-London sewage disposal system built in the 19th century to serve the City of London, one of the grand-scale civil engineering conceptions of the Victorian heyday. The sewer runs above ground and its embankment constitutes a walkway or cycle route through several miles of East London. Our first stretch along the sewer is only a brief one, but it is by far the richest section for wildlife. The banks slope down into adjacent waste land and weedy factory yards covered with a thick growth of shrubs and of wild flowers; campions, melilots, spurges, toadflax, bird-sown sunflowers and three different types of rose.

The real speciality here, however, is a smelly but nonetheless intriguing shrub known as Danewort. This nationally uncommon plant has become well established in East London and covers a large area of these embankments. It is a relative of the elder but unlike its larger woody relative is herbaceous and dies back each winter. According to English legend it sprang up from the blood of slaughtered Danes as they were driven back by the armies of King Alfred. It is often a relic of mediaeval herbal usage – of the nearby Stratford Langthorne Abbey perhaps – and herbalism gives us a different account of the origin of its name. Danewort bears profuse, but poisonous, black berries. A dose of them induces severe diarrhoea or, to use the old name for it, of 'the danes'. Could this be why it is growing so abundantly on a sewer?

From Pudding Mill to Three Mills

ROUTE:
- Follow the sewer embankment and immediately after the second bridge take the steps leading down the slope on the right hand side.
- Of the two roads in front of you, take the further one which curves round over a bridge. At the junction beyond the bridge turn left.
- Continue ahead and after crossing the river take the towpath on the left on the far side of the bridge.
- Follow the towpath past the lock to steps leading up onto a road. Turn right to join the busy High Street.
- Cross High Street using the subway. Pick up the path on the opposite side which leads all the way along the riverside to the Three Mills Complex.

LOOKING AT WILDLIFE: More rich and varied waterside and towpath flora, including giant hogweed and biting stonecrop.

H ere below Hackney Marshes, where the Lea is less than three miles from its confluence with the Thames, it ramifies into a confusion of tidal channels. They fan out over the broad flat valley which once carried masses of melt-water south from the retreating glaciers of the ice age. City Mill River, Pudding Mill River, Three Mills River, Waterworks River, Channelsea River, Abbey Creek and Prescott Channel together constitute the Bow Back Rivers, finally re-unifying at Bromley-by-Bow to wind a tortuous last half mile into the Thames. It has been the struggle of centuries to control and direct this unruly water.

Pudding Mill was one of the many mills along these stretches and operated from medieval times through to the 19th century; but the mill is gone now and the channel which operated it is reduced to a disconnected relic stagnating between Marshgate and Pudding Mill Lane. Its rubble-strewn mudbanks support celery-leaved crowfoot and bur-marigolds which somehow thrive in the scum. Continuing along the next stretch of channel we come to the abandoned City Mill Lock, which was one of the junctions between the navigable channels and the tidal Lea. Its battered and leaking gates, its grey mud banks and accumulated debris, are brought back to life by angelica, hemlock water dropwort, lesser skullcap and gypsywort. An isolated lock cottage stands on the opposite bank, white-painted, inward looking, but with a well cared for vegetable patch alongside. Despite its surroundings of industrial dereliction it is the sort of cottage that is the setting for secret childhood fantasies.

Historically it was never easy to find a crossing over the flat marshlands of the Lea. First to build one was Queen Maud, wife of Henry I, who round about 1100 erected a causeway here which bridged 5 water-courses within 600 yards. It is Queen Maud's route which is still followed today by Groves Bridge and the busy thoroughfare of Stratford High Street. Crossing this main road, our route follows the footpath known as 'Short Wall' which continues to follow the river. Towards Three Mills a water-borne alder seed has lodged itself in the concrete river wall, and has grown to tree size in this seemingly inhospitable surrounding. It sticks out from the vertical bank overhanging the river, its roots obviously penetrating far enough not only to feed its rapid upward growth but also to counterbalance its weight. There are several self-sown seedlings of false acacia attempting the same feat and a wealth of wildflowers staging a colonisation; biting stonecrop, angelica, procumbent marshwort and common osier. Giant hogweed is beginning its spread on the opposite bank and mallard rest on the tidally-revealed mud.

The end of Short Wall brings us to Three Mills, the only mills in the area which have actually survived to the present day, though even here there are two mills and not three. Mills have stood on the site for at least 900 years, for in 1134 they are recorded as having been endowed to the newly founded Abbey of Stratford Langthorne. The concentration of tidal mills in the valley led to many disputes as various millers attempted to capture a head of water for their own wheels. The illicit practices of damming or of digging new cuts either reduced the flow for other mills or raised water levels to such a height as to block the wheel altogether. To settle these disputes a 'Court of Sewers' was established, and enforced a legal depth of 4½ feet for the millers' channels. The mills ground corn for the local bakeries until 1734 when a new trade was established. In that year Peter Lefeuvre agreed with others to become 'co-partners, joint traders and dealers together in the several arts, trades or mysteries of mealmen, cornfactors, millers and distillers.' From that time on the mills ground corn to serve the distilleries.

Daniel Bisson was one of the partners in this enterprise and built the present House Mill in 1776; we approach it from behind, passing a yard overgrown with the pink-flowered Himalayan balsam. The mill has suffered neglect for many years but now the Passmore Edwards Museum Trust has bought the site and is setting about the lengthy and expensive business of restoration. Clock Mill, facing it across the flagstone way, is in better condition. It stands beside two broad channels of the Lea where mute swans swim under the old sack hoists and a causeway carries the towpath down to Bow Locks and the Limehouse Cut. Clock Mill dates from 1817, though the handsome, octagonal clock-tower is older and may well have survived from an earlier weather-boarded mill. In the 1970s the building was restored as offices for Bass Charrington, ensuring not just its survival but a historical continuity with brewing.

Mill Meads

ROUTE:
- On reaching Three Mills cross the little road to take the passage immediately opposite between Clock Mill and the distillery.
- Follow the path (Long Wall) alongside the river and then over a footbridge into Mill Meads.
- EITHER: Enter Mill Meads ahead through a gap beside the concrete piping sections. Carry on more or less ahead, keeping parallel to the river and the concrete fence off to your right. The route rejoins the riverside in the opposite right hand corner beside a pylon. Turn left to follow the path leading up to the sewer embankment. OR: On crossing the footbridge bear immediately right and follow the path between the concrete fence and the riverside. The footpath leads eventually up onto the sewer embankment. This path avoids the trail bikes on Mill Meads but becomes very overgrown in summer.
- Turn right on the North London Outfall Sewer embankment. (You might want to detour left first for another view of Abbey Mills Pumping Station.)
- After a road intersection the embankment crosses a bridge over railway and road. Immediately after the bridge look for a path and steps on the right hand side.

LOOKING AT WILDLIFE: Mill Meads has a good variety of bird life. A wide range of species including pheasant and warblers have bred here and winter visitors include finches and thrushes. Heron, grey wagtail, common sandpiper and other birds might be seen on the channels. There is an interesting flora including marshland, meadow and wasteland species and a particular plant to look for is the flixweed *Descurainia sophia*.

A hidden passage leads us on to 'Long Wall', the name of an ancient footpath which runs alongside the Channelsea River. We cross a footbridge that takes us over the Prescott Channel, an artificially created waterway which was dug as part of a major programme of flood prevention measures in the 1930s. This leads us into the open space of Mill Meads; they were once the meadows of the Stratford Langthorne Abbey, but the Abbey has long since disappeared, and the Meads are no longer the rich waterside meadows suggested by their name. Today they are a large and rather eccentric open space with the scruffy air of abandoned allotments. Trail-bikers have defeated every attempt to deny them access and roar around tracks over hummock and hollow. Despite this disturbance fox and pheasant stalk the thickets and a wide range of wild flowers occur wherever they can escape the strangling spread of bramble or Japanese knotweed. Among them are vetches, campions and cranesbills, and a number of relics of old allotment use such as tansy, asparagus and evening primrose. Along the muddy banks of the riverside are stands of yellow flag iris, Himalayan balsam and great hairy willow herb. Common sandpiper can be seen flying along the channel in the autumn migration period and later, in the winter months, the whole site will be visited by flocks of redwing, fieldfare, yellowhammers and sometimes brambling.

All this is made the more remarkable by its setting in the midst of a dense industrial concentration, a landscape of pylons, sewage works, chemical plants, gas works and tube lines. On the opposite bank are the seven 19th century gas holders of the Bromley-by-Bow gasworks. Their site has a peculiar history. In 1817 the East India Company built a factory here for the production of the first military rockets, the invention of William Congreve, designed for use by the British army in India. From 1813 there were two regular Rocket Troops in the British army supplied with Congreve's weapons and they even played a minor part in the Battle of Waterloo. Here, from the East End, came the very beginnings of rocket technology, a technology which just over a hundred years later was to send the V1s and V2s back again in far more deadly fashion.

The gas holders are listed buildings but they are cast into shade by a building on the opposite side of the Meads which has been described in its grandeur as 'the cathedral of sewage'. This name is misleading for, with its dome, coloured bricks, fancy tile-work, dressed stone, piers and columns and carved capitals, it has more the atmosphere of one of the great mosques of Istanbul. It even had minarettes once, but these outlying two-hundred foot, octagonal chimneys were demolished in World War II when it was feared they were serving as landmarks for enemy bombers. All this – and the famous interior iron work – was built to Joseph Bazalgette's design in 1865 to 1868. Its job is to pump the sewage down the Outfall Sewer to Beckton – at a rate which can rise to 600 million gallons a day in storm conditions. It is the story of this North London Outfall Sewer which begins our next walk.

To complete Walk 3:
Follow the steps down onto Manor Road and turn left to reach West Ham BR and underground station.

WALK 4: West Ham to North Woolwich

Getting Started

From Walk 3:
    Continue along sewer embankment.
From West Ham BR and tube station:
    From the station exit turn right under the railway bridges. After a short distance take the path on the right, just before another bridge, leading up to the sewer embankment.
    Turn right along the embankment.

The North London Sewer Embankment

ROUTE:
• The route follows the embankment for approximately 2½ miles, crossing several road intersections en route. The embankment path terminates at High Street South, next to the large flyover.

LOOKING AT WILDLIFE: There is little wildlife along the sewer embankment, though kestrel sometimes hover overhead and there are occasional plants of fennel or wild hop.

In 1858 as June temperatures reached 95°F the smell of raw sewage in the vicinity of the Houses of Parliament became so intense that sheets soaked in disinfectant had to be hung at all the windows. It became the 'Year of the Great Stink', brought about by the growth of the population of London, by the increasing amounts of industrial effluent and, paradoxically, by the invention of the water closet or 'flush' lavatory.

Before 1850 human waste went into cesspools which were emptied from time to time by 'nightmen'. After this year all new houses were required by law to have WCs and the contents of London's lavatories were flushed direct and untreated via storm drains into the Thames. The banks of the river were deep in sewage solids and people were said to flee in panic whenever a paddle steamer approached for fear of the stench it would produce as it stirred up the putrefying water. This was the

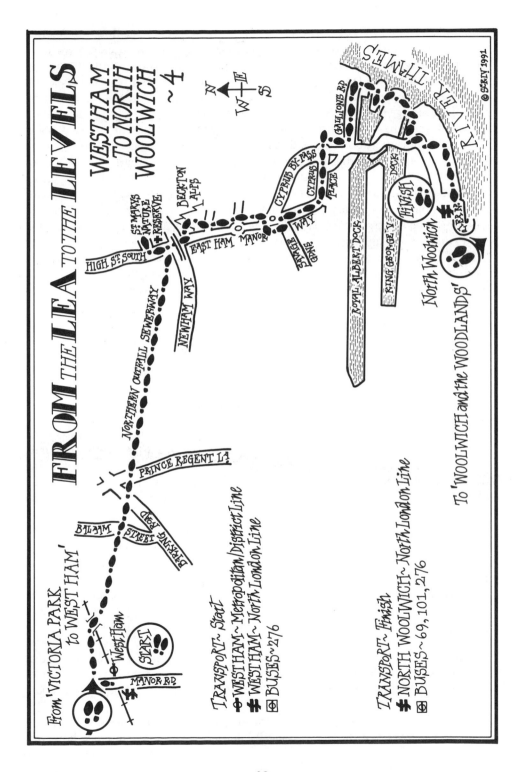

FROM THE LEA TO THE LEVELS

WESTHAM TO NORTH WOOLWICH ~4

RIVER THAMES

© SSKIY 1991

N
W — E
S

St MARYS NATURE RESERVE
BECKTON ALPS
CYPRUS BY-PASS
CYPRUS PLACE
HIGH ST. SOUTH
EAST HAM MANOR
SAVAGE WAY
GALLIONS RD
ROYAL ALBERT DOCK
KING GEORGE V DOCK
FINISH
North Woolwich

NEWHAM WAY

NORTHERN OUTFALL SEWER WAY

PRINCE REGENT L ᵅ

BALAAM STREET

BARKING ROAD

From 'VICTORIA PARK to WEST HAM'

West Ham
START
MANOR RD

To 'WOOLWICH and the WOODLANDS'

Transport~ Start
✠ WESTHAM~ Metropolitan/District Line
✚ WESTHAM~ North London Line
⊞ BUSES~276

Transport~ Finish
✚ NORTH WOOLWICH~ North London Line
⊞ BUSES ~ 69, 101, 276

– 29 –

situation when Joseph Bazalgette, engineer to the Metropolitan Board of Works, came up with his plans for the redesign of the whole system. He proposed a scheme of intercepting sewers picking up the contents of the existing storm drains and conveying them away to the east of London to a huge disposal works at Beckton, East Ham. Through three miles of roof tops and terraced housing, our route follows that of the sewage along the North London Outfall Sewer.

West Ham, where this journey starts, was originally a hamlet in the countryside beyond London. Between 1841 and 1911 it saw its population grow from 13,000 to 289,000. It became, during this period, the eighth largest town in the whole of England and Wales. The greatest impetus for the development of industry in the area had been the 1844 Metropolitan Buildings Act, which placed severe restrictions upon 'noxious trades' within London. West Ham was just outside the jurisdiction of the Act so the noxious trades came flocking here instead, further encouraged by the cheap price of land and the availability of water transport.

By the end of the century 335 firms in chemicals, gas, engineering, shipbuilding, sugar refining, metalwork and confectionery had established themselves in a belt along the Thames from the Lea to North Woolwich. The first waves of residential development to house the increasing numbers of workers were the small townships of South West Ham – Canning Town, Hallsville, Silvertown, North Woolwich. Each one was tied to a particular industry or even to an individual works. The development of the northern part of the Borough came when the building of the railways made commuting possible – to and from the City or the industries alongside the Thames. The arrival of a slightly better-off class of skilled workman encouraged the building of terraced housing in this part of the Borough, and with this came the break-up of the last rural estates.

The line of the sewer embankment is a line right through West Ham's social history. To the south is the concentration of industry and the earlier, poorer, shabbier shanty-towns. To the north are the slightly later, slightly better-off working class communities such as Plaistow, West Ham and Forest Gate. But being outside the City boundaries, none of the Borough was connected to the great sewer line which had cut it in half, and 'bubbling and seething cesspools' remained a feature of the area. The construction of the West Ham Pumping Station, to lift the local sewage into the Northern Outfall system, marks the eventual rectification of this injustice. Unpretentious but quietly handsome, it can be seen back to the left where our route first joins the embankment.

Continuing to our right, we soon pass two adjacent areas of open space; the Memorial Recreation Ground and the East London Cemetery. The flat expanse of playing fields here was originally laid out on a site known as Pigswell Fields, by Arnold Mills, the last President of the Thames Ironworks. This great shipyard below Canning Town, which closed in 1912, once supported several football teams. One of these teams was to evolve into West Ham United who played the first four years of their professional life here until moving to Upton Park in 1904. The site was taken over by West Ham Council in 1924.

The East London Cemetery, except for the fairly wild strip alongside the sewer embankment is one of the more scenically dull of London's cemeteries; however, financially it must have been more attractive. It was developed by the East London Cemetery Company in 1872. 'The population of the surrounding neighbourhood,' they pointed out with some relish in their share prospectus, 'is 150,000, and the death returns for the year 1868 was over 3,000.'

Particularly good for business was the Princess Alice disaster, one of the worst civilian disasters in British history. On 3 September 1878 the Princess Alice, a pleasure steamer, was returning from a day trip to Tilbury laden with holiday makers. At 7.40pm it rounded Tripcock Point into Gallions Reach, and turned directly under the bows of the Bywell Castle, a collier. The Princess Alice was cut in two and sunk within five minutes. The full number of dead was never ascertained but it exceeded 650. The official monument to the incident is in the Woolwich Cemetery, but the graves of many of the victims are here at West Ham.

There is a monument in the Cemetery to the victims of another of the many disasters which have afflicted the working people of East and West Ham. Opposite the main entrance is a large slab bearing a ship's anchor, which commemorates the events at the Thames Ironworks in June 1898 when thousands gathered to watch the launch of the battleship HMS Albion. As the ship hit the water the ten foot wave it threw up swept away part of the staging erected around the slip. Two hundred women and children, the families of the men who had built the ship, were swept into the water with it.

There is yet another, and even more central, chapter in Newham history for which this graveyard is significant. During World War II 3221 'devices' were dropped on West Ham alone. It was almost the first target for enemy bombers flying in from the Channel, attempting to smash both the industrial base and civilian morale. The docks burnt for days on end. The shipyards and gasworks were ablaze. Even the sewer line was hit and spilt out its contents onto Manor Road, and 27 per cent of all West Ham housing was destroyed. Among the acres of simple slabs erected here are many for the victims of that period.

Looking out across Newham from the elevation of the embankment a whole new generation of slabs reveals itself beyond, echoing those in the cemetery. They are the tower blocks, themselves a secondary consequence of the blitz. The post-war councils were faced with an enormous problem of rehousing. The answer, to some, seemed to be to build high. This idea was opposed by residents and by sections of the Council but by the early 1950s the first ten-storey blocks were going up. In 1952 the Housing committee of West Ham had written to Harold Macmillan, then Minister for Housing, enquiring whether government subsidies 'could not operate to favour low rise rather than high rise housing'. Macmillan replied that; 'there is an unwarrantable prejudice against flats so that excessive amounts of land are being consumed in the provision of low densities of ordinary housing. The national interest demands that this should be curbed.' By the 1960s the Council, encouraged by government subsidies and a new Borough Architect, was espousing the idea with enthusiasm and building blocks of up to 22 storeys. In 1965 the process was speeded up still further with the introduction of prefabrication and the new Lars-Nielsen system of factory production. Eventually 21,000 people were living in 110 tower blocks making this the most dense concentration of such homes in London.

One of these tenants was Mrs Ivy Hodge. On 16 May 1968 she got up at 5.50 am on the 18th floor of Ronan Point and lit her gas-cooker. The explosion which followed blew out the load-bearing wall. Like a collapsing house of cards the corner rooms of Ronan Point, from floor 22 downwards, flipped one on top of the other. Five people died and seventeen were injured.

Amazingly, tenants were moved back into a repaired Ronan Point and it took many more years of campaigning by the Tower Blocks Tenants Campaign and their consultant architect Sam Webb, to bring an end to high-rise housing. In 1984 cracks began to appear in the load-bearing walls of the blocks and walls began to part company with floors. In order to put tenants' minds at rest the Council used an empty flat to carry out what they called a 'controlled fire test'. After twenty minutes the fire brigade were called in to bring the test to a premature close. Within a few weeks the tenants had been moved out again, and this time it was for good.

Ronan Point was just the first. Now more and more of Newham's tower blocks are evacuated and awaiting demolition. At the cost of 5 deaths, 17 injuries, millions of pounds and years of campaigning the people's 'unwarrantable prejudice' has been recognised as real.

St Mary's and the Beckton Alps

ROUTE:
- The embankment route ends at High Street South, the busy main road with a flyover to the right. Cross the road and turn left up the High Street and take the first right into Norman Road to reach East Ham Nature Reserve.
- After visiting the reserve and churchyard, retrace your steps down High Street South, continuing under the flyover into East Ham Manor Way.
- Take the path on the left which zig-zags to the viewing platform at the top of Beckton Alps.
- Retrace your steps down the path to the junction near the bottom and carry on straight ahead here to reach Alpine Way beside the ski centre.
- Cross the road (Alpine Way) and follow the path opposite, ignoring the subway to the right, to reach a roundabout on the main road. Cross Winsor Terrace and continue ahead along East Ham Manor Way.
- Just before a second roundabout, curve right along a cycle/pedestrian track. Go straight across a mini-roundabout back into East Ham Manor Way.
- Continue ahead to next roundabout and turn left into Cyprus Place. Where the road bends left, follow the path off to the right, to reach the large roundabout with a pumping station on the central island.

FACILITIES: There is a pub and restaurant in the ski centre at the base of the ski run. Pub on Cyprus Way.

LOOKING AT WILDLIFE: A wide range of plants, birds, insects and bats in the inature reserve and panoramic views from the top of Beckton Alps. East Ham

Nature Reserve is open during daylight hours on weekdays and from 2 to 5 at weekends. The Interpretative Centre is open Saturdays and Sundays from 2 to 5.

Beside the East Ham High Road, with its graveyard overshadowed by the fly-over, the church of St. Mary Magdalene manages to retain an atmosphere of village calm and parish prosperity. So long as even a hint of the marshes remains, there persists here that dark sturdiness of the churches of Romney or the Isle of Grain. The church was established in the 12th century, and much still remains from that time, making it one of the most complete Norman churches in London. It is constructed, as a 1931 survey describes it, of 'rubble walling held together by Norman mortar – Kentish rag, flint and chalk from Purley, Caen stone from Normandy and ancient Roman tiles'. From this structure arises a low, solid tower supported by five foot thick walls with a buttress at each angle.

The parish of East Ham had no more than 70 households when it was built, yet it was prosperous enough to support not only the church but also a resident hermit. In the north west corner of the church exterior are the remains of an anchorite cell – a small door cut through the original Norman stonework of the sanctuary. Over the opening of the door three holes were found containing the remains of wooden pegs which once would have supported a basketwork screen. The supplicants of East Ham would have come down to this church on the edge of the marshes to make their confession through the lowered screen, or to deposit gifts of food for a hermit who was to leave here in neither life nor death. In the course of time, and in accordance with tradition, he was buried beneath the earthen floor of his own cell.

This large, peaceful churchyard was declared a nature reserve in 1976 and has been administered since by the Passmore Edwards Museum Trust. Within its 9 acres bats, foxes and 17 species of butterfly have been recorded. Lesser whitethroat have bred here, spotted flycatchers nest every year and goldfinches raise large numbers of young from nests in the lime trees along the High Street boundary. Other visitors include kestrel, pheasant, bullfinch and greenfinch, with long-tailed tits, redpoll and linnet in winter. The large stands of rose-bay willow herb, which are home to the caterpillars of the elephant hawk moth also provide one of the few locations for a tiny and undramatic but nonetheless rare moth, known as *Mompha nodicolella*. Its larvae cause small swellings or galls in the stems of the willow herbs while the adult moth, according to the Nature Trail booklet, may be seen during the summer months 'doing a sort of circular dance on the tombstones'.

In 1983 the Nature Reserve opened its own Interpretive Centre. In the same year, on the other side of the flyover, the Docklands Development Corporation was landscaping, at the cost of £2.4 million, the 'highest man-made hill in London'. The 246 foot slag heap formed from the waste products of the Beckton Gas Works was being turned into the 'Beckton Alps'. From the top, on a clear day, you can scan London from Epping Forest to Shooters Hill while to the east the river valley opens up to form the industrial Thames estuary and an ever-broadening approach to the sea. You can also see something of the planners' dream for docklands: the 'district' parks, the 'luxury' housing, the water sports 'complexes', the traffic 'interchanges', the 'amenity' areas and the superstores – those now familiar features which attempt to create a community yet which can never give a sense of place or time.

Beckton gets its name from Samuel Adams Beck, or more properly, from the gas-works which he founded. It was one of the mightiest of industrial undertakings, the largest gas-works in the world. From the slag heap it stretched east to the river and south down to the Royal Docks, occupying a space larger than the City of London. In 1860 Beck was appointed governor of the Gas, Light and Coke Co, and used the powers made available by the newly passed Metropolitan Gas Act to buy up numerous small gas companies and establish a local monopoly. Beginning with four retort houses adjacent to Gallions Reach, where colliers ships unloaded direct from the Thames, it grew to the point where one million tons of coal were being imported annually to supply fourteen retort houses producing 63 million cubic feet of gas a day.

For the workers there was a model village, a 'busy if not altogether lovely colony', according to an 1870 *Illustrated London News*, 'often enveloped in its own private fog'. This was the fog of the retort-house furnaces where temperatures reached 2000 to 3000°F. The work of the stokers at their doors was described in *Pearsons Magazine* in 1896:

> It is terrible work this incessant stoking at the furnace doors ... simultaneously three retort doors are thrown open. A wave of tremendous heat rushes forth and with long rakes the silent strenuous figures of the men draw forth the glowing coke. The fiery shower at once falls onto the floor beneath, the furnace being instantaneously refilled with coal, shovelfull after shovelfull being hurled inside, to be apparently at once consumed, so terrific is the heat.

One of these young gas stokers was Will Thorne, who went on to become an outstanding working class leader. He had little formal education and was reputedly taught to read by Eleanor Marx, the daughter of Karl. He was a founder of the National Union of Gas Workers and General Labourers, which had 30,000 members within six months of its inaugural meeting in West Ham. He led the unsuccesful gas workers strike of 1889 – a forerunner by only a few months of the national dock strike – and was elected to West Ham Council in 1894. In 1906 he became Labour MP for South West Ham by which time West Ham had become the first ever socialist-controlled local authority in the country.

Competition from electricity and the introduction of North Sea gas spelt the end for Beckton Gas Works and the last of the retort houses was closed in 1967. The remants of the buildings are rapidly being reduced as the dockland development proceeds, though at the time of writing there still remains a jagged and half-demolished collection of pinnacles and spires, like some eccentric architect's conception of a cathedral. During the years of its decay the gas-works site became home to a wealth of wildlife. Black redstart and little owl nested in the abandoned buildings; short-eared owls hunted here in winter, while pheasants wandered over the wasteland and skylarks sung overhead; wormwood and toadflax, poppies and stonecrops, orange hawkweed and mignonette bloomed on the clinker and among them lived a species of beetle completely new to Britain. Bit by bit they have all been driven away as the sterility of a highly-planned human reclamation swallows up the vibrance and abundance of an unplanned natural one.

The Royal Docks

ROUTE:
- Follow the roundabout to the right. Ignore the first exit immediately to your right and also the second exit, to take the small road beyond it. Follow ahead and then to your left along Gallions Road. NOTE: The footpath through the docks is still a public right of way, though not all the security personnel may be aware of this. There are plans to extinguish this right of way and to open up new paths along the riverside and the situation is continually changing.
- At the end of Gallions Road the footpath begins on the right between two concrete posts, alongside the fence.
- The footpath crosses the dock gates and continues on the other side between two wire fences. It then bears left to reach the river, crosses a second set of dock gates and bears right to regain Woolwich Manor Way.

LOOKING AT WILDLIFE: Waders, wildfowl, grebes, gulls, heron and cormorant along the river and sometimes in the dock basins. An interesting flora along the path.

The docks of the 'Royal' group belong to a second great period of dock-building in London. The first, up-river, docks were built in the age of sail by sea-faring or city men. The new docks were built by a new generaiton of tycoons, who were exploiting the possibilities of steam, railways and telegraph. Among them was George Parker Bidder, who had been the engineer for the scheme which brought the railway from the City to North Woolwich. In the course of this project he and his contractor-associates had acquired large areas of marshland from Barking Road down to the Thames.

In 1850 work began on this land for the Royal Victoria Dock, and by 1855 it was already a flourishing concern. By 1870 however even this new dock was proving too small for the newest vessels. Furthermore it was on the west side of a broad peninsula and by building to the east four miles could be cut from the journey into London. Bidder's original intention was to link the Victoria Dock to Gallions Reach by canal but, the original contractors having gone bankrupt, it was not until the 1870s that the London and St Katherine Dock Co took up the scheme again. At this point the idea of the canal expanded to become the Royal Albert Dock, which opened in 1880 and was, in its day, the finest and largest in the world. It was the first dock to be supplied with electricity, had its own direct rail link to the City, and made the dock basin accessible to ships of up to 12,000 tons.

The earliest docks had been built of stone and were intended to be durable; however, under the new doctrine of 'progress', implying rapid change, the Royal docks were built with a definite and limited life-span in mind. The emphasis was to be on a fast 'turn around'. Instead of the multi-storeyed warehouses which provided the storage facilities of the traditional Port of London, these docks were lined with single-storey transit-sheds through which goods were to pass for immediate dispatch. The Royal Docks group was completed by the building of the King George V Dock in 1921. One of the first works of the newly established Port of London Authority, it could accommodate ships of over 30,000 tons. Together the group constituted 10 miles of quays and 250 acres of water, one of the largest areas of impounded water in the world.

Gallions Road, on its route down to the river, passes the attractive eccentricity of the Gallions Hotel. This stands in a haunted semi-dereliction, its tall red-brick chimneys decorated with hand-cut mouldings, its walls with plaster friezes and hung red tiles; it has domed turrets, roof gables, dormer windows and a mounted weather vane. It was built to serve passengers leaving on P & O liners from the Royal Albert Dock, who arrived at 'Gallions Station' on boat trains from the main line. A subway led direct from the hotel onto the quay. Nothing could have been more romantic than setting out for a long sea journey from here.

The strange and winding footpath from Gallions Road passes right through dockland territory and crosses the lock gates at the entrance basins of both the Albert and the George V docks. This stretch of the river is known as Gallions Reach because of the Venetian galleys which once sailed up here. From the foreshore you can see across to the little light which marks Tripcock Point where the Princess Alice went down. Behind it are the grounds of the Royal Arsenal, largely abandoned but still littered with unexploded ammunition and protected by the Official Secrets Act.

The journey along the foreshore passes many good spots for 'Thames watching' and an ever-increasing variety of gulls, waders and wildfowl are using the river right up to the Pool. Heron sometimes stand on the mudflats whilst shoveler, teal, wigeon, pochard, tufted duck and shelduck are all present at times. The ubiquitous mallard and coot are there too, their numbers sometimes reaching the thousands. Among the waders redshank, spotted redshank, greenshank, common sandpiper, ringed plover and little ringed plover occur, as do all the commoner species of gull, Canada geese, great crested grebes and mute swans. The birds have the river much to themselves now. The dock trade has gone and even the future of the ferry is uncertain. At dusk, with the tide on the turn, the river can be quiet as a pond and sparkling with the reflected lights of industry. Small brown waders run about like automatons on the mud-banks, gradually becoming indistinct, while little groups of duck gather nervously about the lock gates and the occasional greater black-backed gull looms large and dramatic overhead. This is when the cormorants fly purposefully up-river keeping low over the water and making for their roosts on the reservoirs.

The path is also interesting botanically, supporting wild parsnip, wormwood, asparagus, white campion, everlasting pea, toadflax and at least two species of stonecrop. From the two dock entrance basins it leads us alongside the derelict site of the old Harland and Wolff shipyards and hence back onto Woolwich Manor Way.

North Woolwich

ROUTE:

● On reaching Woolwich Manor Way a short detour to the right leads onto a bridge with an excellent panorama of the dock basins and the City Airport. The main route is to the left.

● Follow Manor Way and take the first turning on the left (Barge House Road). Follow it to the end to gain the riverside path and follow the path to the right and then into the Royal Victoria Gardens.

● Follow the riverside through the gardens and leave them beside the Royal Pavilion pub. Climb the steps beyond the pub to reach North Woolwich BR station and buses. To join next walk take the subway under the river from its entrance near the station.

FACILITIES: Royal Pavilion Hotel public house is at the end of the walk.

LOOKING AT WILDLIFE: More views of Thames wildlife from the riverside path.

North Woolwich is a strange and isolated area of industry and housing cut off from the rest of London by the river and the huge expanse of the docks. For hundreds of years it was also a geographical anomaly. In 1086, Hamon, a Norman noble, became Sheriff of Kent. He happened to own two properties on this, the opposite side of the river, in what was then Essex, and succeeded in redrawing the county boundaries to add these two detached segments of his manorial estate into the county over which he had control. Thus they became North Woolwich, and remained administratively part of Kent, and then of Woolwich Borough Council, until 1965, the year of the major reorganisation of the London boroughs. Only then was North Woolwich put back properly onto the north bank and incorporated with East Ham and West Ham into the new borough of Newham.

The area was in fact nothing but marshland providing cattle grazing until Bidder brought the Stratford and Thames Junction Railway here in 1847. By connecting his railway to the steam ferry he planned to provide the fastest route from South London into the city but in 1849 the opening of the Greenwich and Woolwich Railway took away much of his trade, and he proposed instead the residential development of the area. In 1850 he came up with another idea and opened the Royal Pavilion Gardens as an inducement to visitors to use his railway.

The Thames-side walk from the end of Barge House Road leads us through the Royal Victoria Gardens and on to the Royal Pavilion Hotel. Now a public house it was originally an integral part of the Pavilion Gardens, once a major entertainment site for working-class Londoners. Inside it still retains, though in a very down-at-heel way, the air of the music hall and supper-club. In the adjacent gardens up to 17,000 people might arrive by train or steamboat in a single day to see such events as 'Henry Coxwell's balloon ascents', 'Jean Price and Gevani' on trapeze, the Volunteer Band on the esplanade or the ballet 'Le Démon de Paradis'.

By the 1880s the gardens were in decline, and they were put up for sale in 1885. A movement arose to save them as a 'breathing space for the occupants of these very dreary localities'. and they were eventually purchased on the proceeds of the City of London's coal and wine duties, and with donations from a variety of charities and private individuals including £50 from Queen Victoria herself. They were re-opened by the London County Council as the Royal Victoria Gardens in 1890, and still provide a quietly pleasant conclusion to this stretch of the walk – though not the climactic one we might have expected in the days when this was the site of splashing fountains, flashing illuminations, a rifle gallery, a ballroom, a marquee, several stages, refreshment rooms, an Italian garden, and a dancing platform complete with its own full orchestra.

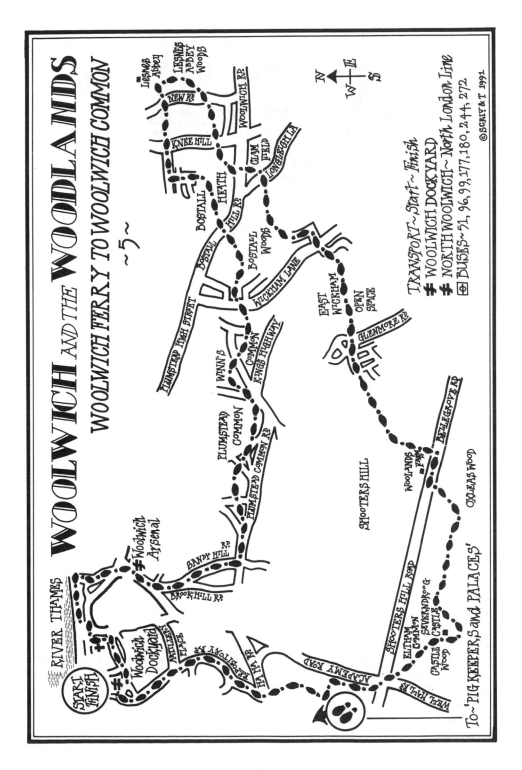

WOOLWICH AND THE WOODLANDS

WOOLWICH FERRY TO WOOLWICH COMMON

~5~

TRANSPORT~ Start ~ Finish

Woolwich Dockyard

North Woolwich~ North London Line

BUSES~ 51, 96, 99, 177, 180, 244, 272

©SCRIV & T 1991

To~ 'PIG KEEPERS and PALACES'

3. WOOLWICH AND THE WOODLANDS

WOOLWICH, PLUMSTEAD AND ABBEY WOOD

I t was the Thames that shaped Woolwich: a little fishing village set below a bend in the river and surrounded by marshes. In prehistoric times it had been a bigger, shallower river set in its own huge flood-plain. Gradually, as the river aged, it cut deeper and straighter, down to its present course and level, leaving a line of steep terrace slopes behind it. They remain a distinctive part of the topography today, running up from the river levels, through Greenwich, Charlton, Woolwich and Plumstead, to plateaux topped with estuarine sands and gravels. It is the soils of these terrace tops which have given rise to the line of commons running from Blackheath to Bostall Woods.

If the first great influence was geography, the second and more recent was the military. It was war and the threat of war which turned Woolwich from a village into a town and gave it a period of prosperity. It began with the navy. In 1512 Henry VIII chose this site for his royal dockyard and within two years this previously insignificant village became the launching place of the greatest ship in the world, Henry Grace a Dieu or Great Harry. For three hundred years thereafter Woolwich was our great naval dockyard until sail and oak gave way to steam and iron and Woolwich gave way to Tyne and Clyde. By 1869, and with great consequent unemployment, Woolwich was finished as a shipyard. But by this time the army had arrived in the Borough.

Throughout the 18th century the Royal Arsenal at Woolwich grew to become the largest munitions works in the country. The whole economy of Woolwich became dependent upon it. The Royal Artillery Company moved here, the Royal Military Academy and the military hospitals were sited here, the marshes were taken over for testing and storing munitions, the commons for drilling and exercising the troops. Even the coat of arms of Woolwich was military: a shield with three cannons.

There is a less-well known story which runs alongside this, a story which turns the history of Woolwich into something more than a set of regimental memoirs. It is the story of the people whose lives and work were dependent upon the Arsenal, of the 'dust hole' and the 'smoke hole', of the 'peace Arsenal' and of the formation of one of the country's most successful co-operative organisations. For these people the commons were their countryside. Yet this unique area of heathland, a treasure of London's open space and one of its most important wildlife sites, was only saved for the public after a long-running battle with the War Office. It was a battle which culminated in riots, arrest and imprisonment.

Today the area is again under threat. The Ministry of Transport intends to build here the approach road to the East London River Crossing. This will decimate heaths, woods, parks and the nearest working farm to Central London. The government attitude seems to be that open space is space without value and, despite the findings of their own official enquiry, successive Secretaries of State have refused to sanction even the compromise proposal of tunneling under sections of the woodland. Thus, this chapter takes us through a unique corner of London which, for the second time in its history, is under threat of imminent destruction.

This chapter covers a single walk beginning and ending at Woolwich. From Woolwich Ferry it covers 9½ miles and links directly into the next chapter at Woolwich Common. There are some steep ascents and sections of the walk can be muddy. It can however be treated as a single circular walk, 10½ miles long, beginning and ending at Woolwich Ferry.

Sections of this walk will be very much affected by the building of the proposed East London River Crossing Route. At the time of writing the future of the road is under consideration following an appeal to the European Court. Walkers should be aware of the possibility of very significant changes to the route described, but it has been retained both because it is unique in character and because it illustrates so much of what this book is about – the struggle for the future of London.

WALK 5: Woolwich Ferry to Woolwich Common

Getting Started

From Woolwich Dockyard Station:

Turn left from station entrance along Belson Road. At the end take a left and a right onto St Mary's Street.

Carry on ahead to find entrance to St Mary's Gardens on the left.

Fork right in the gardens and carry on past the church to reach the gate in the far corner. Turn right on the walkway and descend to the roundabout.

Cross the main roads to the diametrically opposite corner of the roundabout and continue ahead for a few yards up Woolwich High Street.

Turn left down Glass Yard to reach the foot tunnel entrance and the riverside.

From buses:

Alight at roundabout at Ferry Approach.

Walk a few yards along Woolwich High Street and turn left down Glass Yard beside the Leisure Centre to reach the foot tunnel entrance and the riverside.
From North Woolwich (buses and BR) and from Walk 4:
Take the foot tunnel under the river.

From the Dust Hole

ROUTE:
- From the foot tunnel follow the riverside path, until it reaches the brick wall of the Royal Arsenal perimeter and turns inland.
- Turn left at the road (Warren Lane).
- Carry on to the main road (Beresford Street) and cross by the pelican crossing and enter Beresford Square through the old Arsenal gateway.

FACILITIES: Toilets, pubs and cafés on Beresford Square.

LOOKING AT WILDLIFE: Duck, waders and cormorant on the Thames.

'**T**he dirtiest, filthiest, and most thoroughly mismanaged town of its size in the kingdom'. This was Woolwich in 1847 and its dirtiest, filthiest, and most notorious quarter was the maze of little streets squeezed into the space between Woolwich High Street and the river. Here in a jumble of dilapidated homes, pubs and low lodging houses, up to five families were living in a single room using blankets as partitions for their only shred of privacy. This was the 'Dusthole', where soldiers were forbidden and police afraid to enter. The only solution the authorities could come up with was demolition, and by 1912 it had all gone, making way for Ferry Approach and a new power station. Today the site is a neat riverside path and leisure complex – the stock in trade of 20th century planning replacing the chaos of unplanned streets. One or two of their names, like Bell Water Gate and Ship and Half Moon Passage, is all that remains.

It is Ship and Half Moon Passage which leads us inland from the river, along the high brick boundary wall of the Royal Arsenal and onto Warren Lane. The Warren was the original name for this area of marshes, which being only half a mile from the Royal Dockyards was convenient as a site for military stores. During the reign of Charles II, when the Dutch fleet was penetrating the Thames Estuary, the site was fortified and from then it was to grow in both size and importance. The Royal Laboratory for the 'manufacture of fireworks and gunpowder', established earlier in the century, moved here in 1695, and by 1717 the government had established a brass foundry and was also manufacturing its own guns here. From this time the character, if not yet the name, of the Royal Arsenal was established.

There were major extensions to the Arsenal throughout the 19th century and many of the new buildings erected during this period were the work of convicts housed in hulks on the river. These men and women, who lived and died on the hulks, and whose graves dotted the adjacent marshes, gave their name to a flower.

The little purple dead-nettle grows abundantly on disturbed ground and from its frequency on the prisoners' graves it earned the local name of 'convict's flower'.

The growth of the Arsenal mirrored the growth in the size and scale of warfare. It reached its greatest size during the Great War. By 1918 it covered 1,200 acres, with a multitude of buildings, its own canal and railway and a workforce of 75,000. The ups and downs of the industry had a profound effect upon the economy of Woolwich. During the Napoleonic Wars the local population grew by 73 per cent; during the Crimean Wars nearby Plumstead tripled in size; and during the Boer War the grand Town Hall was erected. Conversely, the end of the First World War was to lead to unemployment, poverty and recession. Dismissals at this time were so rapid that the Superintendant of Women Workers shook farewell with 30,000 hands in a week. He had to wear his arm in a sling for a fortnight.

It was amidst the turmoil of this time, with columns of the newly unemployed women workers marching on Whitehall, that the Peace Arsenal campaign was launched. It was based, as workers testified to a government committee, on the wish to change from 'the manufacture of the instruments of death to the repairing of the colossal wastage caused by the greatest tragedy of all time'. The campaign had some success and for a time alternative work was undertaken. Railway wagons and lorries were repaired, GPO equipment, milk churns and dairy appliances, penny blanks and medals, and most importantly 100 locomotives were built here. But it was not enough, and the government's commitment to the scheme had been superficial, its purpose being to reduce the threat of public upheaval. Within a few years workers were being laid off again, including the disabled ex-servicemen who had been promised employment. The total number of workers dropped to 20,000 and by 1922 the brave experiment was discontinued.

The workers made other and more lasting contributions to peacetime pursuits. The engineers, for example, ran their own professional football team. By 1912, it had become too expensive for them to support, and moved as an independent club to Islington. There, as the Arsenal, it became one of the great clubs of British soccer. The workforce also founded its own co-operative trading organisation with the name of the Royal Arsenal Co-operative Society. This society wielded an influence over the whole of South East London and its story recurs several times in the course of this chapter.

The shrunken Woolwich Arsenal of today is divided into two areas. The older, finer buildings are all on the western fringe and good views of these can be had from the old gateway on Beresford Street where a plaque marks out the main buildings, including the Royal Laboratory and the brass foundry. From this area of official buildings the major part of the Arsenal stretches away onto the marshes to the east. In twenty 'Danger Huts', built of light iron sheeting lined with matchwood, workers stuffed shells with gunpowder. This was high-risk work and in the worst incident in 1903 sixteen workers were killed when one of the Danger Huts exploded. Beyond these were the moated 'tumps' where the munitions were stored. From this area, 500 acres were handed over to the GLC in 1967 and used for building the Thamesmead New Town. 'Tump 53' survives and has been transformed into a nature reserve administered by the London Wildlife Trust.

The Master General of Ordnance under George IV was the Marquis of Beresford and both Beresford Road and Beresford Square are named after him. The fine but dilapidated archway leading into the square was once the Arsenal's main gateway and thousands of workers poured out from here every evening into the market. The original Woolwich market was sited in the old town and the Beresford Square market grew up as a popular unoffical alternative. The local Board made various attempts over the years to crush it but it was their own market which disappeared while the unofficial version prospered. Its heyday was in the years before the First World War, and in his book *The Woolwich Story*, E. Jefferson gives a brilliant and detailed account of an evening in the market at that time. Among the hundreds of stalls lit by swaying oil lamps there was, for example, old Ebenezer Gunter:

> ... a man whose life ambition was apparently to eliminate the hacking cough and eradicate pimples on the face. Short and bearded, he was a wily old bird who really enjoyed his weekly swindle. He had a humour which suffered him to be the butt of witty hecklers in the audience because he knew that in the end he would sell them cough sweets or ointment at a price out of all proportion to their costs ... His ointment compounded of petroleum jelly with a little almond oil and a lot of beguiling speech met with an equally good reception and while doing nobody any harm did Mr. Gunter a lot of good. That is why we do not see him this evening - he now spends his days in comfortable retirement at the seaside.

From the smoke hole

ROUTE:
- Cross Beresford Square to leave on the left on the far side of the Ordnance Arms. Turn right onto Woolwich New Road.
Keep straight ahead through Gordon Square and a short distance beyond it turn left into Anglesea Road then immediately right into Brookhill Road.
- At the next junction bear left again into Sandy Hill Road. At the junction at the top of the hill carry on straight ahead and continue to the major junction (Plumstead Common Road/Edge Hill).
- Turn left and continue ahead to reach Plumstead Common on the left. Take the first path onto the common and keep straight ahead, following it to the first road across the common (Green Chain Walk signs).
- Cross the road and continue on the footpath through a second section of common and a recreational area.
- Cross a second road and a small section of common ahead to reach the corner and the stump of the windmill above the pub.
- Follow Old Mill Road along the side of the common and at the corner of Chestnut Rise take the path heading off diagonally on the right towards the hollow.
- Follow the path down into the Slade and up the other side. Turn left on the road then right, following the Green Chain Walk posts across the grass, around the perimeter of the children's play area and through a smaller hollow ahead.
- Follow parallel to the main road across this part of the common (Winns Common

Road) to its end. Turn right along Grosmont Road and carry on ahead at the end of the terrace of houses until reaching the signposted, gravel path leading down through trees on the left to reach Wickham Lane. (Proposed East London River Crossing Route follows line of Wickham Lane.)

FACILITIES: Pubs and toilets on Plumstead Common.

LOOKING AT WILDLIFE: Tits, finches, kestrels and jays on the commons. Many indications of the gravelly Blackheath beds. 'Fairy rings' of field mushrooms on Winns Common.

The enlarged Gordon Square, fronting the solid and worthy offices of the Woolwich Equitable Building Society, was for many years not so much a square as a hole in the ground. It was an open-topped railway cutting through which steam trains ran into Woolwich Arsenal Station. It was named the 'smoke hole' by the surrounding traders whose wares were constantly being coated with soot. Eventually tailor Thomas Brown organised a protest petition which was signed by 20,000 people. By 1928 the campaign had been won, the 'smoke hole' was covered over and the newly created square named after General Gordon, who had been born in Woolwich.

From the square the streets take us up to the steep slopes of the Thames terraces. The lower parts of the slopes are chiefly composed of Thanet sands, a fine loamy sand, pale grey to buff in colour, which was dug for the manufacture of bottle glass. It gave its name to Sandy Hill Road and the water, which sank through the sand to emerge as a spring at the bottom, to Brookhill Road. These steep river-cut slopes of London are always attractive, airy places with fine views. What is unusual about this one is, as Charles Booth noted in 1902, 'it is one of the few districts in London where the workman has made the sides and crests of the steep hills his own.' Elsewhere they were all colonised by the city's wealthier inhabitants.

The beds of Thanet sands are topped by the stonier Woolwich and Reading beds and these in turn by the Blackheath beds, a mixture of sands and shingle. They gave rise to stony, acid soils which were unsuitable for cultivation and remained instead as heathland covered with gorse and broom and tough wiry grasses. Their status as common lands was unchallenged for hundreds of years. Until, in fact, the 1870s.

This was the era of the Franco-Prussian War and a time therefore of further military expansion. The War Office had already acquired Woolwich Common for drilling and exercising the Royal Artillery Company and was now on the lookout for more land. The rights to the Plumstead Commons were held by Queens College, Oxford who, having already failed once that year to enclose the land now entered into a private deal with the War Office. The commons were fenced off, the public excluded and the boots of marching feet turned the grassy tracts into a waste land. All protests to the War Office and the Metropolitan Board of Works were ignored and on 1 July 1876, 10,000 Woolwich citizens assembled in Beresford Square and marched under the leadership of John de Morgan up to the common. The new fences and gates were torn down and thrown onto a bonfire. The Fire Brigade arrived to put it out, were greeted with a hail of stones and retreated. John de Morgan was arrested and taken away to Maidstone Jail. Seventeen days later his sentence was revoked and he was out again. Within a few weeks he was at the head of another march onto the common and this time it was effigies of public officials which were burnt. Within 18 months Parliament was passing the Plumstead Common Act and the common lands were saved.

There are actually two areas of common here, separated from each other by a hollow known as the Slade. To the west is Plumstead Common proper and its most interesting feature today, apart from the views, is the sail-less stump of one of London's few windmills. The first mill here was built in 1636 but in 1763 during a violent storm it was tailwinded and toppled over. The miller narrowly escaped with his life but a visiting customer was blown from a ladder and subsequently died. When James Groom opened the present mill in 1764 he also obtained a licence to sell ale from his house, part of which he converted into a drinking parlour. The mill closed in 1847 and the turret was removed in 1853, but the ale-house remains more or less intact today and is still open for business. Beyond it the common falls away into the Slade where the River Wogebourne cut a deep coomb on its way from Shooters Hill down to the Thames. Only the somewhat neglected pond now testifies to its existence.

The second common is Winns Common named after a one-time tenant of the Old Workhouse. Here there are dark green circles in the grass created by the 'fairy rings' of the field mushroom, and a prehistoric tumulus incongruously surrounded by rugby pitches. Beyond, the path dips down the attractively wooded slope of Bleak Hill – not bleak at all – into the valley which separates the commons from the long stretches of Bostall and Lesnes Abbey Woods.

From the dene hole

ROUTE:
- Cross Wickham Lane to follow the green corridor almost opposite, leading up to the woods. On entering the woods turn left at the first crossing (leaving the Green Chain Walk signs).
- Follow the broad track which climbs and then descends towards a road. Where the path finally curves round onto the road leave it to climb the grassy slope opposite.
- On reaching the first crossing of paths turn left down a flight of steps to the road.
- Turn right and cross the main road and just before the bus shelter take the trodden path on the left which runs steeply up the hill. Follow the path to the distinct grassy plateau at the top of the hill. Bear left across the open space to the bench in the far left hand corner.
- Follow the path which leads down through the woods from here. At the bottom, just before the road, turn right on the path along the backs of houses.
- Leave the main path which swings to the right, keeping straight ahead to a T junction. Turn left here. You will have passed a low concrete retaining wall off to your left.

- Follow the path ahead which runs along the side of the slope, keeping parallel to the backs of houses, until you come to a path on your left which leads between the houses to the road.
- Turn right on the road (Commonwealth Way) and at the end turn right again onto Federation Road. Pass the entrance to the campsite to reach Knee Hill.

FACILITIES: Co-operative Woods Camp and Caravan Site is on Federation Road, Abbey Wood, SE2 OLS (tel 01 310 2233). It is open for camping from Easter to the end of October.

LOOKING AT WILDLIFE: There is a good selection of native tree species, though with disappointingly little understorey. There is some relic heathland flora, a variety of woodland bird species and a good selection of fungi in early autumn.

W ickham Lane runs down the deep valley once formed by the Plumstead River which cut down through the clay, gravel and sands and reached chalk, the bottom layer of the geological soup-bowl that makes up London. Chalk was a valuable commodity and the valley was dotted with the pits and quarries from which it was extracted before being burnt in kilns excavated from the valley sides. The resulting lime was sold for a variety of purposes – for building, for agriculture and for the chemical industry. But there is a more surprising side to this story: the chalk was not only quarried, it was mined. The land below Wickham Lane and its surrounding streets is riddled with more than 2 miles of lost passages and chambers.

Mining here was a feature of the 1800s and lasted into the beginning of the 20th century. According to annual returns filed with the Secretary of State, 49 men were employed in 1905, 35 of them working below ground. The chalk thus extracted was mixed with the overlying brick earth for the manufacture of London stock bricks. By 1920 the industry had collapsed; the mine entrances were sealed, maintenance work ceased on the passageways and consequently it was not long before the mines began to collapse as well. In 1937 a crater suddenly opened in a children's playground in Rockcliffe Gardens and the swings disappeared into a pit thirty feet deep and eighty foot across.

In the following year a garden collapsed in Alliance Road and the Council decided to call in a company to drill bores to locate the exact line of the passages beneath. A group of Council workmen were filling in these boreholes, since they had fulfilled their function, on 2 June 1938. Samuel Morgan was standing 10 foot from a bore when the ground disappeared beneath him. Two colleagues scrabbled in the newly opened pit in an attempt to save his life – they were later to receive awards for bravery – but their efforts were to no avail. The sides of the pit caved in and Samuel's head disappeared underground. His body was recovered next day from under thirty foot of soil.

There were so many collapses after this that during the 40s and 50s the area was described as looking like a battlefield, with craters in the roads and cracks in walls and buildings. Residents were given no advice except to leave their homes, and were eventually forced to form an association to secure rehousing or compensation. After a furore which reached as far as the Prime Minister's office, action was taken. The mine entrances were opened and fly ash blown into them. As water naturally percolated through the chalk the ash set hard forming a solid plug in the shafts and chambers.

The mines are only one set of the underground holes riddling the rock of this region. An even more puzzling phenomenon is the deneholes. These are vertical shafts penetrating from 20 to 40 foot into the ground and ending in a domed chamber with side passages leading off to sets of smaller chambers. They are found in various parts of South East England, always on chalk, and no-one knows their origin. Theories abound however: they are places of religious ritual or 'oubliettes' for captured Danes; prehistoric flint mines or pits dug by the Romano-British for the storage of grain. None of the explanations is completely convincing, though some support for a Roman connection was lent by the 30 foot dene hole to be found off Wickham Lane. Remains found here included seven Roman vases, a knife, a bell and a tile. Dene holes were found in the whole of the region from here through to Bostall Woods and Lesnes Abbey. Whatever their origin they have all now been filled in – and their secret has been buried with them.

Bostall Heath and Woods remain, as they were described by E. Cecil in 1907, 'one of the most thoroughly rural spots within the London area'. They have a sense of isolation which at times is almost menacing. Steep slopes lead up to a plateau of former heathland where birch, beech and oak surround quiet, almost secret, grassy clearings. There are sessile oaks and a few conifers, both of them trees of lighter, sandier soils and therefore comparatively uncommon in London. In 1906 the pines were ravaged by a species of beetle but a few still stand, alongside holly and sweet chestnut in the woods and sorrel, heather, gorse,and bracken on the grasslands. Altogether, it is an area as outstanding as Hampstead Heath, but far less frequented. At dusk, when rabbits come out to graze and darkness settles amongst the trees it could be a hundred miles from anywhere.

The eastern half of Bostall Heath now goes under the separate name of Co-operative Wood. The members of the Royal Arsenal Co-operative Society were keen to follow the ideals of the Rochdale Pioneers and to extend the concept of mutual aid for the working classes as far as they could; hence the RACS developed into an organisation including shops, a pig farm, a dairy, a bakery, an abbatoir, a jam factory, a funeral service, a motor coach service, a convalescent club, an educational service and a variety of loan and savings clubs. With a support network reaching into every aspect of their members' lives it was not surprising that they turned their minds to one of their members' greatest needs: housing. In 1899 they purchased the Bostall Farm and building began in 1900, the laying of the first stone being an occasion of great rejoicing. A procession of the Society's vehicles with accompanying bands paraded the principle streets of Woolwich and Plumstead and finished at the Bostall Estate for an official ceremony. Workers on the project were paid ½d an hour above the union rate and 1052 houses had been completed by 1915. They are arranged in streets bearing the characteristic names of the movement: Rochdale Street, Owenite

Street, Congress Road and Commonwealth Way. Twenty-six acres were maintained as improved woodland and in the early days these were on hire for outings at 7s 6d per day. In the summer of 1907 the LCC organised the first open-air school in England in Co-operative Woods. The land was eventually rented out and in 1968 became the most attractively sited campsite close to central London.

From the Abbey to East Wickham

ROUTE:
- From Federation Road cross Knee Hill and walk directly ahead up the bank and over the grass for about 100 yards to reach a track in a hollow between trees. Turn left and follow the track until it reaches a road (New Road).
- Cross New Road and follow the path straight ahead to the Abbey.
- On leaving the Abbey take the path marked with Green Chain Walk posts which leads through the gardens and through the hedge into the woods.
- Follow the path ahead and turn right following the Green Chain Walk signpost to Bostall and Oxleas Woods.
- Continue to follow the frequent Green Chain Walk marker posts through three sections of woodland and across three roads until emerging on a main road opposite the football pitches of Clam Field.
- Turn right then left across the field, just after the line of trees, to pick up the line of Green Chain Walk marker posts again.
- Follow the posts through Bostall Woods and then alongside Plumstead Cemetery to reach Wickham Lane.
- Turn left on Wickham Lane then right alongside the pub to follow the markers onto East Wickham Open Space.

FACILITIES: Toilets beside the abbey.

LOOKING AT WILDLIFE: Lesnes Abbey Woods are primarily known for the spring display of wild daffodils. There is a large stand of sessile oak with some mature sweet chestnuts, and a better variety of shrubs and wild flowers than in Bostall Wood. The smaller pond supports waterside plants and dragonflies. There is a good range of woodland bird species including woodpeckers and warblers. The stones of Lesnes Abbey support an excellent collection of ferns.

Whern Henry II cried out in his calculated rage, 'Will no-one rid me of this turbulent priest', it was probably Richard de Luci who took him at his word. Richard was the Chief Justiciar of England, the man who acted as Regent when Henry was travelling abroad. He had been excommunicated for his support of Henry in the dispute with Thomas à Becket, and was definitely implicated in the plot to murder Thomas in Canterbury Cathedral. Thereafter he seems to have lived in fear for his immortal soul. In 1178, two years before his death, he undertook an act of penance by donating land and money for the building of an abbey and church. He dedicated them to the Virgin Mary – and to St Thomas à Becket. Subsequently, he retired from active life and became the Abbey's first Prior.

This was an Augustinian abbey, built just above the flood plain of the Thames. One of its responsibilities was the maintenance of the dykes and river walls on the Plumstead marshes, and after it was suppressed by Cardinal Wolsey in 1524, both the abbey and the river walls fell into decay. In 1537 the banks burst and 2000 acres of marsh were flooded. They were to remain under water for another seventy years. For a time ownership of the abbey changed hands with monotonous regularity, one of the less lucky owners being William Brereton whose association with Anne Boleyn was to cost him his life. In 1633 it became the property of Christ's Hospital and remained with them until it was purchased by the London County Council in 1936.

What remains of the abbey today is a neat and well-maintained ground plan surrounded by attractively organised flower beds, lawns and a mulberry tree. It reveals the foundations of the chapter house and cloisters, the dormitory, refectory and kitchen and above all the abbey church with its 132 foot nave. The stones which held up the abbey buildings now support a rich and attractive variety of wild plants. There is thyme-leaved sandwort, black medick and wall barley, and a particularly good assortment of ferns including harts tongue, black spleenwort, maidenhair spleenwort, polypody, and male fern.

Perhaps the plants rather than the ruins provide the best sense of continuity with the days when this was a busy working community. In 1506 William Bayse, sub-prior of the abbey, compiled a notebook which listed plants with healing properties to be found in the vicinity of the abbey. There are references to 'sharpburrs, daffodyll, fumytory, endyvs, dragen' and to 'celyndyn (which) is good to drink for the jaundy', especially, apparently, 'if yt be gathered on Lammesday, fastyng'. Beyond the abbey gardens and beneath the woodland trees, at least one of these species is still flourishing. Abbey Woods have probably the finest display of wild daffodils in London. The fenced areas of woodland are carpeted with them in early April. No sooner are they over than the floor of the woods is white with the massed star-like flowers of wood anemone. Later still, as spring gives way to early summer, it is the massed ranks of bluebell which cover the ground, like a blue haze, a mist of flowers rising from the woodland floor.

The oddly named Clam Field leads us back to another corner of Bostall Woods. This time we follow the boundary marked by Goldie Leigh Lodge and the Plumstead Cemetery. This part of the estate was acquired by the Woolwich Poor Law Guardians who opened an orphanage here in 1902. It was a Dickensian institution in the prevailing 'barrack' style and was rapidly rebuilt after a damning government report of the same year decried the conditions in such homes. Today the Goldie Leigh hospital is a home for children with very severe handicaps, many of whom attend their own school on the site.

The Green Chain Walk which we have been following for much of our route is part of a pioneering project created by four London boroughs – Bexley, Bromley, Greenwich and Lewisham – in response to development pressures in London.

Beginning in 1977 they jointly designated 4,500 acres of open space as the 'Green Chain' and set about linking them with signposted Green Chain Walks. The network now covers some 40 miles linking places as far apart as Crystal Palace, Chislehurst Common, the Thames Barrier and Erith.

Over Shooters Hill

ROUTE:
- Cross the large East Wickham Open Space keeping roughly ahead. Keep the cemetery and then the allotments off to your right and keep in line with the tower on the Shooters Hill horizon to eventually emerge between houses onto the road.
- Turn left on Glenmore Road then immediately right onto Dryden Road.
- Carry on ahead at the crossroads and where Dryden Road bends to the left take the path which leads off ahead across another open space.
- Follow the path alongside the brook and the line of trees. Keep on this path as it curves left through the fields of Woodlands Farm and eventually joins Shooters Hill Road. (Proposed East London River Crossing route runs through Dryden Open Space and Woodlands Farm.)

FACILITIES: Turn right at the crossroads on Dryden Road to reach a pub.

LOOKING AT WILDLIFE: Shaggy ink caps on East Wickham Open Space. Hedgerow birds and plants on Woodlands Farm.

E ast Wickham Open Space was previously a Council tip and was later grassed over to provide a rather dull expanse of mown grassland. Much has been done in recent years however to improve it, with extensive tree planting and wide expanses of the grassland thankfully left uncut. A short stretch of road leads us onto another unimaginatively named 'Open Space' which has even more to offer. The path running alongside a small wooded brook leads us soon between open fields. Quite unexpectedly we are in the midst of a farm, the closest working farm to central London. This is another product of the expansion of the RACS, purchased by them as Woodlands Farm in the 1920s. Its main function was to supply pork and bacon to the co-op's butchers and over the fields to the right can be seen the 'model' pig unit and the abbatoir. The fields supply barley for feed and straw for bedding. Here is preserved an isolated piece of the Kentish countryside. There is wych elm, elder, oak, hawthorn, osier, crack willow and crab apple in the hedgerow, with white bryony scrambling up shrubs and flocks of greenfinches flighting from tree to tree. Carrion crow and wood pigeon pick their way over the brown furrows of the surrounding fields. London has continued its relentless march outwards, surrounding and separating all this from the rest of the agricultural world by miles of suburbia; it creates a strange sense of displacement as you walk from a Council estate onto open farmland and up towards the summit of Shooters Hill.

The Hill is 432 feet high and has for several thousand years carried over its crest one of the main routes into London. Here the Romans built their Watling Street on the site of an ancient trackway and by the 13th century it had become part of the Pilgrim's Way to Canterbury. This important route ran up the steep slopes of a hill surrounded by dense woodland, the remnants of which survive today. Not surprisingly it was also the notorious haunt of footpads and highwaymen who held up travellers and took collections for what they called the 'highwaymans benevolent fund.' During Elizabethan times it became known as the Hill of Blood and the vestry book of Eltham Parish Church shows several entries like that of 1616: 'Paid to a poore man that was robbed at shouters-hille of all that he had a 100 mile (from) home ... 6d.'

As a warning to the highwaymen a gibbet was erected at the summit; however the bodies, left to rot where they hung, failed to deter the highwaymen but put the fear of god into everyone else. 'A filthy sight it was to see', wrote Samuel Pepys in his diary, 'how his flesh is shrunk to his bones'. Dominating the skyline today instead is the 1910 water tower, an octagonal building in multi-coloured brick and stone. Shooters Hill once had a considerable reputation as a spa with waters containing magnesium sulphate and during the 1760s grandiose and fanciful plans were being put forward to develop a whole new spa town here. The first few houses of the scheme were erected and remain today, but the complexities of land ownership – involving both the crown and the military – ensured its eventual collapse.

Another scheme, floated in 1847, was that of turning the hill into a huge terraced cemetery with accommodation for 10,000 catacombs. This too came to nothing. Shooters Hill and its surrounding woodlands has survived these and many threats across the years – but it is now in danger of succumbing to the Department of Transport's implacable determination to devastate a place of beauty. Despite massive opposition from local people, the local authorities and organisations like the Nature Conservancy Council and the London Wildlife Trust, the government is intent on pushing through its plan for the East London River Crossing, which would involve six miles of highway, sweeping through Falconwood Field, Shepherdleas Wood, Oxleas Woods, Shooters Hill Golf Course, Woodlands Farm, Plumstead Common and Bostall Woods. This destruction of ancient woodland, of open fields, of a precious part of country London, is scheduled to take place to serve the short-term interests of the road haulage lobby and the motor car. The government appointed inspector who sat at the public enquiry reported in favour of a tunnel under Oxleas Wood, but even this has been unacceptable to successive Secretaries of State for Transport who have insisted that for the sake of cheapness the road must plough directly through the trees.

Oxleas Wood to Eltham Common

ROUTE:
- Cross the main road and turn right. After a few yards turn left into the woods.
- Follow the Green Chain Walk signs on a path which leads initially

parallel to the main road and then turns into the woodlands.
- Follow the broad ride to the second crosspaths and a Green Chain Walk signpost. Turn right here following the route for the Thames Barrier.
- Follow the marker posts through the woods until emerging onto Oxleas Meadow. Walk straight across the front of the café and ahead to pick up the markers on the Woolwich Common branch of the Green Chain Walk.
- Follow the markers through the woods and passing Severndroog Castle, to emerge onto the main Shooters Hill Road on Eltham Common, just behind the police station. (The proposed East London River Crossing route runs across the eastern side of Oxleas Wood.)

FACILITIES: Café on Oxleas Meadow. Toilets at Severndroog Castle.

LOOKING AT WILDLIFE: There is a wealth of wildlife in the woodland complex of this section. Specialities include guelder rose, wild cherry, wild service tree and butcher's broom. As well as a wide range of woodland flowers there is a large number of fungi including many edible species. Bird species include woodpeckers, nuthatch, tree creeper, spotted flycatcher, the wood warbler and on occasions the woodcock. Butterfly species include small tortoiseshell, comma, peacock, speckled wood, meadow brown, holly blue and orange tip.

Oxleas Wood, Shepherdleas Wood, Jack Wood and Castle Wood together constitute one of the most extensive areas of long established woodland in London. Such is their significance that they have been declared a Site of Scientific Interest by the Nature Conservancy Council. Unlike the woodlands we have already passed through they are on the London clay rather than the sand and gravel and for this reason the sessile oak is replaced here by the pedunculate oak, the oak more usual in Southern England.

Among the thirty species of tree and shrub to be found here the wild cherry and the wild service tree are particularly interesting as indicators of ancient woodland. Wild service was once used in the brewing of an alcoholic drink known as chequers and it is from this that many country pubs – and the Prime Minister's country residence – get their name. The drink was supposed to be an effective cure for colic or the 'torments'.

The trees of Oxleas Wood were coppiced up to the Second World War and the Greater London Council returned to this form of management, which was an eminently sensible arrangement. It kept the trees in good condition, setting back the process of ageing, while at the same time providing wood for baulking timber, benches and fencing. Coppicing also has the effect of exposing the woodland floor to more light and thus increasing the range of wild flowers that can grow there. Oxleas boasts a long list of species including bluebell, yellow pimpernel, wood sage, hedge woundwort, wood anemone, wood violet, yellow archangel, and common cow-wheat. One of the specialities is butcher's broom. This strange prickly plant with tiny greenish-white flowers is another indicator of long-established woodland. It derives its name from the fact that switches from it were cut and used to clean butcher's chopping blocks. The 210 fungi species so far counted include the famous fly agaric or 'magic mushroom', *amanita muscaria*. Its red cap with white spots is the familiar illustration of fairy stories and it has a long association with folklore, religion and mythology.

The latest discovery to cause excitement at Oxleas was made in July 1987 when spider expert Edward Milner found a rare green hunting spider with the name of *Micrommata virescens*. This was the first time the spider had been found in London for 250 years and the event made the headlines of the local paper. The *Bexley and Eltham Leader* raised the hope that where all else had failed a 2½ inch spider might hold up the East London River Crossing.

Jack Wood and Castle Wood to the west of the complex are a strange mix of wild wood with council flower beds and formal planting. There are terraces and parterres, with grand views of South London out as far as the North Downs; these are remnants of disappeared villas and their grounds. One strange folly which remains is Severndroog Castle. This eccentric triangular tower was erected in 1784 as a monument to Eltham resident Sir William James by his widow. As a castle it seems rather a sad affair and has to be approached up the steps from the west to retain its grandeur. James himself was a romantic figure, born the son of a tenant miller in Pembrokeshire in 1721. By the age of 12 he was at sea and the various tales that are told about his early days include his escaping from a prison in Havana and surviving 20 days in an open boat by drinking from a snuff box. In 1747 he joined the East India Company, his job being to patrol the Malabar coast between Bombay and Goa, protecting company convoys from Arab pirates, most of whom were based on the island fortress of Severndroog. In 1755, exceeding his orders, James led a direct attack on Severndroog. The fortress was bombarded and laid waste and one thousand fleeing pirates were captured after the main magazine had blown up. In later days James became an MP and a wealthy man. He bought the Park Farm Estate in Eltham, and is buried in Eltham churchyard.

Woolwich Common

ROUTE:
- At the major road junction ahead turn right into Academy Road. After a short distance take the gravel path on the left running along the edge of the common.
- Turn left at the crosspaths following the tarmac path across the common.
To join Walk 6:
- Join Walk 6 here.
To complete circular walk:
- At the next crosspaths turn right following down the common and eventually round to the left and onto the road.
- Follow Stadium Road then go straight across Ha Ha Road into Repository Road.
- At the next crossroads go straight across Artillery Place into Frances Street.
- Go down Frances Street, passing the old entrance gates into Cambridge Barracks

and Red Barracks, taking the fourth turning on the right (Belson Road) to reach
Woolwich Dockyards Station.
- To continue to buses and North Woolwich, follow Belson Road to the end then turn
left and right into St Mary's Street.
- Take the entrance on the left into St Mary's Gardens. Walk through the churchyard
keeping the church on your left.
- Turn right out of the churchyard down the slope to the roundabout and buses.
- For the foot tunnel to North Woolwich, cross to the diagonally opposite corner of
the roundabout and walk a short distance up Woolwich High Street. Turn left up Glass
Yard alongside the Leisure Centre.

LOOKING AT WILDLIFE: There is a varied flora on Woolwich Common,
particularly in the vicinity of the covered reservoir. There are some scarce species of
vetch on the south part of the common and the pixy-cup lichen *Cladonia coccifera*,
scarce in London, occurs on the northern section.

'Far away down the avenues of time we discern the beginning of our ancient
common. A wild heathland under the wooded slopes of Shooters Hill, from
whose recesses the skin-clad savage emerges to survey the desolation of the
marshes and the heights of Hampstead Heath ...'

So began *The Story of Woolwich Common*, jointly published in 1928 by the
Chamber of Commerce, the Regional Town Planning Committee, the
Council of Social Services, the Rotary Club and the Kent County Playing
Fields Association. What had drawn all these bodies together was the fight to save
the common.

Until the 19th century this was open land with gorse growing between ponds and
alongside a running stream. Then, in 1802, the Board of Ordnance purchased the
areas now known as Barracks Field and Repository Ground, and rights over the rest
of Charlton and Woolwich Commons. The landowners received £57,000, Woolwich
Vestry received £3,000 and Charlton Vestry, which objected to the whole scheme,
received nothing. As for the commoners, their rights were 'extinguished'.

The Board of Ordnance wanted to use the Common for a drill ground for the
troops of the Royal Artillery Regiment – whose barracks had just been built on the
edge of the common. Very soon however the open grassland was being put to a
different use; the barracks were not big enough and many soldiers began to build
their own shanty town on the common. It soon became rife with cholera, and
remained a public scandal until 1804.

The War Office having done nothing it was left to Lady Maryon-Wilson, whose
family name is commemorated in two local parks, to knock down the hovels at her
own expense and have them replaced with new huts. These remained on the
common till 1875. Meanwhile, other military buildings were rapidly eroding the rest
of the open land. In 1806 the Royal Academy buildings went up and these were
followed by the two military hospitals, one of which destroyed Charlton Common

altogether. It was the proposal to build a nurses home, again on common ground, which finally proved too much. The Woolwich Common Joint Committee was formed, published the history of Woolwich Common, and launched a public appeal. Battle, albeit in a gentlemanly sort of way, was joined. The outcome was an uneasy compromise. The 'common' remains the property of the Ministry of Defence but it has agreed so far to refrain from any further erosion or development.

Woolwich Common, like many others, is largely a flat expanse of grassland. Yet unlike others, it retains considerable wildlife interest. The richest area is undoubtedly the site of the old covered reservoir, just where we enter the Common on Academy Road. The Reservoir was dug by convict labour in 1848 but it was never really needed since water was plentiful locally. Today the sloping sides constitute an artificial wetland with their own little reedbed watered, presumably, by the leaking reservoir. The top of the reservoir is a bright display of pink and white flowered goats rue, deep red everlasting pea, and bright yellow hawkweeds. Meadow browns, blues and other butterflies feed from flower to flower, grasshoppers sing and a large colony of well-fed diadem spiders sit on webs stretched between the high stalks of the hawkweeds.

Half way down the length of the common there is a sudden dip. We are confronted with a five foot drop and a marked transition in the flora. Looking south over the higher ground, the grassland is lush and green, looking north it is lower and thinner and has a purplish haze. The southern part of the common is on the London clay, rich in nutrients and supporting a wide variety of grasses and of vetches. The north section, by complete contrast, is on the Blackheath beds. The soil is sandy and hence acidic and low in nutrients. The pebbles which constitute the Blackheath gravels can easily be seen in the bare patches on the surface. Such a soil creates a truly heath-like section of the common, where common bent makes up 85 per cent of the ground cover and where sorrel, broom, gorse and birch add to the typical heathland flora. The transition between the two parts of the common marks a return from the slopes of Shooters Hill onto the level of the old river terrace which we followed through Plumstead Common and Bostall Heath. Ahead of us the terrace dips down again to the Thames and to Woolwich town centre where our walk began.

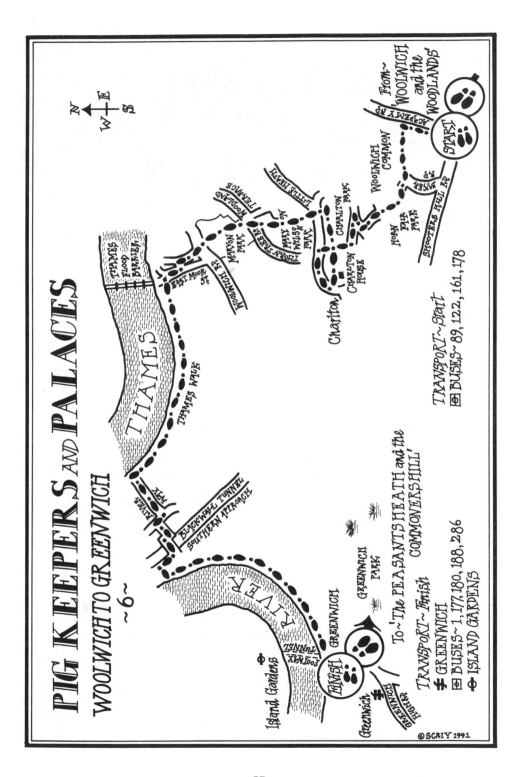

PIG KEEPERS AND PALACES
WOOLWICH TO GREENWICH
~6~

N W E S

THAMES

THAMES FLOOD BARRIER

WOODLAND TERRACE

THAMES WALK

No.1 THORN TREE RD

MAYON PARK

LITTLE HEATH

EAST MOOR ST

WOOLWICH RD

BLACKWALL TUNNEL SOUTHERN APPROACH

RIVER WAY

Island Gardens

FOOTWAY TUNNEL

FINISH GREENWICH

GREENWICH PARK

GREENWICH PIER

To ~ 'The PEASANTS HEATH and the COMMONERS HILL'

Transport ~ Finish
⚓ GREENWICH
🚌 BUSES ~ 1, 177, 180, 188, 286
Φ ISLAND GARDENS

RIVER

ASTON WISE PARK

CHARLTON PARK

CHARLTON HOUSE

Charlton

CHARLTON PARK

WOOLWICH COMMON

HORN FAIR PARK

START

ACADEMY RD

from ~ WOOLWICH and the WOODLANDS

BYERS RD

SHOOTERS HILL RD

TRANSPORT ~ Start
🚌 BUSES ~ 89, 122, 161, 178

© SCRIY 1991

4. OF PIG KEEPERS AND PALACES

FROM WOOLWICH TO GREENWICH

When the Saxons settled around London they gave us our 'tons' – Brixton, Kennington, Islington and Paddington. Charlton, or Cerletone, was where the cerls or free churls lived, raising their pigs along the riverside and owning allegiance to no-one. From this community arose the village on the hill above the river: a cluster of houses surrounding the inn, a manor house, the parish church of St.Luke's, and its adjacent village green, home of the gloriously anarchic 'horn fair'. Nineteenth century rationalism and the demands of 'public order' swept away the horn fair but despite this, and all the other changes of the centuries, Charlton has managed to retain a distinct identity and a definite village atmosphere.

The Village is really one of two Charltons. Below the hill is Lower Charlton or Charlton Riverside, where the fishermen and barge dwellers and river people lived. Always a race apart, their homesteads in the marshes developed after the 1850s into a tight-knit working-class community separate from, and somewhat suspicious of, the world beyond its boundaries. This was the area of the 'Four Streets', fringed by wharves, barge-works, rope-walks, cable-layers and all the paraphernalia of the riverside.

Two miles, as the fish swims, from these two communities is a portion of London which stands at the completely opposite end of the social and political spectrum: Greenwich, one-time centre of the 'known' world, of imperial ambition, naval adventure and merchant expedition. It was here that monarchs from Henry VIII to James II built their palaces and conducted their courts, dynasties were made or broken, and the fate of thousands decided.

The links between Greenwich, with its pomp and its palaces, and the two Charltons, home of the working class and the free churls, is the link between all the diverse elements of London's history – the river. This stretch of the walk takes in a long section of riverside path and illustrates in many ways the complex relationship between the city and the river. It is the river which gives the city its unity. The river is the very reason for London's existence – and as dockers' leader, John Burns put it, 'every drop is liquid history'. It was alongside the river that the Celtic settlement of Llyn-din was established, which rose to prominence under the Romans as Londinium, the first fordable point on the river between Dover and the capital at St. Albans. By 1594 the river gave employment to at least 40,000 people and by the 1870s 2000 vessels might be gathered at any one time in the four miles of reaches between London Bridge and Deptford. By the beginning of the 20th century it was the location of the largest and busiest dock complex in the world.

Yet within a few decades of the ending of World War II all this was over. The docks had closed, the big ships had gone and with them the trade of the lighterman, the waterman, the docker, the stevedore, the coal heaver and the pilot. Now the miles of abandoned quays and the acres of industrial dereliction are designated as 'free enterprise zones'; they are the site of mega-development with office towers, shopping malls, yachting marinas and fashionable homes and town houses for the wealthiest of Londoners. Any genuine connection between a city and its river has been lost. For the new docklanders the river is no longer a central part of their lives and their livelihoods, no longer the link between their past, present and future. It is simply a 'feature' which adds to the value of property.

Meanwhile, the old riverside community of the Four Streets has disappeared under the works for the Thames Barrier, which was planned to save London from flooding for at least a hundred years. In fact, by the latest calculations it will be ineffective in 50 and the area most under threat will be the low-lying areas of the new docklands development. It seems that the river may, after all, have the last word.

This chapter covers a single 6 mile walk from Woolwich town centre to the Cutty Sark at Greenwich.

WALK 6: Woolwich to Greenwich

Getting Started

From buses:
> From the major junction of Academy Road, Well Hall Road and Shooters Hill, turn down Academy Road to reach Woolwich Common.

From Walk 5:
> Continue from point where Walk 5 reaches Woolwich Common.

The Horn Fair

ROUTE:
- From Academy Road turn left onto the gravel path beside the covered reservoir (Green Chain Walk sign), following the edge of the common.
- At the cross-paths turn left along the tarmac path crossing the common.
- At the Y junction close to the road, bear left along a gravel path to reach Baker Road.

- Turn left for a short distance on the road to find the path on the right which begins immediately beyond the car parking area.
- Follow the path through a gate and turn left and right to follow the perimeter of the fenced football pitch (Green Chain Walk signs) and emerge at the far side onto a road.
- Walk straight ahead up Inigo Jones Road. At the end turn right and then left alongside Charlton Park.

LOOKING AT WILDLIFE: There is a varied flora on the common, particulary in the vicinity of the covered reservoir. There is a good variety of vetches and grasses and a speciality on this part of the common is the pixy-cup lichen *Cladonia coccifera*, unusual in London.

While out hunting one day from his palace at Eltham, King John crossed Shooters Hill and came across a mill. He decided to stop there for refreshment. The miller was out and the king, finding the miller's wife alone, decided to seduce her. The seduction was in process when the miller returned. He drew his knife rushed at the king and then recognised who he was and fell to his knees. The king led the miller to the door and in recompense granted him all the land he could see between there and the river – together with all the revenues from an annual fair. His neighbours mockingly christened the river boundary of his new property 'Cuckold's Point' and the annual fair became the 'Horn Fair', horns being the symbol of a cuckold.

Like many of the best stories, this account of the origin of the Horn Fair is apocryphal. It was held each year on the green outside St Luke's, the parish church of Charlton, on 18 October, St Luke's Day. The saint is traditionally depicted composing his gospel beside a cow and an ox with large horns, which has led to the suggestion that the fair was held in honour of St Luke. However, christianity has a well-tested habit of taking over older legends and festivals turning them to new account. Herne, the horned god of the woods, was a very important pagan deity and given the ribald nature of the Horn Fair festivities, it is very likely that they are of much older origin.

The 'horns' were always a central part of the fair, which began with a procession from the riverside in which horns would be worn on hats, men would dress as women and a mock king and queen would take part. On reaching the parish church they would walk round it three times then take to the adjacent village green where they 'fell to lecherie and songs, daunces, harping, piping and also to glotony and sinne and so turned holiness to cursydnesse'. A 1711 report describes the 'Ancient Guild Of Fumblers' who assembled at the Fair to sing popular songs and to hit each other with ladles. Perhaps the ladles were made from horn for there was always a large number of stalls and peddlars selling a wide variety of articles made from horn. The Fair was notorious for licentious and unbridled behaviour and was described as 'the rudest fair in England'. It lasted for three days and was attended by upwards of 15,000 people who, according to an 18th century newspaper account, were 'so fond of spirituous liquor that it is sold publickly at Hornfair by people with wheelbarrows'.

In 1819, in an effort to disassociate the celebrations from the church, the fair was moved away from the village green and onto a site known as Fairfields. By the 1870s the development of the rail network brought Eastenders to the Fair in ever larger numbers, and eventually the authorities decided to suppress it. It was banned by a parliamentary Order in Council of 1872.

Hornfair Park, where our walk begins was originally part of the Maryon-Wilson estate. It was purchased by the London County Council and opened as a public park in 1936. When the LCC acquired the adjacent Blue Cross Kennels for new housing development in 1958 the animal cemetery from the kennels was designed into a small enclosure and included in the park. Prince Henry Road and Inigo Jones Road, which link Hornfair Park and Charlton Park, both bear names recalling aspects of the history of the area. Inigo Jones is said to have lived for a time at Cherry Orchard in Charlton and was traditionally, though erroneously, credited with the design of Charlton House. Prince Henry, son of James I, was regarded as the model prince, but he died at 18. By this age he had already gathered around himself a brilliant circle, among whom Inigo Jones was a leading figure. It was for his personal tutor, Adam Newton, that Charlton House was built.

Charlton House and Park

ROUTE:

• Turn right through the first gate into Charlton Park. Follow the path across the park and turn left to reach the front of Charlton House.

• Turn right on the road in front of the house and follow it past St Luke's and along The Village. Take the gate on the right, immediately opposite Charlton Lane, back into the park.

• Retrace your steps back along this path to reach the junction of paths at the corner of the running track, close to a shelter. Turn left here.

• Follow the path and turn left beyond the changing rooms to find the exit onto the road (Charlton Park Road).

FACILITIES: Toilets and refreshment kiosk in Charlton Park. Pubs and cafés in The Village.

LOOKING AT WILDLIFE: The park has some fine old trees including an ancient mulberry, large horse chestnuts, and avenues of holm oak and yew. There is a resident population of squirrels, tits, finches and jays.

The palaces and royal buildings of Greenwich receive millions of visitors every year. A short distance away Charlton House must be one of the most determinedly overlooked buildings in London. Yet it is one of the finest Jacobean houses in the country, rising red and massive above Charlton Park and the surrounding suburbs. It is built in the shape of a shallow H with an impressive tower on either flank topped with a cupola and spire. Its rooves carry a collection of chimneys like twisted candy and its soft red brickwork is complemented by white ashlar blocks on every cornice, mullion and frame. There is an especial exuberance however about its main entrance, a slightly projecting porch extending up the whole height of the building. It carries elaborate workmanship in a mixture of styles bearing columns, scrolls, human and animal masks, coats of arms and the bust of an unidentified woman. This together with its interior detail is described in *Nairn's London* as 'sinister poetry ... the most undisciplined ornament in all England'.

The site was completed for Adam Newton in 1612, though the architect is unknown. John Evelyn suggests in his diary that it was built for Prince Henry himself, and not for his tutor, but if this was the case his early death prevented his occupancy. Newton died around 1630 and is buried in Charlton Church. He was succeeded by Sir Henry Newton who lost most of the family fortune as a result of backing the wrong side in the Civil War. He was forced to move from here to Warwickshire and later sold the house to Sir William Ducie. Ducie, according to the records, paid £8,500 for it in 1658 and sold it for £5,468 in 1680 – a re-assuring reminder that house prices do not always rise, but also part of a continuing story of ill-luck for those connected with the house. This was to continue under the next owner, Sir William Langhorn, a retired East India merchant. He was twice married but was never able to beget an heir, something he bitterly regretted. After his death in 1714 his ghost continued to inhabit the house, and is still reported to appear, either pursuing women visitors about the building or as an unspecific 'presence in the bedrooms'. Even unluckier was one of the subsequent and most famous tenants, Spencer Percival, who became Prime Minister in 1809. Four years later, while still in post, he was assassinated in the lobby of the House of Commons. Like Adam Newton, he is buried in Charlton Church.

The feeling of ill-omen surrounding Charlton House can only be heightened by the strange detail of its decoration. The grand entrance porch and much of the interior bear a grotesque ornamentation unique in English houses. There are representations of the devil, horned heads, grimacing wolves, leering faces with lolling tongues and a menagerie of outlandish half-human, half-animal creatures. Adam Newton himself had a somewhat mysterious history and when this is put together with the suspicious death of the Prince – who died of an unidentified fever – and the proximity of the house to the pagan Horn Fair, all the ingredients exist for some fascinating speculation. In *Charlton House: A Hidden History*, local historian Ron Pepper traces a link between Newton and the powerful, occult, European-wide, secret society of the day, the Prieure de Sion. Newton, he suggests, may have been a member of the Society uniquely placed to bring the future King of England under its influence. Pepper speculates that the Prince may have been less malleable than the Society expected and that they accordingly disposed of him.

Charlton House passed eventually into the ownership of the Maryon-Wilson family, whose name occupies a central place in the history of Charlton and will figure again in the story of Hampstead Heath. The last member of the family to occupy the house was one Sir Spencer Pocklington Maryon Maryon-Wilson, 11th Baronet. He sold the house with 108 acres of land to Greenwich Borough Council who opened it as a public library.

During World War Two the building was fitted out with a gas chamber for testing gas masks and also with a model living room to demonstrate how a room could be made gas-proof. It suffered severe bomb damage in this period and during rebuilding workmen discovered the body of a baby boy in one of the chimneys. This leant credence to another of Charlton's complement of spectres – the ghost of a servant girl who wanders through the grounds with a baby in her arms. Today, as a public library and community centre, it must be one of the most spectacularly located such facilities in the country. Just beyond the house is an even more spectacularly located lavatory. Originally a summer house, it is the only part of the Charlton buildings attributable to Inigo Jones, and has an attractive Dutch appearance and a curious keel-shaped roof. With supreme disrepect the Borough Council converted it into public toilets in 1936.

After a detour through Charlton Village our route returns to Charlton Park, which is an uneasy mix between the stately grounds of a historic home and a municipal recreation site. Its oldest surviving feature is a mulberry tree reputedly planted in 1608, one of 200 mulberry trees planted here by order of James I who was keen to establish a silk industry in England. In this however he made a serious error. The larvae of the silk moth feed entirely on the leaves of the white mulberry, but James mistakenly introduced the inedible black mulberry. It seems that even the king had bad luck at Charlton.

Hanging Wood and Happy Valley

ROUTE:
- Cross the road (Charlton Park Road) and enter Maryon Wilson Park to the right. In the park bear right at the first fork and continue ahead to the animal enclosures (Green Chain Walk signs).
- Turn right between the enclosures and carry on up the hill to the road.
- Cross the road and follow the path ahead leading to steps into Maryon Park.
- Part way down the steps turn left to follow the path along the hillside. Follow this to its end and then take the bridge over the railway.
- Cross the main road and turn left. Take the first turning on the right (Hardens Manor Way) and continue ahead to reach the Thames Barrier and the riverside walk.

FACILITIES: Toilets in Maryon Wilson Park. Toilets, children's playground and café (summer only) in Maryon Park. Pubs on Woolwich Road and Hardens Manor Way.

LOOK AT WILDLIFE: There is a wide variety of trees and of commoner woodland and garden birds in the two parks. Maryon Wilson Park has animal enclosures with ponies, sheep, fallow deer, waterfowl, bantams and peafowl.

Beyond the walls of Charlton Park, and flanking the village to the north, was the dense Hanging Wood, notorious retreat of robbers and home of the highwaymen who roamed Shooters Hill. It was 32 acres of this site which Sir Spencer Maryon-Wilson donated to the LCC in 1924, and on which the Maryon-Wilson Park was opened. It is a cheery park with sloping lawns, animal enclosures and a sort of makeshift stream running down through dells of oaks, willows and birches. Some of these oaks may be all that's left of Hanging Wood.

Maryon Park on the other side of Thorntree Road – previously Hanging Wood Road – has a different atmosphere. It is one of the most beautiful of London's small parks and spans the slopes of the steep Thames terraces. The heavily wooded banks wrap around it to north and west giving a sense of seclusion and perhaps of some rather disturbing mystery. Perhaps this is why Antonioni chose it for some of the most haunting scenes in his film *Blow-Up*.

This park was also a gift from Sir Spencer Maryon-Wilson to the LCC and was opened in 1891, with several subsequent additions of land including acres of disused sand pit; much of the park is made up of worked-out sand, chalk and gravel quarries. The sand pits remained a feature of Charlton life into the 20th century, the sand being dug for ballast, for scouring and for the glass industry – in particular the local bottle factory. It was also used for spreading across parlour floors in the days before carpets were in widespread use. Some of the sand pits on the western side of the park have been declared a Site of Special Scientific Interest for their excellent sequence of geological beds.

The view from the top of the terraces must have contributed to the choice of this site for early settlement. The famous Egyptologist, William Flinders Petrie, who was born in Maryon Road, was the first to survey the site in 1891. Then in 1915, major excavations revealed a Romano-British settlement covering 17½ acres from the present Thorntree Road entrance northwards. There was a double bank and ditch surrounding a group of hut dwellings, which had been in occupation for four hundred years ending in the 4th century AD. However, after 1915 it was progressively destroyed by quarrying. Detached from the main terrace is Cox's Mount, an isolated pinnacle to the north of the park, named after a local eccentric who built a summer house on the top in which to entertain his friends. The Mount was rented by the Admiralty in the 1850s as a measurement point for the adjustment of ship's compasses.

The Maryon-Wilsons were lords of the manor of Charlton for over 200 years, their land mainly in Upper Charlton. Beyond, in Lower Charlton along the riverside, their place was taken by the Roupels, and these two families owned 60 per cent of all the land and properties in the area. Conrad Rupell arrived in the country in 1689 as Captain to the bodyguard of William of Orange. His descendants obtained prominent positions as salt-tax collectors, customs officers, lawyers and masters in Chancery. By the 19th century they had acquired the chalk and sand hill slopes between Victoria Way and Charlton Lane and much of the marshland fronting the river; they then set about the major industrial development of riverside Charlton, aided by the arrival of the railway. From 1850 the marshes were infilled for factory sites and housing. Farmer Samuel Harden's market garden – which gave its name to

Hardens Manor Way – gave way to factories such as Siemens, the electrical and telegraph engineers and cable layers, which once employed 17,000 people.

Many of them would have lived in the adjoining community known locally as 'the Four Streets'. Jo Anderson, whose family came from the area, describes it beautifully in her book *Anchor and Hope* published by Hodder and Stoughton in 1980. 'The Woolwich Road,' her uncle had told her, 'might have been the Brandenburg Gate.' On one side lived the city clerks and other white collar workers, on the other the riverside people: 'My wife, as is now, lived over on the other side, and was never allowed to cross the road to the Waterman's Arms area. All the boys over her side wore school uniforms and neat little caps. They never walked past us, they sped past.'

The Four Streets was a tight-packed huddle of 'two up and two downers' with little corner shops 'sweet with the smell of barreled beans and new baked bread, home-made toffee and fresh herring.' The small back gardens with their roses and cabbage patches were a cacophony of chickens and ducks, and housed rabbit hutches, pigeon coops and kennels for the greyhounds. Within the area was the East Street Mission which, in 1903, initiated a weekly football match on the meadow near Siemens. The team which played here became known as the Charlton Reds and after several changes of venue found itself a home on the fields just off Hanging Wood Lane where Benson the Butcher fattened his cattle. By now they were Charlton Athletic, top of the second division, and their ground was 'Happy Valley'.

Most of the area disappeared under the works for the Thames Barrier, and one of those new and sterile industrial estates regarded as 'urban renewal'. Almost the only remaining building is the Lads of the Village pub. Surrounded for a hundred years by small terraced streets it now stands in unsplendid isolation, and is known, prosaically, as the Thames Barrier Arms.

From the Barrier to Ballast Quay

ROUTE:
- At the Thames Barrier turn left along the riverside. The path leads through a tunnel under the Barrier buildings and then along Nagasaki Walk.
- Follow the Riverside Walk signs along several sections of roadway or path until it turns inland along River Way.
- Bear right at the end of River Way then take the first left into Boord Street to reach the main road (Tunnel Approach).
- Cross the footbridge and walk towards the tunnel entrance. Turn left on the footpath returning to the riverside.
- Follow the riverside route to Ballast Quay.

FACILITIES: The Thames Barrier has a souvenir shop, café, toilets and disabled toilets and a visitor's centre (entrance fee). There are some attractive riverside pubs en route.

LOOKING AT WILDLIFE: The variety of bird life along the tidal Thames has been increasing. Cormorant are common and a variety of duck, swans, gulls and waders may be seen. There are some interesting wild flowers, including species such as toadflax and wood sedge along the footpath and stonecrop and pellitory-of-the-wall growing on structures.

When surge and storm conditions hit South East England in 1953 they brought tides which were 18 foot higher than normal sea level at London Bridge. Sea defences all along the East coast and the Thames Estuary were overcome. In the ensuing floods 309 people drowned.

Forty-five square miles of Central London lie below the level of those 1953 tides and the threat of flooding since then has been steadily increasing. There are a number of causes. The greenhouse effect is melting the polar ice caps and inexorably raising the level of the world's oceans. Britain itself is slowly tilting to the south east at the rate of about 30cms every hundred years, whilst London, resting on a bed of clay, is sinking. If – or when – surge conditions combine with high tides and strong winds, the city could be inundated. Tens of thousands of homes would be lost, gas and electricity cut off, the underground flooded, the water supply contaminated, and the work of the capital grind to a halt. It was to avoid such a scenario that the Thames Barrier was planned.

It straddles the river with a series of curving hooded piers, each thirteen stories high and containing the operating machinery for the barrier. They resemble nothing so much as a solemn procession of silver-cowled monks making their way between one bank and the other. Between these piers are slung the gates, the central ones over 200 feet long and 70 feet high. When they are in the open position they are not visible, being embedded in the river bottom but when flood conditions threaten they swivel upwards presenting their rounded fronts to the surge. They are known as 'rising sector' gates, and the idea is said to have occured to engineer Charles Draper while he was at home, turning on the tap of his gas fire. The Barrier was opened on 8 May 1984, having taken 4000 men and women eight years to build at a cost of nearly £500 million. But the sea level continues to rise; London will very soon have to come up with another, larger, and even more expensive, solution.

From the Barrier the riverside path runs as far as Greenwich, with a brief excursion inland cutting off the great loop of Blackwall Reach. This route is the beginning of what the Countryside Commission and the Ramblers Association hope will eventually be a 180-mile Thames Path linking London with the source of the Thames near Kemble in Gloucestershire. The path would not only provide direct walking access to the countryside but would be a major step towards securing what has so long been denied to Londoners – the right to walk along much of their own riverside.

As recently as the early 1960s this riverside would have provided a fascinating scene of noisy, busy and diverse Thames industry. Moored along the Charlton Roads just here would have been sugar boats, cable-laying ships, small tankers, jute, flax and hemp carriers, rafts of floating logs and a whole flotilla of barges. On-shore were the bottle works, the brick company, the coal carriers, the rope works, the barge builders and the large ships' fittings yard of Stone Manganese. The story of the Thames in the last twenty years is the story of the loss of this industry, the employment that went with it and the communities that depended upon it. The scene today is of wastelands where ragwort blooms amongst burst rubbish bags, and grass grows between abandoned railway lines. There are scrap paper yards whose merchandise blows along the paths and over adjacent plots, rusting cement hoppers, and disused overhead conveyor belts – once used for carrying gravel from ship to shore. The path winds through all this with the occasional modernised section serving only to heighten the feeling of emptiness. The riverside path too is losing much of its interest and eccentricity as well-meaning planners 'tidy' it up. Where once it ran through the middle of yards, sometimes under the heaving and clanking of overhead machinery, it now skirts around them. Where once it ran in a tunnel right through the heart of a factory, it now follows a municipal paved deviation around it.

The end of the old Four Streets area is marked by the Anchor and Hope pub. There has been a beer-house on this site for centuries and alongside it sailing barges and brigs would moor to load ballast before heading out to sea. If conditions turned nasty the skipper might be forced to 'anchor and hope', waiting sometimes several days for the weather to change. This attractive pub, with its lantern roof, is reputedly the place where Hogarth, that chronicler of English dissipation, printed his 'Idle Apprentice'.

The stretch of river from here along the Charlton roads to Blackwall is known as Bugsby's Reach and curves up one side of the industrial peninsular of land which culminates in Blackwall Point. This peninsular, isolated by the river to the north and by Greenwich marshes to the south, was known as 'the marsh'. It became the site of refineries, gas works, power stations and a whole concentration of unhealthy industry, afflicting the residents with one of the highest incidences of industrial diseases in the country. It was officially declared at one stage as the unhealthiest place in London.

There is currently no riverside path around the peninsular and our route turns inland along River Way, previously known as Ceylon Place. Here a row of early 19th century two-storey cottages stands next to an attractive 18th century pub, The Pilot, with a canted bay running from ground to first floor. This dainty scene is framed by moving hoppers, pipe lines hissing steam, scruffy waste land, huge gas holders and a blackened London School Board building. There is a ceaseless dull roar of traffic, the heady smell of gas, and the thick sweet odour of malt and grain. There is one further indignity – the motorway, which ploughs through the remnants of the marsh on its way to the Blackwall Tunnel.

Blackwall itself, which is on the north bank of the river, opposite Blackwall Point, was home to the great Blackwall Shipyards where wooden sailing ships, Navy frigates, and the tea and cotton clippers were built. As the Isle of Dogs docklands developed on the north bank, schemes were drawn up to dig a linking tunnel under the Thames. The first of these was by Joseph Bazalgette whom we have already met as the designer of the great new sewage system for London. Despite his earlier successes some experts, most notably Alexander Binnie, Chief Engineer of the Metropolitan Board of Works, had serious doubts about the soundness of his tunnel scheme. The Board of Works was about to be dissolved to make way for the new London County Council and, largely to prevent the Board placing a contract for Bazalgette's scheme, Parliament agreed to the LCC taking over its powers ten days before the appointed date of 1 April 1889.

Binnie became the chief engineer for the LCC and re-designed the tunnel. Its construction marked a major advance in tunnelling techniques for it was driven below the river using the combination of a tunnelling shield and compressed air. The 800 people who built it advanced at the rate of only 100 feet a month along the total length of 6,200 feet. Since it was designed for use primarily by horse-drawn carts and waggons, it was essential to avoid steep gradients, and the tunnel roof had to be taken as close as possible to the bed of the river – at one point they are seperated by only five feet. The tunnel was opened in 1897 and had justified its construction within the first year when, 335,425 vehicles and over 4 million pedestrians passed through it. By the 1950s it was almost permanently congested and to relieve the flow the GLC built what is now the southbound tunnel between 1960 and 1967.

From the tunnel entrance we follow the river back to the south along Blackwall Reach. Opposite there are good views of the Isle of Dogs, during the 19th century another thriving docklands area, but by the 1960s in the terminal stages of decline. The abandoned acres of dockland here became an experiment in 'enterprise culture', the Isle of Dogs Free Enterprise Zone. The remnants of the old dockland community were displaced or surrounded by the ensuing developers' free-for-all. The beautiful and expensive new homes of the Free Enterprise Zone, some with their own beaches, can be seen lining the river all the way from Compass Point to Island Gardens.

Along the south bank meanwhile, the path leads through East Greenwich to Ballast Quay, which takes its name from the Blackheath gravel which was loaded here onto departing ships, fetching a very good price on the continent. The work was supervised from a Harbour Master's Office which still stands alongside the Cutty Sark public house and a pretty row of late 17th century houses.

Ballast Quay to the Trafalgar Tavern

ROUTE:
• Follow Ballast Quay and Crane Street along the riverside route to reach the Trafalgar Tavern.

FACILITIES: Several attractive riverside pubs.

The great and blank-walled bulk of Greenwich Power Station built in 1906 sits astride the riverside path. In its shadow, in one of the strangest juxtapositions of architecture in London, is the little 17th century Trinity Hospital. The two buildings create a fascinating combination, the power station looking like a big brother to the hospital, towering above it with a glowering protectiveness as if daring anyone to disturb the tranquility of the hospital precincts. It has even allowed the ivy from the Hospital gardens to cover expanses of its huge west wall.

The Trinity Hospital, or Norfolk College, was founded in 1613 by Henry Howard, Earl of Northampton, as a home for 20 pensioners, eight of whom were to come from Norfolk where Howard had been born. Its white castellated walls are topped by a clock tower and weather vane and if the wooden gates are open you can see through to the tiny courtyard where a fountain tinkles into a central pool. It has a sense of inviolable peacefulness and would be suggestive, were this not a Christian foundation, of the outer courtyard of an Islamic heaven.

In front of the hospital is a short stretch of road known as High Quay. Its name comes from the quay which was specially constructed here in the 15th century to facilitate unloading from the high Venetian galleys. The plaque set into the wall, however, commemorates not high galleys but a high tide. The last major inundation of central London came on 7 January 1928. Seventy five foot of this wall was demolished by the water which swept through the Hospital and into Greenwich.

The last stretch of road before the path reaches Greenwich itself is Crane Street. On the corner here, with a balcony over the river, is the Trafalgar Tavern. Wilkie Collins, Captain Marryat, Thackeray and Dickens all dined here and Dickens used it for the setting of Bella Wilfer's wedding breakfast in *Our Mutual Friend*. Despite its illustrious place in literary history the tavern closed in 1915, but it has the unusual distinction of having been saved rather than destroyed by the Second World War, for it was the onset of war which scotched the planned redevelopment of the site. It is now open for business again.

The Woolwich and Blackwall reaches of the river were regularly worked by whitebait fishers whose catch was off-loaded at waterside inns and the Trafalgar was the scene for several special whitebait events. One was an annual ministerial whitebait dinner held at the end of each parliamentary session throughout the reign of Queen Victoria. Another was an annual whitebait festival when decorated barges would ply between Swan Stairs and Greenwich Pier and unload their catch straight from net to pot.

Whitebait was probably the last fish to be caught commercially in the river. Long gone were the days when oysters were sold at 1d a dozen and London apprentices petitioned that 'they be not fed salmon so often'. Throughout the 19th century the level of pollution was continually increasing, to the detriment of Londoners who died of regular outbreaks of cholera and typhoid. In the 20th century the cocktail of human sewage, domestic waste and the effluvient from fish markets, tanneries and slaughter houses was compounded with a growing quantity of industrial pollutants. By the end of the Second World War it was said that the hydrogen sulphide released by the river was tarnishing the silver in ship's saloons, the buttons on uniformed jackets and the brass on ships' fittings. Suicides died of poisoning rather than drowning, and the stomach pump had become a standard part of rescue equipment. Nothing could live in these poisonous waters. In 1957 investigators found the forty-three miles of the Thames between Kew Bridge and Gravesend to be completely devoid of fish, bird or any other 'significant aquatic organism'.

The recovery of the tidal Thames between 1950 and the 1980s is one of the most often-told success stories of London. Improvements in sewage treatment plant, greater regulation, improvement in industrial processes and the determination of organisations like the GLC, the Thames Water Authority and the Port of London Authority, reduced pollution in the Thames by 90 per cent in 30 years. And this led to a return of the wildlife. In 1967 the riverside power stations of the Central Electricity Generating Board combined in a scheme to monitor the return of fish to the Thames. By 1974 their list of species had grown to 91 and included salmon and a sea-horse. This was followed by the return of the birds, beginning with large flocks of wildfowl during the cold winters of the early 1960s. Ducks, swans, geese, waders and heron all use the river today and one of the commonest sights is of cormorant, perched on buoys or the masts of boats or skimming low over the water in their evening flight upstream.

This great improvement of the river is, however, not an irreversible phenomenon. Between 1980 and 1985 Britain's rivers in general deteriorated for the first time in 25 years. In 1987 reported pollution incidents rose from 12,500 to 23,353. Along the Thames the number and variety of birds has already declined with the development of the dockland sites and in 1987 the Thames Water Authority was itself prosecuted for discharging raw sewage into the river upstream of London. With the great changes taking place within the water industry and in the regulation of rivers, Londoners will have to keep close watch to ensure that the Thames remains a living river.

Into Greenwich

ROUTE:
- Continue along the riverside route in front of the Royal Naval College buildings to reach Greenwich Pier and the Cutty Sark.

FACILITIES: Greenwich has toilets, cafés and pubs – and an eel and pie shop. There is a particularly wide choice in the Market area. The Cutty Sark and the Gipsy Moth are open to the public (entrance fee).

In 1427 Humphrey, Duke of Gloucester, brother of Henry V and Regent to the infant Henry VI, built Bella Court, a palatial residence on the riverside. The court of Henry VI, when he came to power, was riven with internal divisions. When Gloucester became a possible focus for public opposition his enemies moved against him. He was arrested in 1447 and murdered, one week later, in his prison cell. Margaret of Anjou, Henry's Queen, became owner of Bella Court.

For four hundred years this site remained the home of monarchs. As the Palace of Pleasaunce and later, the Palace of Placentia, it was the birthplace of both Henry

VIII and Elizabeth I, both of whom ran their courts from here. James I came to live here too and it was he who first enclosed the neighbouring hunting grounds of Greenwich Park. James I also began the construction of a new summer palace for his wife, Anne of Denmark. Queen Anne died before it was completed but it was continued under the instruction of Charles I for his own wife Henrietta Maria. Designed by Inigo Jones – another link between Charlton and Greenwich – the Queen's house was the first house in the country to be built in the new classical style. A cool, white villa, restrained and elegant, it can be seen set back across the main road between the blocks of the Royal Naval College. The building inspired many others, including the White House in Washington, and even the generals of the Commonwealth seem to have respected it. While they despoiled the great Palace of Placentia, stripping it of all its treasures, stabling horses in its halls and quartering troops about its buildings, the officers had their quarters in the Queens House and Oliver Cromwell himself was brought here to lie in state after his death.

By the time of the restoration the main palace was in ruins. Charles II planned to build a new palace on the site but only one block was ever completed. It was around this block, and the ruins of the great Palace of Placentia, that the present Royal Naval College buildings arose.

They were not originally built as a Naval College. After the British fleet had defeated the French at the Battle of the Bay of La Hogue, Queen Mary, wife of William of Orange, came down to Greenwich to greet the victorious returning sailors; what she saw of the sick and wounded disembarking shocked her profoundly and she decided to build a Royal Hospital for Seamen, appointing Christopher Wren as architect. He waived all his fees wishing 'to have some share in this great work of mercy.' The Queen rejected the initial designs on the grounds that they blocked the view of the river from the Queens House; Wren had to come up with new plans which divided the buildings into separate blocks, leaving a clear view down the middle. To this caprice of Queen Mary we owe the continuity of a magnificent vista, clear from the top of Greenwich Park through to the Isle of Dogs on the opposite bank of the river,

The hospital was finally completed in 1750 and became the home of several hundred naval pensioners. By 1814, after Nelson's death at Trafalgar and the end of the Napoleonic Wars, it had reached its capacity of 2710 inmates. After this it went into decline until eventually the hospital was closed in 1869 – the same year in which, on the banks of the Clyde in Dumbarton, the Cutty Sark was launched.

The listed 'buildings' of London include sewage works, gas-holders, underground stations, twenty-two concrete prehistoric monsters and a ship. The ship is the Cutty Sark, and it was a showpiece in its own day. Built to a revolutionary new design from America, it is sleeker and sharper than anything that went before. Its innovatory raked masts give it an air of jaunty self-confidence and there is something unmistakeably sensuous in its lines. As soon as she was launched the Cutty Sark was racing the other clippers on the long run to and from China. With its streamlined shape and its 30,000 square feet of sail the Cutty Sark could reach maximum speeds of 17½ knots – 360 miles in a day. But despite all these advantages, the shipyard which built it went bust from the expense and the Cutty Sark itself was overtaken by another, and more significant revolution, the coming of steam. The first steam ships were no faster than the clippers but they could use the new Suez Canal whilst the sailing ships had to travel the whole length of Africa and round the Cape.

The Cutty Sark was transferred to the Australian wool run and held her own for another 25 years, but this was putting off the inevitable. With their deeper holds and more regular services the steam ships came to supplant her even there.

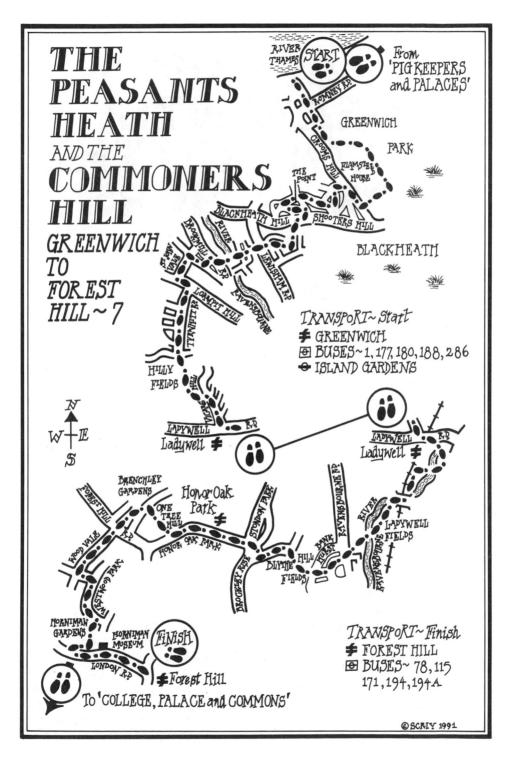

THE PEASANTS HEATH AND THE COMMONERS HILL

GREENWICH TO FOREST HILL ~ 7

RIVER THAMES

START

From 'PIG KEEPERS and PALACES'

GREENWICH PARK

ROMNEY RD

CROOMS HILL

FLAMSTEED HOUSE

THE POINT

BLACKHEATH HILL

SHOOTERS HILL

BLACKHEATH

ST JOHNS VALE

BROCKLEY RD

RIVER

LEWISHAM RD

RAVENSBOURNE

LAMPIT HILL

TURNPIKE

HILLY FIELDS

HILL

SHEAL

LADYWELL RD

Ladywell

LADYWELL RD

Ladywell

TRANSPORT ~ Start

🚆 GREENWICH
🚌 BUSES ~ 1, 177, 180, 188, 286
🚇 ISLAND GARDENS

N W E S

BRENCHLEY GARDENS

Honor Oak Park

ONE TREE HILL

FOREST HILL RD

WOOD VALE

HONOR OAK PARK

HORNIMAN GARDENS

HORNIMAN MUSEUM

FINISH

LONDON RD

🚆 Forest Hill

To 'COLLEGE, PALACE and COMMONS'

STONDON PARK

BLYTHE HILL FIELDS

BROCKLEY RISE

BANK

FOREST

RAVENSBOURNE RD

RIVER

LADYWELL FIELDS

RAVENSBOURNE

FORESTWOOD PARK

TRANSPORT ~ Finish

🚆 FOREST HILL
🚌 BUSES ~ 78, 115
171, 194, 194A

© SCRIY 1991

5. THE PEASANTS' HEATH AND THE COMMONERS' HILL

FROM GREENWICH TO FOREST HILL

The southward sweep of the London suburbs has inundated farms and fields, woods and hills and rural riversides. The huge area of housing which now covers so many square miles of what was once Kent and Surrey developed over a comparatively short period of time, the product of a Victorian building boom made possible by a transport revolution. The great 19th century period of railway building gave South London the busiest and most complex suburban network in the world, and it made it possible for the ever-growing army of clerks and scribblers who served the City to live further and further from their places of work, thus producing the dormitory suburbs of London.

Some of this piecemeal and rather chaotic development has both come and gone. Between Greenwich and Forest Hill we cross a string of urban nature reserves based on abandoned sidings or embankments whose rail lines have long since disappeared. A nature reserve on a railway site is a particularly appropriate development – as well as bringing people into London, the railways played an interesting and important role in the spread of urban wildlife. It was along the rail corridors that foxes were able to colonise the whole of South London and that Oxford ragwort reached the inner city. It is on the railway embankments that bank voles and wood mice feed and that ox-eye daisies, horse radish and escaped garden lupins have made their stand.

But the railway banks and the railway reserves are just a relic of a countryside which has been lost. Even before the housing arrived to replace the farmland, enclosure had seen the disappearance of commons and of the huge area of forest known as the Great North Wood. The great interests in this section of the walk today lies in uncovering the remnants of a rural history – in street name, in story and in the surviving fragments of heath, wood and field. Blackheath, transformed from a wild, undulating heath into a flat plain for footballers, still has its precious corners. There are reminders of the farmlands at Hilly Fields and Ladywell Fields and Blythe Hill Fields; and best of all there is that fragment of the forest that remains today as One Tree Hill. What all of these places have in common is that people have had to fight for them – sometimes quite literally. Contained in this chapter, and in this corner of London, are stories of struggle from the first recorded fight for commoners' rights anywhere in Britain, through to the 1897 'Battle for One Tree Hill'. Included along the way are the great peasant gatherings at Blackheath, and Octavia Hill's campaign to save Hilly Fields. These stories remain an inspiration at a time when unfettered development again threatens the open spaces and character of London and when, sometimes on the very same sites, ordinary people are having to struggle to preserve all that is best in their environment – space in which to stretch, breathe, look and be.

This chapter covers 6½ miles from the Cutty Sark at Greenwich to Horniman Park at Forest Hill. It can be split into two walks by using Ladywell Station (BR) but has been considered here as a single walk.

WALK 7: Greenwich to Forest Hill

Getting Started

From Greenwich Station:
  Turn left onto Greenwich High Road and continue onto Greenwich Church Street to reach the Cutty Sark.
From Island Gardens Station (Isle of Dogs):
  Take the foot tunnel under the river.
From buses:
  Follow King William Walk or Greenwich Church Street and signposts to Cutty Sark and the riverside.
From Walk 6:
  Continue from end of previous walk.

Greenwich Park

ROUTE:
- From the Cutty Sark walk up King William Walk past the college gates and continue ahead across the main road to reach the park.
- On entering the park bear left and follow the paths which lead up the hill to the prominent Observatory buildings.
- From the top of the hill follow the main park avenue alongside the Observatory buildings. At the junction of roads cross to the right and pick up the path which leads off between rows of ancient trees and beside a covered reservoir.
- Leave the park by the little gate beside Macartney House.

FACILITIES: Greenwich has pubs, cafés and an eel and pie shop. There is a particularly wide choice in the market area. There are toilets beside the Cutty Sark. There are toilets in Greenwich Park and a café near the Observatories. The Cutty Sark, the Gipsy Moth and the Observatories are all open to the public (entrance fee).

LOOKING AT WILDLIFE: There are over 60 species of bird recorded for Greenwich Park and breeding species include stock dove, coal tit, jackdaw and spotted flycatcher. The high ground around the Wolfe statue is also a good observation point for autumn migrants. There is an excellent collection of trees including ancient oaks and sweet chestnuts and exotic species such as prickly castor oil, Pride of India, Chinese yellow wood, foxglove tree, paper birch, Lebanese and Deodar cedars. There is a wildfowl collection in the formal gardens and next to these, the Wilderness has herds of red and fallow deer.

Whe the Duke of Gloucester built Bella Court by the riverside in 1427 (see chapter 4) he also obtained a Royal Licence to enclose 200 acres of Blackheath for hunting. This area of rough pasture, woodland and heath forms the basis of the Greenwich Park of today, but not without a major transformation in its appearance. Whilst in exile in France Charles had become familiar with the work of the great landscape artist Le Notre, which he would have seen at Versailles and elsewhere. In 1601, shortly after the restoration, he decided on a similar grand geometric design for the grounds of the palace at Greenwich, Although his exact involvement is uncertain, Le Notre was certainly consulted on the plans. The particular problem for the designers was the split nature of the site, the sudden drop in levels constituted by the Thames river terraces. It was solved by the layout of a system of avenues and vistas culminating at the highest point, where the Wolfe statue now stands; below this a series of earthworks, known as the Giant Steps led down the steep slope to the river level. These steps remain in only a degraded form and the slope has become a favourite site for tobogganing in winter, or for dizzy children to roll down in summer. This was the first place in England where a complex network of avenues was used as the main feature in a park design, and it was a direct forerunner of the development of landscape gardens during the 18th century.

Blackheath Avenue, the centrepiece of the design, provides a strong and historic central axis which subsequent developments have served to emphasise. From the spire of All Saints Church on the other side of Blackheath, the vista runs along the avenue to the 1930 statue of General Wolfe, the work of Tait Mackenzie. From here it continues down the slope to the Queens House, between the blocks of the Royal Hospital and across the river to Island Gardens and the Isle of Dogs. It previously continued to the spire of another church, St Anne's Limehouse; today it terminates in the phallic monstrosity of Canary Wharfe. This huge monument to money is the centre of the docklands development and has thrown everything else in London out of scale. Not only have the Greenwich buildings lost much of their former grandeur but the whole of London has had its focal point pushed several miles to the east. The view from the park demonstrates clearly how the skyline of London no longer centres on its churches or cathedrals but on the banks and office blocks which have come to dwarf them.

The 1660 planting plans for the park included 1000 elms and a large number of sweet chestnuts. Many of the chestnuts survive, ancient rugged trees with deeply ridged bark sweeping in great curves round the broad boles. A mature sweet chestnut is one of the most beautiful of trees and these specimens represent the oldest surviving ornamentally planted trees in England. They predate the first of the Observatory buildings by 15 years. In 1675 Charles II commissioned Wren to design a building 'for the Observators' habitation and a little for Pompe.' Charles however, wanted his 'pompe' on the cheap; he cut the budget for the building and decreed that it be paid for from the sale of old gunpowder. In Flamsteed House Wren nonetheless produced a beautiful building, an octagonal red-brick tower rising directly from the top of the hill. Closer examination reveals one of the economies forced upon the builder; some of the 'stone' facings are actually made of wood.

The Rev John Flamsteed, after whom the building is named, lived and worked here as the first Astronomer Royal. He continued to experience problems with the king's stinginess. He received an 'incompetent allowance' of £100 a year for himself and his staff and was obliged to take up private tutoring to make ends meet. The king failed even in his commitment to provide instruments for his 'Royal' Observatory.

Flamsteed's main work was in the detailed plotting of stars, from which he was attempting to make a perfect computation of longitude. Isaac Newton, one of the people who depended on these observations for his own work, seems to have abused his relationship with Flamsteed by publishing, under the title of 'Historia Celestis', a pirated version of Flamsteed's work. Flamsteed was understandably bitter. 'How unworthily, nay treacherously, I am dealt with by sir Isaac Newton', he wrote; and three years later he managed to obtain all 300 copies of the book and burnt them as 'a sacrifice to Heavenly Truth'.

When Airey's Meridian was finally accepted as longitude zero for the world in 1884 it was only sixteen yards from the location fixed for it by Flamsteed 200 years earlier. In the same year an international conference in Washington accepted Greenwich mean time as the basis of the world's time-keeping system. The atmospheric pollution around London, especially the output from the Greenwich and Deptford power stations, eventually made the area unsuitable for astronomic observation and the Observatory moved from here in 1948.

The Park was first opened to the public in the 18th century and became a firm favourite on the London tourist itinerary. It now receives over 2 million visitors a year and this, combined with the earlier effects of pollution, has caused extensive damage and a serious erosion problem. Both wild flowers and breeding bird species have decreased in numbers, though foxes are common and the ubiquitous grey squirrels were feeding from the hand here long before they were such a familiar sight elsewhere. The animals most closely connected with the history of the Park are no longer wild at all: deer were first introduced here in 1510 and for many years they ranged freely, but now they are enclosed in 'The Wilderness', a fenced area adjacent to the formal gardens. Here, no longer the 'monarchs of the glen' or the prey of kings, they doze in the dappled shade of trees or try to beg food from visitors, despite the signs forbidding it. They have become, said Henry James, describing a visit to the park, as 'tame as sleepy children'.

Blackheath and The Point

ROUTE:
• From the park gate cross the road and continue ahead, descending the grassy hillside to reach the curving road below (Hyde Vale).
• Turn left along Hyde Vale and take the first turning on the right (West Grove). Walk between the houses and the narrow heath extension and continue ahead along West Grove Lane, descending to Dartmouth Row.
• Cross the road and follow the path opposite. Turn left up the steps to reach the grassy plateau known as The Point.
• Walk straight ahead across the plateau to reach Point Road. Turn right along the paved path to reach Blackheath Hill, the main road across the heath.

LOOKING AT WILDLIFE: Blackheath has been largely denuded of its wildlife but a number of visiting birds still occur. Meadow brown butterflies can sometimes be seen and the stag beetle is said to be endemic. There is a variety of grasshoppers on the longer grass, including the lesser marsh grasshopper, a coastal species which has spread from the Thames marshes. Stagshorn plantain, is generally a maritime plant species, but this can also be found, in trampled areas, especially around benches.

In 1381 the peasantry of South East England occupied London. It was the culmination of the Peasants' Revolt which saw uprisings in no less than 28 counties. After years in which landless labourers had struggled against subsistence wages, and half-freed villeins against manorial oppression, came the final provocation – the first attempt in this country to impose a poll tax. In order to pay for its French wars, the government of the boy-king Richard II had levied a charge of 3 groats per person on everyone over the age of 15.

From Kent and Essex huge contingents of peasants marched on the capital. They were inspired by the popular Christianity of hedge preachers and itinerant friars such as John Ball, who preached the revolutionary doctrine of the equality of all in the eyes of God. Their largest contingent marched from Kent onto Blackheath. Led by Wat Tyler, a blacksmith from Dartford, they arrived here 10,000 strong on 12 June. Using the heath as their camp they sortied into London, where they found the gates opened before them by the London poor and a sympathetic party amongst the aldermen. As they streamed through London, the 'impregnable' Tower was surrendered, the Fleet and Marshalsea prisons opened, the Monastery of St John of Jerusalem burnt and the Temple library destroyed together with all the hated lawyer's rolls.

King Richard – still only 14 years old, went to meet the rebel force at Smithfield.

During this meeting William Walworth, Lord Mayor of London, pulled Tyler from his horse and stabbed him to death. The rebels dispersed, most of them returning to their lands where they were met with revengeful punishment by their 'lords'. The leaders of the revolt were executed and the uprising seemed to have been defeated. But it was to leave an indelible mark on history. In the short term, the hated poll tax was abolished. In the longer term, the peasantry had shown what a potent force it could be when roused; and it was 600 years before anyone attempted to levy a poll tax again.

Only 70 years later Blackheath was once again the focus of rebellion. Almost bankrupted by its years of wasteful war, the government of Henry VI attempted to make good its deficit by imposing higher taxes on a country already simmering with discontent. In 1450 Jack Cade led 20,000 Kent and Essex yeomen onto the heath, where they set up camp. They laid the 'Blackheath Petition' before the Royal Council, calling on the king 'to punish evil ministers and procure a redress of grievance'. The state pretended to consider the demands whilst sending Sir Humphrey Stafford with a force to crush the rebels. But it was Stafford who was defeated and killed and the rebels entered London in triumph. After occupying the capital for three days the rebels received an offer from the government to consider their demands and began to disperse to their homes. Promises however were not enough for Jack Cade who continued to demand real concessions. But his support had melted away. He was forced to flee into hiding in Sussex where the kings forces eventually caught up with and murdered him. His name is commemorated in Cade Road on the heath.

By 1497 the rebels were back, in what was to be the last and most tragic of the great peasant rallyings on the heath. This time they had marched all the way from Cornwall, 6,000 of them led by Thomas Flannock and Michael Joseph, in protest against taxes levied to pay for the Scottish wars. This time there was to be no treating or negotiating. Henry VII dispatched his army and in the 'Battle of Blackheath' up to 2000 of the rebels were killed and their bodies unceremoniously dumped in mass graves. The survivors surrendered and their leaders were taken for execution. Whitfield Mount, behind the Whitfield pond on Goffers Road, is the remains of one of these burying places.

For thousands of years Blackheath was a wild tract of heathland covered with gorse and heather. In the 18th century the great Swedish scientist Linnaeus arrived here on a visit and is said to have been so struck by the masses of yellow gorse blossom that he fell to his knees in wonder and offered up thanksgiving to the 'great Creator of Nature'. It was Linnaeus who devised the scientific binomial system which remains the basis of taxonomy. Should he turn up on the heath today he would find very little wildlife left to label. As late as 1859, its fauna was listed as including weasel, stoat, polecat, hare, harvest mouse and even the rare natterjack toad. At one time there were more species of grass to be found on Blackheath than anywhere else in Southern England. But its animals are gone; its grass the tough imported strains of football pitches. Blackheath is, for the most part, a tired and barren green waste. Even its one-time undulations were infilled with rubble from the blitz. Litter floats in its remaining ponds and the whole plateau has been reduced to a dreary uniformity, a flat expanse of football and rugby pitches sliced up by an excessive network of roads. The main interest of the Heath now lies in its history, in the architecture of its surrounding houses, and in the one or two surviving corners that have escaped over-regulation. These include the old gravel pits around Vanbrugh Park and the slopes of Hyde Vale. It is at this latter point that our own route emerges from Greenwich Park.

The rambling red-brick range beside the Croomshill Gate is Macartney House, built around 1676, and from 1751 to 1758 the home of General James Wolfe. Further up Chesterfield Walk is the stylish villa known as the Rangers House. Lord Chesterfield, who inherited it in 1748, wrote here the book which became famous as *Letters to his Son*. The letters are full of pompous homilies: 'There is nothing so illiberal and so ill-bred as audible laughter' wrote Chesterfield, and 'women ... are only children of a larger growth'. The recipient of such wisdom was Phillip Stanhope, Chesterfield's natural son. Perhaps the most revealing feature of their relationship is that Stanhope married and raised a family – and kept it a life-long secret from his father. Rangers House, later the official residence of that royal sinecure post, the Park Ranger, is today a museum housing paintings and musical instruments.

Across Hyde Vale from here we reach The Point, a small Westward extension of the Blackheath plateau, in an area of elegant 18th century housing. From here there is an uninterrupted panorama of London taking in Greenwich, Deptford and the City. The Point is in fact a hollow hill: in 1780 a local builder chanced across a vertical shaft which led down into three caverns, the largest of which was 58 foot long, 30 foot wide and 12 foot high. The origin of the caverns is unknown but it is likely they were chalk excavations of some kind for here layers of chalk are nearer to the surface than anywhere else around Blackheath.

The entrepreneurial Victorians subsequently put the caverns to use. The public were admitted for viewings at 4d a time and, once a bar had been fitted, they became a regular venue for drinking parties, balls and dances. No doubt the local residents were continually disturbed by the revellers attracted to their neighbourhood and in 1853 came the final outrage: a practical 'joker' doused all the lights in the course of a masked ball, panic ensued and there was a stampede for the exits. The outcry about this led to the closure of the caverns and the entrance passage was filled in so effectively that it became impossible to re-locate. In 1938, when the local authorities commissioned a report on the possible use of the caverns as air-raid shelters, they were unable to find the entrance, and were forced to sink a new shaft down. Their conclusions were that the caverns were unsuitable for shelters but a passage in their report describes the main chamber, still with half-burnt candles standing on the abandoned bar. The site has become a sort of sealed time capsule, remaining just as it was left late one night by the revellers of 1853.

The Valley of the Ravensbourne

ROUTE:
• Go straight across Blackheath Hill into Dartmouth Row and turn right at the junction with Dartmouth Hill.

- Descend Dartmouth Hill and turn left into the unmade lane beside Montague House. Half way along the Lane turn right onto the paved viewing area.
- Follow the wooden steps down the hill and onto the estate. Bear left at the end, between the estate and the steep bank, keeping to the left at the childrens' playgrounds to reach the main road.
- Cross the main Lewisham Road and, a few yards to the right, take the path which runs down through the Orchard Estate.
- Cross Coldbath Street into Ravensbourne Place and then bear left alongside the river to find the footbridge leading into Brookmill Park.
- The path ahead leads to Brookmill Road across which is the Brookmill Nature Reserve. The main route leads through the gate on the right into Brookmill Park.
- Leave the park by the gate onto Brookmill Road, just before the main lake. Cross the road and take Bolden Street opposite. Turn right at the end into Albyn Road.
- Turn left into St Johns Vale to reach Lewisham Way.

FACILITIES: There is an attractive pub, the Ravensbourne Arms, on Coldbath Street. Toilets in Ravensbourne Park. Pub and cafés on Lewisham Way.

LOOKING AT WILDLIFE: Alkanet, salad burnet and giant hogweed all grow along Morden Lane. Brookmill Park lake attracts some wildfowl and there are goldfinches and greenfinches in the formal gardens. The Nature Reserve has a variety of native trees and wild flowers.

The smart houses of Dartmouth Row and Dartmouth Hill were an illegal encroachment on common land. Building began on the Heath in 1690 and continued in a piecemeal way until 1866, when those already living there decided to prevent anybody else doing what they had already done by founding a preservation society. Within a year they had already managed to get an Act through parliament preventing any further development on Blackheath. It was part of the first national legislation giving protection to common land.

From Morden Lane – named after one of the major landowners in the area – we drop down the steep sides of a tributary valley cut by the River Ravensbourne. What looks today a tame and restricted little stream has, over thousands of years, cut down through forty foot of sands and gravels and into the underlying chalk. The steep slopes at the back of the Lethbridge Estate were the site of Loats Pit where chalk was quarried and burnt in kilns. According to Duncan's 1908 *History of Lewisham*, they provided much of the lime required for the rebuilding of London after the Great Fire. The slopes continue in gentler fashion down through the Orchard Estate, once the site of the 'Home for Fatherless Girls', to Coldbath Street and the river itself.

According to legend, Julius Caesar was campaigning in Southern England when his forces ran out of water. They were forced to encamp whilst sending out detachments in search of a supply. They were unsuccesful but Caesar himself had noted ravens regularly flying to and from a spot not far from the camp. He sent out more men to investigate and they came upon the small spring on Keston Heath still known as Caesar's or Raven's Well. Legend does not relate how everyone else had missed so obvious a source. From this spring arises our river, the Ravens Bourne, flowing 10½ miles to reach the Thames at Deptford.

The Ravensbourne's channel, particularly above Ladywell, is confined and tortuous and particularly liable to flooding. In September 1968, after a week of heavy rain, the river burst its banks from Loampit Vale through Lewisham and all the way upstream to Beckenham. The tributaries of the river were overflowing too, the Poole River up as far as Bell Green, and the Quaggy inundating Kidbrooke. The normally insignificant Quaggy rose in a few hours from 6 inches to 14 foot in depth. There was another fourteen foot of water filling the Odeon Cinema in Lewisham. The High Street became a river four foot deep, whilst basement flats in the area were inundated almost to their ceilings. Hundreds of people were evacuated to emergency centres, 40,000 phones were cut off, firemen took to boats and the Mayor toured the area, not in his Mayoral limousine, but in a dinghy.

Following the tradition established by Julius Caesar, the Ravensbourne was long a source of drinking water. In 1701 the Ravensbourne Water Company founded, on the site of today's Brookmill Park, the Deptford Waterworks. In 1809 this became the Kent Waterworks and an engine house of this period survives in the park as the grey stock brick storehouse. Next to the engine house the water company sunk a well through 272 foot of chalk to reach the artesian basin under London. Water trapped in the porous chalk beds was forced up to the surface by the weight of the rock above. These 'artesian wells' were the main source of drinking water for Londoners for many years. Even the fountains in Trafalgar Square at one time operated on the natural pressure of artesian bores. Over the years however so much water was withdrawn from the basin that it became inoperative as a source of supply and the water authorities turned to reservoir building, a process which was to have a big impact on the wildlife of London. Here, the lake, with its Canada geese, coot and moorhen, and the inevitable weeping willow, is the last remnant of the reservoir which once covered much of the site.

As the waterworks declined so the park expanded. Beginning in 1880 as a small recreation ground around the now bombed Emmanuel Church it grew through a series of stages to reach its present size in 1951. It is a well maintained and attractively laid-out little park with those gaudy bedding displays beloved of the municipalities, a peat bed with azaleas and rhododendrons, a rose pergola and some more natural landscaped beds thick with bluebell and forget-me-not. Along the south end of the park runs a wooded embankment which marks the route of the old Greenwich Park branch line railway, which opened in 1888. By which time the route had lost much of its potential importance and despite some traffic from outings to the park it was never very succesful, and by 1917 it had already succumbed to competition from the tramways. The line crossed Brookmill Road, named after the silkmills which once stood in this vicinity, and the remains of the embankment on the opposite side have been turned into the Brookmill Nature Reserve.

Hilly Fields to Blythe Hill Fields

ROUTE:
- Turn left onto Lewisham Way and cross it to take Tyrwhitt Road, the first turning on the right.
- At the end of Tyrwhitt Road take the path straight ahead up Hilly Fields. Just before reaching the summit fork to the left of the red-brick toilet block and carry on straight ahead, passing the trig point and following the path which curves around left to meet Vicars Hill.
- Turn right down Vicars Hill and at the end turn left onto Ladywell Road.
(WALK SEVEN CAN BE BROKEN INTO TWO WALKS BY STOPPING AT LADYWELL STATION OR BY CONTINUING AHEAD TO LEWISHAM HIGH STREET FOR BUSES.)
- Cross the railway bridge and after it take the second footpath on the right.
- A short detour straight ahead leads to the Church. For the main route fork right at the first junction of paths to cross the footbridge.
- Turn left in Ladywell Park and follow the riverside. Cross the river at the second footbridge and take the footbridge over the railway.
- Carry on along the riverside beneath a railway bridge and across the river for a third time, to emerge onto Ladywell Fields. Take the middle path of the three facing you to reach the road (Ravensbourne Park).
- Turn left on the road. Take the first right (Ravensbourne Park Crescent) and the first right again (Montacute Road). On reaching the T junction the passage immediately opposite leads onto Blythe Hill Fields.

FACILITIES: Ladywell Park has toilets, childrens playgrounds and a refreshment hut (summer months only). There are toilets and and a children's playground in Blythe Hill Fields.

LOOKING AT WILDLIFE: There are yews and turkey oak in St Mary's churchyard. Nearby, Himalayan balsam grows on one of the few natural stretches of the Ravensbourne. The trees in Ladywell Park include walnut and a weeping wych elm.

O ctavia Hill was one of the many remarkable women of the Victorian era. Born in 1838 she originally trained as an artist and became a protegé, and later a close friend, of John Ruskin. In early adulthood she developed a passionate interest in the housing conditions of the London working classes; her idea was to buy up areas of housing herself and then to improve them for the tenants. She made her first purchases through Ruskin in 1865 and by 1874 had the plan on a firm business footing, raising funds through friends and devoting her time to housing reform. In 1884 the Ecclestiastical Commissioners, one of the largest property owners in London, began to put her in charge of some of their own areas of housing and it was in this way that she assumed responsibility for 133 homes in Deptford and began her connection with the area. 'Poor Deptford, our black sheep' she called it, finding it an area particularly resistant to her brand of reforms. In a poorly furnished room in one of the Deptford houses she one day noticed a vase of freshly picked wild flowers. She was told they had been picked on Hilly Fields, and set off the same day to locate the place.

Octavia was concerned not only with the housing conditions of the London poor but with the quality of the environment in which they had to live. In 1875 she had campaigned unsuccesfully to save her beloved Swiss Cottage Fields from development and thereafter became an executive member of the Commons Preservation Society. Time and again she found herself campaigning against the building developments that were devouring the open spaces enjoyed by Londoners, especially those for whom the opportunity to walk across common or field was one of the few reliefs from atrocious living conditions. 'The thousands of rich people,' she said in 1883, 'who owe their wealth to London, or who avail themselves of its advantages, have not, as far as I know, given one single acre of ground, that could have been sold for building over, to Londoners for recreation ground or Park, if we except Leicester Square.'

The Hilly Fields discovered by Octavia Hill was a London clay outcrop above the Thanet sands, a beautiful hilly prominence rising to 175 feet with extensive views over London. Somehow it had so far escaped the development which was swallowing up Brockley all around it. The area then was mostly farmland, with an area of game shooting common to the south. This latter part had already been leased to developers for building and Octavia realised that none of the site would be spared for long. She helped establish a committee to save the Fields and set about raising funds for its purchase. The recently formed London County Council soon lent its support but it was not without a difficult and protracted campaign that the fields were finally secured for the public. They were 'opened' on 16 May 1896, by which time Octavia Hill had moved on to other campaigns, among them that abiding monument to her work, the National Trust, which she co-founded in 1885.

Our route to Hilly Fields takes us across Lewisham Way where the establishment Anglican Church stands next to the Ewglys Presbyteriad Cymru. The parish church of St John is Gothic revival, its restrained and suburban white stone contrasting with the dark-leaved evergreen holm oaks in its grounds. Built in 1855 it served a growing congregation as the farmlands of Lewisham and Brockley disappeared beneath street after street of housing, among them Tyrwhitt Road, named after the Tyrwhitt-Drakes, previously one of the area's major land-owning families.

After crossing Hilly Fields we descend into Ladywell, which is named after not one well but two. The 'lady' in question was probably the Virgin Mary, to whom the wells were dedicated, though some accounts suggest it was the attendant who dispensed the healing water. These were chalybeate springs with a high mineral content and particularly recommended at the time for the treatment of eye complaints. One of the springs was beside the river just beyond the Ladywell Bridge and the site was later taken over by the swimming baths. This building, now a community centre, remains one of the most interesting and attractive in the area. It is of red brick with granite window dressings and string courses. Best of all though, is the round water tower with pierced surrounds and pointed windows. The walls of the Baths have a strange adornment; they are pitted with hundreds of vertical grooves where children queueing impatiently for admittance ground their threepenny bits into the brickwork.

From Ladywell Road our route follows the winding course of the river for over a mile through Ladywell Park and the Fields. In the 19th century the rich water meadows were glebe land attached to the parish of St Mary's. In 1889 they were purchased by the London County Council and the Lewisham Board of Works. The meadows were drained and landscaped, the river straightened, its bends cut off to form islands, and the whole opened as the new Ladywell Recreation Grounds. A photograph of 1900 shows it still threaded with a broad and shallow river, children paddling along its banks and sheep grazing in the background. Today the river is controlled and contained and hidden behind fencing. But even with its concrete casing, its backdrop of railways, its islands planted with unsuitable and sickly bushes of aucuba and box, it manages here and there to maintain a rural air, where it is overhung with alders, elms and hawthorns.

At the northern end of the Fields is the Parish Church of St Mary's, a classical, aristocratic structure belonging to a time when Lewisham and Ladywell were much wealthier places. Parts of the tower date back to the 15th century, but most of the church belongs to the 18th and 19th centuries. Its most striking feature is the unusual Grecian porch, four columns supporting a large and rather out-of-scale pediment. The attractive little churchyard between the path and the river contains the grave of the Irish poet Thomas Dermody.

The few short streets which link Ladywell Fields to Blythe Hill Fields are unremarkable but for the name of one of them. Montacute Road leads a short distance from Bankhurst Road to Blythe Hill. It also leads into a story of intrigue, torture and regicide.

Edward II came to the throne of England in 1307. He was not a man who would enjoy or excel at the martial activities – war and the tournament – which would have earned him the respect of the troublesome barons of England. Nor were they impressed by his homosexual relationships. He was defeated at the battle of Bannockburn in 1314, and this seriously weakened his standing. He married Isabella, daughter of Philip the Fair of France, but as their relationship worsened she spent more time back in France. The story goes that there she met Roger Mortimer, one of the great Marcher Lords, in exile after an unsuccessful revolt, and that the two became lovers and began to plot a take-over of the English throne. They landed in 1326 and Edward was usurped with hardly a hand raised in his defence. He was imprisoned eventually in Berkeley Castle where legend has it that, on the night of 21 September 1327, they sent murderers into his cell who killed him by pushing a red hot poker into his bowels.

The new king Edward III, son of Isabella and Edward II, was still a boy. For four years Roger and Isabella were able to rule in his stead, but when Edward III reached his majority the situation suddenly and unexpectedly changed. One night a group of Edward's closest associates entered Nottingham Castle by a secret passage and seized Mortimer. The leader of the band was William Montague, also known as

Montacute. Sir Roger Mortimer was arraigned before parliament and hung at Tyburn. Isabella was placed under house arrest at Castle Rising, and remained there in isolation for the rest of her life. Montacute was rewarded with the Manor of Catford, and Montacute Road, within the bounds of the old Manor, now bears his name.

The Battle for One Tree Hill

ROUTE
- Cross Blythe Hill Fields, bearing to the right at the first junction of paths to reach the road (Codrington Hill).
- Turn left here, then right onto Gladiator Street. Turn left and right again to reach the main road (Stondon Park).
- Cross Stondon Park and continue straight ahead down Honor Oak Park.
- Carry on past the station and the entrance to the sports ground. After passing the allotments take the gate on the right which leads up steps onto a woodland path past the church.
- At the summit of One Tree Hill carry on straight ahead to descend on the other side. Follow the path all the way downhill to reach the road (Brenchley Gardens). Cross the road and enter the gardens by the gate opposite.

FACILITIES: Cafés on Honor Oak Park.

LOOKING AT WILDLIFE: A detour to the left from Honor Oak Park leads down Devonshire Road to the Devonshire Road Nature Reserve. This is a 6 acre London Wildlife Trust reserve of woodland and grassland with a wide variety of bird, plant and butterfly species. One Tree Hill is mixed woodland with oak and ash and introduced species like plane and robinia. It supports a good variety of woodland birds including jays, tits and warblers and there are speckled wood butterflies along the paths and clearings.

Blythe Hill is another in the succession of prominences which we follow across South London. Its modest 200 feet saved it from development and it was opened as a public park in 1935; it is now surrounded by the rather amorphous but pleasant suburb of Brockley. The name comes from two Anglo-Saxon words, broc meaning brook and leah, meaning a clearing or glade. Until the 18th century Brockley was a village set in a clearing in the huge expanse of the Great North Wood, which stretched for miles over much of what is now South London. The wood survives in names such as Norwood, Forest Wood, Forest Hill and Westwood, and in a remaining fragment at Honor Oak.

The 'honour' oak itself stands at the top of One Tree Hill. It is said to derive its name from Elizabeth I who picnicked here in 1662 whilst out 'a-maying' with Sir

Richard Buckley, but the real origin is undoubtedly much older; a large oak tree at the top of a hill has a pre-Christian religious significance. This importance continued into comparatively recent times, for the beating of the Parish bounds, which took place once every three years, always ended under the branches of the honour oak. Traditionally the ceremony would finish with the singing of Psalm 104; it is no doubt a comment on the decline of organised religion that when the ceremony last took place in 1899, the assembled dignitaries could not remember the words of Psalm 104 and were forced to sing the much shorter Psalm 100 instead.

The woodland which now clothes One Tree Hill is secondary woodland, much changed since the days of the great forest. The native oaks and ashes which grow there are mixed with introduced and exotic species from many other parts of the world – flowering cherries, false acacia, sycamore and plane. Similarly the honourable oak surrounded by palings at the summit is not the original ancient tree but a more recent replacement, planted in 1905 in a ceremony which marked the outcome of the 'Battle for One Tree Hill'.

For generations the residents of Honor Oak had regarded One Tree Hill as common land. Then, one morning in 1896, they awoke to find the hill surrounded by a six foot fence. It had been erected by the local golf club which now claimed to have a legitimate lease on the land. Within a few days an 'Enclosure of Honor Oak Hill Protest Committee' was holding its first meeting in the Samuel Bowley Coffee Tavern on Peckham Rye. With the support of the Commons Preservation Society it began the laborious business of researching the legal status of the land. This constitutional mode of procedure was too slow for most local people and public anger boiled over when two local boys faced criminal proceedings from the golf club for alleged damage to the fence.

On the next Sunday, 15,000 people gathered on the slopes of the hill. Directing their attacks from Honor Oak Park and Honor Oak Rise, they tore down the fence and swarmed across the Hill in what the authorities described as a 'disorderly multitude'. The groundkeeper's cottage was attacked and seriously damaged and the crowds dispersed only as police reinforcements arrived.

The following Saturday three disaffected members of the Protest Committee, which had dissociated itself from the demonstration, cut down a section of the fence and, having notified the press, the police and the golf club in advance, invited the authorities to arrest them. The next day, crowds estimated variously as between 50,000 and 100,000 again massed around the hill. This time they were met by large contingents of foot and mounted police. As the crowd stormed the fences the police made a mounted charge. Missiles were thrown, furze bushes fired and a police inspector injured. Nine people were arrested of whom five were sent to prison for their part in the battle to liberate the hill.

In spite of these activities, it was not until 1902 and the establishment of the London County Council that the land was saved for the public. Using its new compulsory purchase powers it took the golf club to court and completed its acquisition two years later. In 1905, in the presence of 30,000 spectators, One Tree Hill was officially re-opened to the public and the latest of the 'oaks of honour' planted on its summit.

At the bottom of the hill stands Brenchley Gardens, built partly on the line of the old Crystal Palace railway. The main part of this attractive but slightly ramshackle park, with its rose pergola, its fragrant cypresses and its shrubberies, was opened in 1928. The Camberwell Borough Council decided to name the gardens after William Brenchley, one time Mayor of Camberwell and the first Freeman of the Borough. The LCC had a policy that sites should not be named after people who were still alive and therefore refused to endorse the name. In an imaginative counter-stroke the Borough Council announced that it was still calling them Brenchley Gardens – after the village of Brenchley in Kent.

The Battle for Westwood

ROUTE:
- Bear left in Brenchley Gardens, walk down through the gardens and the planted woodland area to exit onto the main Forest Hill Road.
- Cross Forest Hill Road and keep straight ahead on Wood Vale, alongside the cemetery.
- Take the first left into Langton Rise and then right at the T junction into Westwood Park.
- At the bend on Westwood Park take the footpath between the houses.
- At the junction of paths:
- EITHER: Turn right to follow alongside the railway nature reserve and connect directly with Walk 8 OR:
- Turn left to complete this walk.
- Follow the path to the park gates. Turn left inside the park and follow the path which curves to the right in front of the animal enclosures. Follow the main avenue ahead to reach the main road, adjacent to the Museum.

FACILITIES: Toilets in Brenchley Gardens and Horniman Gardens.
Ladies toilets in Camberwell Old Cemetery. Pub in Wood Vale. Café in Horniman Museum.

LOOKING AT WILDLIFE: The woodland in Camberwell Cemetery has a population of woodland birds, flowers and butterflies. Horniman Gardens has animal enclosures with bantam, guinea fowl, cranes, wallabies and rabbits. There is a very fine collection of exotic trees including Western hemlock, deodar, mop headed acacia, red maple, snake bark maple, corkscrew willow and red oak. The fine formal gardens include a very attractive water garden and a conservatory. There are three nature trails, one along the railway embankment nature reserve adjacent to the gardens.

amberwell Cemetery, unusually for a cemetery designed for 'the middle, artisan and poorer classes', was laid out in great style. Founded in 1856 it covered nearly 30 acres and was equipped with chapels designed by the great

George Gilbert Scott. Following these promising beginnings however, it soon fell into a state of disrepair. Today, by contrast it is one of the most attractive of the still 'active' cemeteries in London. There is a 'semi-maintained' condition here which avoids that stultifying and sterile conformity of so many of our modern cemeteries where the headstones stand in unrelieved rows, as boring, and as mundane, as a queue at the grocer's. Here jays and finches and speckled wood butterflies fly among ashes, chestnuts, sycamores and thorn trees, and away in the south west corner a large unused area has returned to woodland.

Wood Vale, once the boundary between Kent and Surrey, leads us into Westwood Park. The names recall stretches of the Great North Wood, and Westwood is honourable amongst them. It was the site of the first recorded fight for commoners' rights in Britain. The Westwood once extended over 500 acres and was part of the Manor of Lewisham. The poorer inhabitants of the area had for generations used it for pasturage and for furze cutting, and regarded it as common land; but in 1605 it was granted by the king to Henry Newport, a local member of the gentry and a 'yeoman of ye boiling house to James I'.

The commoners immediately made complaint and the case came to trial in 1606. The Commissioners attempted the impossible by coming down on both sides and saying it was both the 'Kings waste' to dispose of as he pleased, and a common. Naturally this satisfied nobody and the case went on to the Court of Exchequer in 1607. The commoners won their case but Newport and two associates immediately, and despite the ruling, took possession of 347 acres of the common.

The case was brought to court a third time, this time with a jury from the County of Kent, which decided in Newport's favour. He immediately began to make ditches and enclose the common, driving the commoners off and killing their cattle. The commoners responded by demolishing the fences and filling the ditches. As the crisis came to a head the local vicar, Abraham Colfe, led 100 parishioners to London to make a direct appeal to the king who referred the case to the Lords of Privy Council. A retrial was ordered. On 16 October 1615 it came before the Barons of the Exchequer; the rest of the story is told by the Reverend Colfe;

> The Lord's holy name for ever for his great tender mercies be blessed a verdict passed in the behalfe of the poore inhabitants and on the 18th of November following judgement was also granted and a copy of both of the order and of ye judgement taken out under the seale of the Exchequer Chamber which is kept by us.

It was a great victory for the commoners and lasted for two hundred years. In 1810 an Act of Parliament was passed authorising the enclosure of the whole of the common. Westwood, except as a street name, disappeared.

The footpaths from Westwood lead us to the Horniman Gardens and the Horniman Museum, a free gift from Frederick Horniman 'to the people for ever'. Frederick was the son of John Horniman who had founded a tea business and became the first person to sell tea in sealed packets. He had been a keen collector since childhood and was able to indulge his passion with a vengeance in his work for the tea company. He travelled at least twice round the world, taking in Egypt, India,

Sri Lanka, Burma, China, Japan, Canada and the USA. From each of these countries he made a point of bringing back artifacts illustrating either their natural history or their arts and handicrafts.

In 1868 he moved into Surrey House at the top of Forest Hill, where eventually his 'artefacts' filled so much space that there was no longer room for both his family and his collection. It was the family which had to move – and they took up residence in the adjacent Surrey Mount, which stood on the highest point of what is now Horniman Gardens. Its name, though eroding rapidly, can still be seen on the stone pillars of the main gate. In 1890 Frederick, who was by now both Chairman of the tea firm and MP for Falmouth, opened his collection to the public as a free museum. Within seven years it was receiving over 90,000 visitors a year with 3,270 people crowding into Surrey House on a single Bank Holiday. It was obvious that a brand new building was necessary.

Frederick Horniman, and the architect C. Harrison Townsend, have given us one of the most interesting and individual buildings in London. Completed in 1901 in Art Nouveau style it cleverly makes use of the steep slope into which it is set. The arched frontage of the South Hall faces the road and set slightly apart from it is a tower in beautifully grained and honey-coloured stone, with rounded corners from which four little subsidiary towers emerge as naturally as buds. The hall frontage bears a large mosaic panel by Anning Bell, its 117,000 pieces depicting a rather obscure allegory on the course of human life. From the museum, the Gardens, which were originally the grounds of Surrey Mount, slope up through lawns and shrubberies, a sunken formal garden and a water garden to a summit at 300 foot, the same height as One Tree Hill. In the autumn there is a stunning display of autumn colour as the great variety of exotic trees across the grounds turn red, brown, yellow, ochre and golden. There is a miniature zoo, a genuine Dutch Barn and no less than three nature trails.

One of these trails follows the comparatively wild railway embankment adjacent to the park, another remnant of the Crystal Palace Branch line. Another crosses a terrace on the eastern side of the park with extensive views over Kent and London. Here on summer evenings the ghosts of an Edwardian couple are said to appear, dancing arm in arm. There can be no more agreeable way of conducting a haunting.

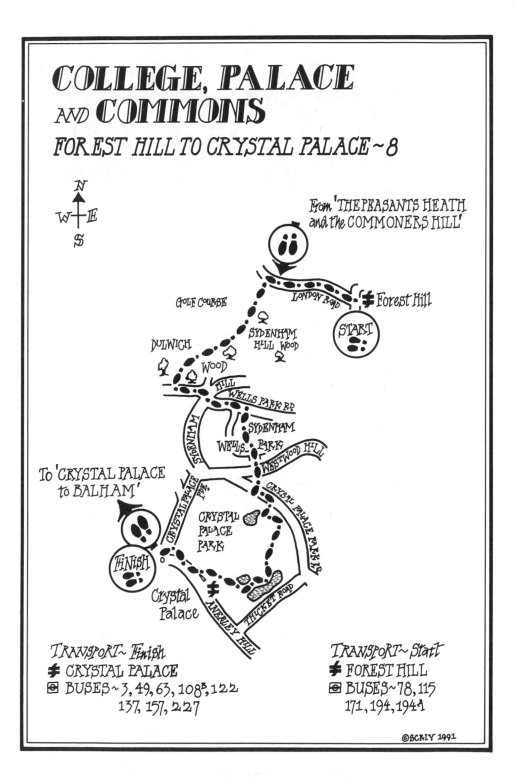

COLLEGE, PALACE AND COMMONS

FOREST HILL TO CRYSTAL PALACE ~ 8

From 'THE PEASANTS HEATH and the COMMONERS HILL'

GOLF COURSE

LONDON ROAD

Forest Hill

START

SYDENHAM HILL WOOD

DULWICH

WOOD

HILL

WELLS PARK RD

SYDENHAM

WELLS PARK

WESTWOOD HILL

SYDENHAM

To 'CRYSTAL PALACE to BALHAM'

CRYSTAL PALACE PDE

CRYSTAL PALACE PARK

CRYSTAL PALACE PK RD

FINISH

Crystal Palace

ANERLEY HILL

THICKET ROAD

TRANSPORT ~ Finish
CRYSTAL PALACE
BUSES ~ 3, 49, 63, 108ᴮ, 122
137, 157, 227

TRANSPORT ~ Start
FOREST HILL
BUSES ~ 78, 115
171, 194, 194A

©BCRIY 1991

6. THE COLLEGE, THE PALACE AND THE COMMONS

FROM FOREST HILL TO BALHAM

Excluding some of the most 'desirable' riverside areas, a general rule could be formulated for the residential districts of London – that income increases with altitude.

The inner layer of the geological phenomenon known as the London basin is comprised of a layer of clay: blue, grey or orange; heavy, sticky and sodden, the London gardener's curse. It is thinnest down by the river but reaches up to 300 feet thick towards its rim. And it is along this rim that many of the most sought-after residential districts in London are to be found: Highgate, Hampstead, and Harrow-on-the Hill in the north, and in the south the suburbs that we follow on this section of the walk: Forest Hill, Dulwich, Sydenham Hill, Crystal Palace, and Streatham Common – where the air was said to come 'straight from Brighton'.

Dulwich owes much of its present shape, and its considerable beauty, to ex-actor Edward Alleyn who settled here in the 17th century and bestowed upon the village most of his wealth. During the same century Sydenham was becoming fashionable; its 'wells' had been discovered and even the king came here to sample the waters. Streatham, which had its own wells, reached its apogee a hundred years later when Hester Thrale was entertaining most of the great names of the day on her estate at Streatham Park. But for this part of London as a whole, the greatest era of development, the high point of the high places, came after the arrival of the Crystal Palace in 1852.

The Palace was a place for all classes. The Victorians came in their thousands to see the exhibitions, to listen to the huge organ and the enormous choirs, to gape at the incredible building, to walk in the grounds, to watch the extravagant water displays, to gasp at the fireworks or to wonder at the concrete dinosaurs. They came, but this being the intensely class-conscious society that it was, they did not mix. From the High Level Station through to the Palace, the upper classes had their own separate platforms, tunnels and entrances. And these wealthy Victorians made the high and healthy eminences around the Palace site their home. Today the surrounding suburbs are still full of their beautiful villas, with tall belvederes, granite porches and grand, stained-glass windows.

In the great fire of 1936 the Palace disappeared overnight. Since then Crystal Palace has declined as a suburb, with many of its villas now in multi-occupation. But all classes meet again in this chapter, from the Whig minister who drafted the Reform Bill in Streatham, to socialist activists like John Burns and Annie Besant; from Hester Thrale, 'queen' of her own Streatham Park court to Margaret Finch, the 'queen' of the gipsies; from Ned Allen of the London stage, Lord of the Manor of Dulwich, to the proud and penniless gardener who lived as a hermit in its woods.

This chapter covers 8½ miles from Forest Hill to Balham. It can be taken as two shorter walks:

WALK 8: Forest Hill to Crystal Palace Parade (3½ miles).

WALK 9: Crystal Palace Parade to Balham High Street (5 miles).

WALK 8: Forest Hill to Crystal Palace

Getting Started

From Lordship Lane:
> Alight from bus at Horniman Museum.

From Forest Hill Station:
> From the station cross the road to join London Road opposite. Follow this for about ⅓ mile to reach Horniman Museum.

From previous section:
> Continue from end of path alongside Horniman Gardens.

The Dulwich Woods

ROUTE:

- Cross the main road at the traffic lights at one end of Horniman Gardens.
- Immediately beyond the traffic lights take Lapsewood Walk running between the houses.
- Follow the path across the estate, crossing two service roads and following a line of lamp-posts. It becomes less distinct but keep straight ahead to reach the entrance to the woods.
- On entering the woods, turn right and go down the slope and over the footbridge.
- Beyond the bridge ignore the first gates on the left and go through the green iron-fronted gate immediately next to them. Follow the main path downhill until walking parallel first to a golf course and then to allotments. Keep to the right at junctions.
- The path swings right around the top of the allotments. Keep right at the first

junction and follow the path running parallel to the allotments at first and then deeper into the woods.

● Ignore turnings and cross-paths to eventually reach a gate in an iron fence. Turn left along the tarmac lane.

● Follow the lane until it ends on Crescent Wood Lane, opposite the Dulwich Wood House.

LOOKING AT WILDLIFE: Dulwich and Sydenham Woods are relict ancient woodland of sessile oak and hornbeam. There is a large variety of tree, flower, bird and butterfly species. Birds include stock dove and all three woodpeckers and a plant to look out for is the shade-loving Solomons Seal.

In 1605 Francis Calton sold the Manor of Dulwich to Edward Alleyn for the sum of £5000, and that, according to Alleyn, was £1000 more than any other man would have given for it. Alleyn was born in 1566, the son of an innkeeper of Bishopsgate, but as Ned Allen, he was to become famous as both an actor and a theatre proprieter. Described as 'the Roscius of his age', he even had a sonnet composed in his honour by his friend Ben Jonson. According to a popular story Ned Allen's life was transformed as the result of a theatrical apparition. The cast of a play in which he was performing contained twelve demons, but one night he found himself somehow confronting thirteen of them, and decided it was time to re-assess his life. He left the theatre and devoted the rest of his time on earth to good works.

This wonderful story has latterly been discounted but the fact remains that Alleyn retired from his theatrical career a rich man and spent the rest of his life in a combination of philanthropy and the pursuit of preferment. In 1519 he became Lord of the Manor of Thirle and in 1604, Lord of the Manor of Kensington. In this same year he bought for himself the title of 'Chief Master, Ruler and Overseer of All and Singular of His Majesty's Games, of Bears, Bulls and Mastive Dogs'. It was in the next year that he bought the Manor of Dulwich, where he moved 1613.

This move was to shape the whole future development of the area: he founded almshouses and schools, including the famous Dulwich College, and endowed the 1200 acre 'Estates of Alleyn's College of Gods Gift'. Dulwich Village remains today one of the most attractive and select of the London suburbs, and much of the village, together with the Dulwich woodlands, remains under the control of the Estate.

Alleyn's original bequest ordered that a portion of his estates should remain a woodland divided into ten equal portions, which would be lopped in rotation to supply the college with fuel. The names of many of these portions still survive in one form or another: Lapse Wood, Low Cross Wood, Sydenham Hill Wood, Kingswood and Peckarmans Wood. Today the 27 acre Sydenham Hill Wood belongs to the London Borough of Southwark and is managed by the London Wildlife Trust; the rest belong to the College Estates and have, until recently, been kept strictly private.

Both of these owners have attempted at different times to build in the woods. In 1985 Southwark Council applied to build 125 flats on Lapsewood but was defeated after a public enquiry, although development was allowed in one small part of the site. In 1988 the same Council turned down the third application from the Dulwich College Estates to build flats in the woods. The Dulwich Village Preservation Society threatened to take the Estate Governers to the Charity Commissioners if they should appeal against this decision. The Governers, they said, were acting like feudal landlords and were contradicting the terms of Alleyn's will. Nonetheless the Estate Governors did take their application to appeal and at a public enquiry in 1989 they were turned down for the fourth time.

It was walking in these woodlands that Browning composed his famous lines:

> The lark's on the wing, the snail's on the thorn
> God's in his heaven – all's right with the world.

Our route through them begins from Lordship Lane which once constituted the Eastern boundary between the Manors – or Lordships – of Dulwich and Friern. The path passes a corner of Sydenham Hill Wood as it crosses a footbridge whose rustic wooden arches give it a vaguely Japanese appearance. The brick peers carry the bridge across a cutting of what was once the railway route to Crystal Palace High Level Station. In 1871 the impressionist painter Pissaro sat on this bridge painting a view of a steam train puffing towards him from the now extinct Lordship Lane Station, through a landscape comprised largely of fields. The painting hangs today in the Courtauld Galleries in the Strand.

From the footbridge we cut across the thickest, stillest, richest part of Dulwich Woods to reach Low Cross Lane, the cross referred to here, being the cut made in a tree or on the ground to mark out the Parish boundary. It is in this section of the woodland that the 'Dulwich hermit', Samuel Matthews, is said to have had his home. Matthews came from Wales to serve as a gardener in Dulwich College but after the death of his wife in 1796 he retired into seclusion. Here in the woods he dug himself a cave in the mud and roofed it with fern, furze and brambles, remaining there until friends heard about his condition and took him back to Wales. He managed to escape their ministrations however and made his way back to Dulwich and his home in the woods, where on 28 December, 1802, he was found murdered. The rumour had arisen that he was a miser guarding a stash of treasure – why else should anyone want to live in solitude in the wild? Samuel was found with a hook in his throat with which the killers had tried to drag his body from the low-entranced cave. The crime remained unsolved until 1809, when, on his death-bed in Lewisham Workhouse, Isaac Evans confessed to being the perpetrator of the 'Dulwich Woods tragedy'.

From the Woods to the Wells

ROUTE:
- From Low Cross Lane turn right onto Crescent Wood Lane.
- Cross Sydenham Hill and take Wells Park Road opposite.
- Continue to reach Sydenham Wells Park on the right. Take the first entrance and bear right to walk downhill. After passing a second entrance gate on your right, go straight ahead at the crossing of paths and continue along the broad tarmac path to reach the ornamental lakes.

- Bear right after the lakes to reach the gate onto Longton Avenue. Go straight across into Ormanton Road.
- Cross Westwood Hill straight ahead into Charleville Circus.
- Go round either side of the Circus, cross Crystal Palace Park Road, turn left and enter Crystal Palace Park through Fisherman's Gate on the right.

FACILITIES: Dulwich Wood House is a pub with garden. Toilets in Sydenham Wells Park.

LOOKING AT WILDLIFE: There is a pets corner in Sydenham Wells Park with tropical finches, waxbills, quail, golden pheasant, rabbits and a very large and noisy colony of budgerigars. There is a variety of wildfowl on the lakes and regular visiting herons.

The Dulwich Wood House, cream-painted with a white belvedere, was built around 1840 and is a local listed building – more deservedly so than the affront next door. 'Six Pillars', a Grade II Historical Building , dates from 1935 and is in the 'International Style', so-called presumably because of its blandness and lack of any cultural references whatsoever.

John Logie Baird, inventor of television, lived at 3 Crescent Wood Road from 1934 to 1936. His TV laboratories were situated in the nearby Crystal Palace, and were entirely destroyed in the fire of 1936. Here, at the height of Sydenham Hill, once the boundary between Kent and Surrey, is a clear view of Baird's 'memorial', the BBC TV aerial atop the Crystal Palace Hill. Sydenham Hill, originally part of the Westwood Common, was an area of weather-boarded cottages surrounded by market gardens and orchards until it became increasingly fashionable following the success of the Crystal Palace. Its high location made it healthy too, so that Upper Sydenham came to consist of large, wealthy, family villas, whilst the working people lived in Lower Sydenham below.

In 1640 the discovery was made on the Sydenham portion of the Westwood Common, of wells whose water was of 'a mild cathartic quality, nearly resembling those of Epsom'. As their fashionable use developed they were said to have 'performed great cures in scrofulous, scorbutic, paralytic and other stubborn diseases' and even, by one contemporary commentator, to be 'a certain cure for every ill to which humanity is heir'. The wells were covered over in the mid-19th century but a scientific analysis of the waters was made many years later during a temporary re-emergence of a spring near Crystal Palace. They were found to contain large quantities of magnesium sulphate – more commonly known as Epsom salts.

The 17½ acres of undulating slopes which today constitute Sydenham Wells Park were purchased by the Metropolitan Board of Works and laid out with broad pathways, ornamental plantations and a succession of small lakes and rivulets. The main speech at the opening ceremony in 1901 was made by the trade unionist and socialist John Burns, an appropriate choice for a number of reasons. Earlier in his life Burns had driven for six months the first electric tram in England, one of the 'features' in the Crystal Palace Park. Burns also had a particular concern for the right of public meeting in parks and commons. As a leader of the Dock Strike in 1889 he was an associate of Ben Tillett and Tom Mann and by 1892 he had become MP for Battersea, sitting as one of the first Independent Labour Party members in the House. Walter Greening heard him give his opening speech and commented that although 'the stentorian-voiced orator, the doughty John Burns,' did not make him a convert to radicalism, he was nevertheless forcedly impressed with the manliness of his utterances and practical common-sense remarks arising from the circumstances appertaining to the proceedings in which he was taking part'.

From Festival to Fire: The Career of a Crystal Palace

ROUTE:

- From Fisherman's Gate turn left then left again after the artificial ski slope.
- Turn right at the next junction passing a yellow brick building and keeping straight ahead to reach the lakes.
- Take any path between and alongside the lakes and at their end turn right up the bank then left (Green Chain sign) between the National Sports Centre and the animal enclosures to reach Crystal Palace Station.
- Finish walk here or pass station and turn right up Ledrington Road and onto Anerley Hill.
- Towards the top of Anerley Hill turn into the park gate beside the museum. Take the flights of steps ahead onto the original Crystal Palace site.
- Cross the herb garden and leave by the gate onto the roundabout at Crystal Palace Parade.

FACILITIES: Crystal Palace Park has toilets, a maze, a children's zoo (open summer months only), children's playground, adventure playgound and two cafés. The Crystal Palace Exhibition is near the top of Anerley Hill, open Sundays from 2 to 5. Toilets, pubs and cafés on Crystal Palace Broadway.

LOOKING AT WILDLIFE: Crystal Palace Park has a good variety of exotic trees, including contorted willow, Monterey pine and Indian bean tree, with a good display of autumn colour. There are wildfowl and frequently herons on the lake, a children's zoo and a number of animal enclosures housing muntjac, flamingoes, rheas, peafowl and cranes.

I t was Prince Albert's idea: a Great Exhibition displaying the power and scope of British imperialism, a monument to Victorian self-confidence and its cultural domination of the world. The design of building which would itself reflect these achievements came about almost by accident. A member of the organising committee whilst reading a copy of the *Illustrated London News* noticed a picture of the green-houses at Chatsworth, built for the Duke of Devonshire by Joseph Paxton.

The idea for the 'Crystal Palace' was born.

The Palace was erected by Paxton in Hyde Park in 1851 but its popularity led the organisers to look for a permanent home for the building once the Exhibition was over. In 1852 road and rail waggons carried 9642 tons of iron, 500 tons of glass, 30 miles of guttering and 200 miles of wooden sash out to the top of Sydenham Hill. The 1,608 foot long palace was re-erected on a site which overlooked London, Kent and Surrey.

The extravagant grandeur of the Palace had now to be matched in the lay-out of its 200 acres of grounds. In a brilliant imaginative stroke the shimmering glass surfaces of the Palace, with their ever-changing play of light, were recreated in the grounds in the shimmering and shifting surfaces of a water park. The whole design of the grounds was to meet this end – 11,788 separate jets and fountains, ten miles of underground piping and a complex system of reservoirs fed from their own artesian well. On its grandest nights the park could put on a display consuming as much as 6 million gallons of water, with its highest jets reaching 250 foot into the air.

Palace and grounds were opened by Queen Victoria on 10 June 1854 before a crowd of 40,000 people. It became a pleasure garden for the nation, a forerunner of the theme park, with exhibitions, choral festivals, funfairs, balloon ascents, aeronautical shows, a pneumatic railway, an electric tram ride, spectacular firework displays and a wide range of theatrical and sporting events. Even the FA Cup Final was staged here from 1894 to 1924.

Victorian architecture, for all its pretensions, is amongst the most exuberant and exciting in the country. But its extravagance was unsustainable by a later age: by the early twentieth century the grand Crystal Palace had become a liability. It must have been a sad and shabby site in its decline, its acres of windows cracked and grubby, its miles of iron girders rusting, its fountains no longer functioning and its grand paths weeding over. The end was sudden. It came on the night of 30 November 1936. The fire which destroyed the Crystal Palace was attended by 90 fire engines and could be seen from as far away as Brighton. A sea of molten glass flowed down Anerley Hill and the great organ could be heard eerily playing itself as fire-heated draughts of air rushed upwards through the pipes. By the morning nothing but two flanking water towers remained. The circumstances surrounding the fire remain a mystery. An official account blames it on a workman's blow-torch igniting a paint store but popular accounts take note of the fact that an 'accidental' fire had conveniently disposed of a loss-making liability.

Today all that remains is the arcaded terrace at the top of the park, the foundation on which the glass edifice once rested. Here the London Borough of Bromley has laid out the ground-plan of one end of the Palace and planted it as a herb garden. The Borough is also working on a plan to upgrade the park, restoring some of the original features such as the maze, and laying out trails which highlight its history. But sadly it remains a fact that Crystal Palace feels more like a park with a past than one with a present. Much of this is related to the presence of the National Sports Centre, plumped down in the very centre of the park in 1964, with athletics stadium, Olympic pool, tower-block accommodation for competitors and all the associated paraphernalia. Whatever its own intrinsic merits, it has taken the heart out of the park, which has lost any sense of unity or landscape, becoming an untidy mish-mash of scattered features, an ambling periphery with no core.

The most interesting remaining feature is undoubtedly the area around the Lower Lake. The lake is so divided by bridges, paths and islands that it actually looks like several lakes; it was the main reservoir for the park and its water levels fluctuated so greatly when the water displays were in operation that it became known as the Tidal Lake.

The largest of the islands now contains the Children's Zoo, opened in 1953. The other two carry creatures more ancient and less caged – the famous prehistoric monsters which form one of the strangest 'listed buildings' in London, and date from the Crystal Palace's heyday. From the incongruously mown grass – for a neurotic municipal tidiness intervenes even here – amidst a backdrop of cypresses, juniper, pines and monkey puzzle, they stick their heads up over rocks, grimace in their green and concrete way and fail to frighten the waterfowl whose only real concern is to get the next handout of white bread from the Sunday afternoon strollers. There is a pterodactyl about to take off, eyes glaring, one paw raised; there are Irish elk with their young among the aucuba; prehistoric crocodiles under the weeping willows with long and narrow snouts whose bulbous ends look like eye-droppers; tortoises with fangs; amphibious dinosaurs with corkscrew necks; and the mighty iguanodon with skin as rough as a lychee, snarling to keep up appearances whilst obviously wondering what the hell is going on.

The display as a whole was intended to illustrate the course of evolution, working from west to east across the park. It was designed by the delightfully named Waterhouse Hawkins, with scientific advice provided by Professor Richard Owen, the man who gave the world the word 'dinosaur'. On New Years Eve 1854, when the work was just completed, they gave a dinner party in the open belly of the iguanodon, its top half being cemented in place later.

TO COMPLETE WALK 8: Crystal Palace Parade is a terminus for several bus routes.

WALK 9: Crystal Palace to Balham

Getting Started

From Walk 8:

From the roundabout turn right onto the Parade and almost immediately left onto Farquhar Road.

To start walk here:

From Crystal Palace Parade find Farquhar Road, close to the roundabout on the opposite side to the park.

COLLEGE, PALACE AND COMMONS

CRYSTAL PALACE TO BALHAM ~ 9

TRANSPORT ~ Start
* CRYSTAL PALACE
BUSES ~ 3, 49, 63, 108B, 122
137, 157, 227

From 'FOREST HILL to CRYSTAL PALACE'

START

© SKTV. 1991

CRYSTAL PALACE PDE
ANERLEY HILL
CRYSTAL PALACE

DULWICH UPPER WOOD
FARQUHAR RD
GYPSY HILL RD
WESTOW HILL

GYPSY HILL
WHITE LEY RD

NORWOOD PARK
ELDER RD
CRESCENT RD
KNIGHTS HILL

CROWN DALE
BEULAH HILL

NORTH CROWN LANE
COMMON
NORWOOD GROVE
GNOSSE TRH
STREATHAM

HILLPATH
THE ROOKERY
VALLEY RD
STREATHAM COMMON
RUSSELL'S FOOTPATH

STREATHAM HIGH RD

GARRAD'S RD
AMBLE SIDE
LANE
STREATHAM LANE
MITCHAM

To 'OF HUSTINGS and HUGUENOTS'

PENALEY RD
EMMANUEL RD
BALHAM
TOOT'NG DEC
BEDFORD HILL
COMMON
TOOTING BEC RD

FINISH

N
W — E
S

TRANSPORT ~ Finish
⊕ BALHAM ~ Northern Line
BUSES ~ 88, 131, 155, 355
* BALHAM

– 100 –

The Vicar's Oak and the Vicar's Wife

ROUTE:
- Follow Farquhar Road and take the second turning on the right (Bowley Lane). Pass the gate on your left and take the path into the wood shortly beyond it.
- Follow the zig-zagging path through the woods and shortly after passing a little fenced enclosure bear left and keep heading downhill to reach a gate back onto Farquhar Road.
- Cross the road into Dulwich Wood Avenue opposite and follow it to take the first left into Colby Road.
- Follow Colby Road to Gipsy Hill.

LOOKING AT WILDLIFE: Dulwich Upper Wood is 5 acres of deciduous woodland with a variety of woodland birds, wild flowers (including common spotted orchid) and fungi.

The Crystal Palace Parade, though a mere 110 foot above sea level, is the highest point on Sydenham Hill. Here, on the 'summit' stood the great Vicar's Oak which at one time gave its name to the area. There are numerous places throughout England named after oak trees and in London alone we have Honor Oak, (see chapter five) Burnt Oak, Gospel Oak and Royal Oak. Though these places are often given a christian or a monarchical connection the special significance of the oak predates both our religion and our royalty. Here, the Vicar's Oak was such a significant feature that the boundaries of five parishes met beneath it. Even today the London Boroughs of Bromley, Croydon, Lambeth and Southwark meet at this roundabout, while a fifth, Lewisham, abuts the opposite end of the Parade.

Farquhar Road, leading off the Parade, gets its name from Sir George Farquhar, the first Secretary of the Crystal Palace Company. From the top of the road we look down on new housing which occupies the site of the old Crystal Palace High Level Station, the terminus for the line which we have come across repeatedly in our walk. Here, at the Crystal Palace, it arrived in style. Like the great central London termini it was completely arched over and its separate first, second and third class platforms stretched the whole length of the Parade. At its peak it handled 10 to 12,000 passengers an hour who made their way in subways, a separate one for each class of passenger, under the Parade, direct to the Palace turnstiles. The 24 bays of these passageways, with their brick built fan-vaulted ceilings are just about all that survives of the High Level Station; the planners concerned with improving the Crystal Palace area will not have completed their job until they find a way of re-opening them to public inspection. The station, built in 1865, fell into decrepitude after the 1936 fire. It was closed in 1954 and demolished in 1961.

Of the Great North Wood which once covered this area, one small fragment survives. Dulwich Upper Wood is 5 acres of mixed deciduous woodland, owned by the Dulwich College Estates and managed by the Ecological Parks Trust as an urban nature reserve. As well as some of the ancient woodland the site covers the basement and garden areas of several Victorian villas, bomb casualties of the Second World War. There is therefore an odd mix of species; of native oaks alongside garden robinias, horse chestnut, damson and bay. In this small but beautiful fragment of woodland blackcap and chiffchaff sing on spring mornings, the foraging nuthatch gives its long, loud piping call, foxgloves bloom in the shade of oaks and the speckled wood butterfly glides along the woodland edges. The Trust for Urban Ecology has established a tree nursery on the site and is gradually carrying out coppicing and other management work to increase the diversity of the wildlife. They should also be applauded for another recent step – that of opening the woods to complete public access rather than treating them as a 'reserve' with restricted visiting hours.

Colby Road, which we reach off Dulwich Wood Avenue, is named after Edmund Colby, who was a fellow of Dulwich College in the 17th century. A plaque above number 39 records that Annie Besant lived here in 1874. After a disastrous marriage to her local vicar, Frank Besant, she left him and moved to Colby Road in 1873. She was an astonishing and versatile woman, a writer, free-thinker, socialist and great orator, with a particular concern for the living and working conditions of women and children in London. She was an active supporter of the striking Bryant and May match girls and founded the socialist paper *The Link*. In 1889 she joined the Theosophists, and eventually moved to India where she became a supporter of Home Rule. Her contribution to the struggle was recognised when she was elected President of the Indian National Congress. She died in Madras in 1933.

Gipsy Hill and Norwood Park

ROUTE:
- From Colby Road turn left onto Gipsy Hill. Pass the station and turn sharp right into Sainsbury Road alongside the railway line.
- Follow Sainsbury Road as it curves round into Bristow Road and continue to the T junction at the end.
- Turn right into Whiteley Road and at the end turn right on the main road to take the first entrance into Norwood Park on the left.
- Follow the path ahead, passing the viewpoint plaque, to the corner of the fenced play area.
- Continue left and right around the play area and then take the first path on the left alongside the fenced picnic area.
- Fork right to descend through the park to the junction of Elder Road and Central Hill.
- Cross Central Hill and turn right up the main road (Crown Dale). Continue to the major road junction at the top of the hill.
- Turn left into Beulah Hill and then take the first right into Gibsons Hill.

FACILITIES: Cafés and pubs on Gipsy Hill. Toilets in Norwood Park beside fenced play area. Café at junction of Crown Dale and Beulah Hill.

LOOKING AT WILDLIFE: There is an interesting, elderly holm oak tree in
Norwood Park, its roots raising it several feet above ground level. Winter gulls
congregate in Norwood Park.

The windmill which once stood at the top of Gipsy Hill functioned until 1853. It was proposed at one time to build a second windmill but the idea, apparently, was opposed by the locals who felt that 'there wasn't enough wind to work two at once'.

The hill gets its name from the gipsies who were encamped in this corner of the Great North Wood from at least the 17th century and probably much earlier. They lived for the most part in poverty, collecting wood and making it into pegs, baskets and butcher's hooks for itinerant sale. Their most famous 'Queen' was Margaret Finch who died in 1740 at the age of 108. It was said that towards the end of her life she remained squatting in one position for so long that when she died her limbs could not be straightened and she had to be buried in a square box. Her funeral was paid for by local publicans in recognition of the custom she had brought them. One of these 'customers' was Samuel Pepys' wife; her visit is recorded in an entry in his diary in 1668. By 1777 the gipsies' reputation had spread so wide that a Covent Garden pantomime, 'The Norwood Gipsies' was based upon them.

Despite this entertainment value and the income they had seemingly generated for the area, the gipsies had, by the end of the 18th century, been deemed a public nuisance. They suffered continual harassment from the local constabulary after the passing of the Vagrancy Act in 1797 and when, in the early 19th century, this harassment was compounded by the effects of enclosure, the gipsies were driven off altogether, leaving only their name behind them.

The enclosures of the 1800s ensured that by the end of the century, the whole of that part of the Great North Wood which gave its name to Norwood, had been clear-felled and developed. By 1903 the only area of any size left was that now forming Norwood Park. As Great Elderhall Coppice it had been part of the Manor of Lambeth and therefore in the ownership of the See of Canterbury. The Ecclestiastical Commissioners, amongst the most ardent in pushing through Acts of Enclosure, sold off this last remaining piece of land to the London County Council in 1903. It opened as a public park in 1911.

Once it was a coppiced common land surrounded by strawberry fields. Along one side ran the now lost River Effra, a row of thatched and white-washed cottages standing along its bank. Today we have instead a rather featureless expanse of grass, a gathering ground for winter gulls, dotted here and there with an older oak or poplar. The most interesting feature is the viewpoint from the top of the hill – although the explanatory GLC plaque has already been made out of date by the Canary Wharf development which impedes the view to the east. Nevertheless Alexandra Park and Epping Forest stand out as distant high ground and the city stretches out below them from Millbank to the Isle of Dogs. In the foreground to the right is the green-capped spire of Dulwich College and looming above that the wooded crest of Sydenham Hill crowned with the Crystal Palace TV mast.

Descending through the park towards the bottom of Central Hill, two distinctive Victorian buildings can be seen on either side. Off to the right on Elder Road – named after Great Elderhall Coppice – is the 'Norwood House of Industry', a school for poor children built in 1815, now a somewhat sombre private housing development. Even more severe is the massive and forbidding pile of the Fidelis Convent off to the left, which is the sort of building that could have inspired Mervyn Peake's *Gormengast*.

There is a more attractive 19th century building at the top of Crown Hill, just a few yards ahead along the main road where our route turns left down Beulah Hill. Like Tower Bridge or St Pancras Station, it is one of those Victorian buildings which, although poaching styles from all over the place, gets away with it because of a supreme self-confidence. Here are columned porticos, a stone-faced front porch which runs the height of the whole building, roof finials, a mass of chimneys, roundels at the gable ends and an orange-red brick that glows in the evening light. Built in 1894 as the British Home and Hospital for Incurables, it was one of the very first such establishments in Britain.

Streatham Common and Russell's Path

ROUTE:

- Descend Gibsons Hill and at the second junction on the right take the gate into Norwood Grove. Turn right up the path which runs parallel to the lane, to reach The Mansion.
- Follow round The Mansion to join the lane and turn left along it onto Streatham Common.
- Follow the path ahead, passing the entrance to The Rookery, and at the top of the hill take the small path off to the right which crosses the end of the car park.
- Keep straight ahead across the grass to reach the main road beside the iron bollard.
- Cross the road to find the opening into Hill Path. At the end of the path turn right on to Valley Road to find the entrance to Russell's Path leading off to the left.
- Follow to the end of the path, crossing another road en route, emerging up steps onto Streatham High Road.

FACILITIES: Café on Streatham Common near the Rookery. Cafés and pubs on Streatham High Road.

LOOKING AT WILDLIFE: Mature parkland trees in Norwood Grove including oak and cedar and an ancient mulberry. Open woodland and heathland flora on the Common including gorse and Scots pine. Grey squirrels are abundant and there is a good variety of woodland birds. Holly, holm oak and yew overhang Hill Path.

From the southern tip of the very urban borough of Lambeth, Gibsons Hill leads down into what looks like the rural fringes of Surrey. At a turn in the road we come into parklands and open fields and a view which stretches out over Mitcham – and the dark bulk of the Beddington Power Station – as far as the Surrey heaths. Gibsons Hill was the home of Stenton Covington, who played a large part in the preservation of this South London countryside.

The sinuous slope of Norwood Grove, dotted with mature trees like an old English estate, leads up to The Mansion, a fine white house with a bow in the middle of the facade and a long conservatory all along one side, topped with little glass cupolas which look like copies from the Brighton pavilion. The house was clearly designed as the family seat of a weighty Victorian 'captain of industry'. Its fine plaster-work ceilings can still be glimpsed through the upper windows and the house was set about with formal features – a trefoil garden, a rose pergola, ponderous cedars and a gnarled old mulberry on a perfectly level lawn. It was built in the early 19th century, the home of Arthur Anderson, founder of the P & O steamship company.

Norwood Grove is just one of several delights contained in this little north east corner of Streatham Common. Here the path runs alongside the only remaining woodlands of the common; a dappled light falls through trees onto hazel, bramble and gorse and the local population of grey squirrels has become cocky enough to steal a picnicker's sandwiches. And beside this is a 'secret' garden, The Rookery, one of the finest municipal gardens in London.

Streatham's common lands were unchallenged for centuries until in 1794 the Duke of Bedford, the freeholder, illegally sold off the fuel rights to a private buyer. The commoners immediately gathered in protest and prevented the sale by the drastic measure of setting fire to all the gorse. The Duke responded by enclosing the grazing areas but the *Gentleman's Magazine* reported that, on the very same evening a hackney coach drove to the spot, and six men, draped in black with crapes over their faces, got out of the carriage, cut down the paled enclosure, returned into the coach, and drove off.

By this date the Common was already fashionable for its three wells. The most important of these had been discovered in 1659 when, according to story, the ground gave way beneath a horse and plough. The waters rose here at a temperature of 52°F and were described as having a slight smell of sulphur and a sparkling taste. They were held to be particularly good for the eyes and for 'the expulsion of worms'. By 1701 hundreds of people were arriving to take the waters and to attend the concerts at Streatham Wells House, which, says Colonel Sexby, 'made the crowds of visitors as gay and frivolous as their ailments would allow'. But by the end of the 19th century the wells had long since fallen into disuse.

In 1888 the major part of the common was sold by the Ecclesiastical Commissioners to the Metropolitan Board of Works for the nominal sum of £5. The Wells House however, now known as The Rookery, was in private hands and went on the market in 1912. It was then that Stenton Covington came on the scene, founding a preservation society that campaigned for the public purchase of the estate. The committee succeeded in raising half the purchase price, the rest was met by the London County Council and the Borough of Wandsworth, and the Rookery was opened to the public in 1913. Eleven years later Mr Covington was back in action when the adjacent Norwood Grove was threatened with development. The committee was re-activated and the LCC, this time with the Croydon Corporation, was persuaded to buy the site for the public. Once again the preservation committee raised a substantial portion of the purchase price.

One of the old medicinal wells can still be seen in the Rookery, in the beautiful setting of the Old English Garden. There is also a White Garden, rock and water gardens and a picnic area in the 'Orchard', all remnants of the days when Councils could afford to invest in the provision of a beautiful environment.

An unusual sequence of footpaths leads from the common into central Streatham. The first of these is Hill Path, which begins next to St Michael's Convent where mature hollies, yew trees and dark evergreen oaks overhang the first part of the way. The convent was previously Park Hill, residence of the Tate family, whose sugar fortune endowed the Tate Gallery. The second of the Streatham wells was to be found in the grounds here, whilst the third is on Valley Road, where we make the connection between Hill Path and Russell's Footpath. This third well, currently being restored, was in the grounds of the old United Dairy Depot and the water, at 1d for 3 pails, was delivered by the dairymen along with the milk. As concerns about the quality of tap water increase perhaps there will soon be door-to-door deliveries again.

Russell's Footpath runs in a long straight line between rows of back gardens. Several generations of Lord Russell lived in Streatham – presumably one of them made this his route to the common, thus giving the path its name. During the 19th century the Reverend Wriothesley Russell was the tenant of the rectory, and one of his regular visitors was Lord John Russell, the Whig Cabinet Minister. Lord John is said to have used a stay at the Rectory to draft the Great Reform Bill which was passed in 1832, greatly extending the right to vote and abolishing the old 'rotten boroughs'. The initial defeat of the Bill precipitated a General Election and Russell campaigned throughout the country often attended by huge and agitated crowds. In the course of one journey to Devon hundreds turned out to see him pass and Sidney Smith wrote to Lady Holland that:

> the people along the way were very much disappointed by his smallness. I told them he was very much larger before the bill was thrown out, but was reduced by excessive anxiety about the people. This brought tears to their eyes.

From the Bec to Balham

ROUTE:
- Turn right onto Streatham High Road then left onto Gleneagle Road, just after Station Approach.
- Cross the road and turn right into Ambleside Avenue.
- Follow Ambleside Avenue across Mitcham Lane and continue ahead to reach Tooting Bec Road and the common.
- Turn left along the edge of the common and just before the railway bridge take the

path on the right. Keep parallel to the railway line through the woods to reach Bedford Hill.

• At Bedford Hill turn left and cross the railway bridge. Turn right onto the common again and walk through the woods, parallel to the other side of the railway.

• At the far side of the common join the path ahead, going under two railway bridges to reach Fernlea Road.

• Turn left and follow Fernlea Road and then Balham Station Road to reach Balham High Road.

FACILITIES: Pubs and cafés in Streatham and again in Balham. There is a café on Tooting Common near the corner of Hillbury Road and Bedford Hill.

LOOKING AT WILDLIFE: The two areas of woodland on Tooting Common support a surprising variety of birds including goldcrest, spotted flycatcher, long-tailed tit and nuthatch. There is also a good variety of autumn fungi including fly agaric, death cap, puffballs, boletus and parasol mushroom.

Tooting has two commons, Tooting Bec and Tooting Graveney. The larger of the two, and the one we cross, is the Bec, which draws its name from the Abbey of St Mary de Bec-Hellouin in Normandy which held the Manor of Upper Tooting in the Middle Ages. This one-time wild stretch of woodland had the usual sad history of incursions until in 1861 the Duke of Bedford put both the manor and the common up for sale.

The commoners immediately met together to discuss the possibility of a joint purchase. They learnt however that Mr W.J. Thompson, a City of London broker who had lived in Tooting for 18 years, had decided to bid for it himself. Since Mr Thompson was known to be opposed to enclosure, it was unanimously decided not to put in any bid against him. However, the commoners were to be disappointed. Henry Warwick Cole takes up the tale in *Fraser's Magazine*:

> Mr Thompson ... as carefully avoided giving any pledge that would bind him on the subject, as he did giving any hint that might disabuse the minds of his neighbours from the conclusion so favourable to himself which they had too hastily arrived at ... his prudence was so effective that he was suffered, at the sale, to become the purchaser of the manor and the houses and cottages for £3,285 only ...
>
> The premises were conveyed to Mr Thompson in December 1862, when a new light instantaneously, and as if by magic, broke in upon his mind as to the extensive nature of the rights of lords and the limited nature of the rights of commoners ... perhaps the circumstance that some of the common was established by himself as worth £1000 an acre for building, may have induced him to study the merits of the legal question with more individualism than impartiality. Under the influence of his new impressions he vigorously set to work to inclose the whole common, and convert it to building-land for his own benefit.

But not without opposition. Every time Mr Thompson put up fences the local people pulled them down again, and the battle continued until 1870 when Mr Betts, the local butcher, obtained a court injunction forbidding further enclosure. Five years later the Metropolitan Board of Works came to the rescue and purchased the commons as public open space for the sum of £17,771, a profit to Mr Thompson of £14,000.

Tooting Bec has two remaining areas of woodland, one on either side of Bedford Hill, and in season they support an interesting variety of fungi. Among them is the sinisterly named Death Cap, *Amanita phalloides*. Fungi in this country are held in an inordinate and undue dread but in this case, at least, it is justified. This one species is responsible for 90 per cent of fatal poisonings. Its cap is olive-green, the colour of someone already sickening, and its toxins are unaffected by cooking. One cap is more than enough to cause death.

One of the early incursions made upon the common, with the Duke of Bedford's express permission, was for the large house and grounds of Streatham Park. The estate was built by Mr Thrale, the founder of Thrales Brewery. His wife Hester was an astute, ambitious and intelligent woman, and their home became the centre of an impressive social circle. Frequent visitors included Goldsmith, Burke, Chambers, Garrick and Fanny Burney all of whom had their portraits painted by another of the regular house guests, Sir Joshua Reynolds. Most regular of them all however was Samuel Johnson who, after his second visit, took up more or less permanent residence for almost 15 years. He wrote *Lives of the Poets* here and had a favourite walk up to the top of Streatham Common and back.

Mr Thrale died in 1781 from eating 'too much quail liver paté'. Johnson, despite his well-known misogyny, had been in love with Hester Thrale for many years, but perhaps it took the death of Mr Thrale for this to become apparent. Hester, for her part, became noticeably cooler towards Johnson and very soon announced her engagement to her children's music teacher, Mr Piozzi. When he received her letter containing the news the 72 year-old Johnson wrote back instantly:

> I who have loved you, reverenced you and served you, I who long thought you the first of human kind, entreat that before your fate is irrevocable, I may once more see you.

Hester went ahead with the marriage however; Johnson burnt all her letters and never saw her again, dying two years later. The new Mrs Piozzi went on to succesfully publish his biography, *The Anecdotes of the Late Dr Samuel Johnson*.

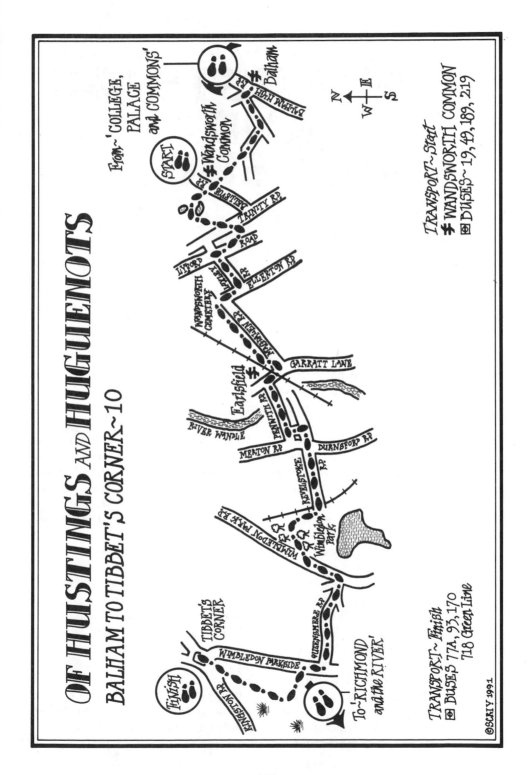

OF HUSTINGS AND HUGUENOTS

BALHAM TO TIBBET'S CORNER ~ 10

From ~ 'COLLEGE, PALACE and COMMONS'

Balham

START

Wandsworth Common

TRINITY RD

SALTERS RD

ILFORD ROAD

ELLERTON RD

LYFORD RD

WANDSWORTH CEMETERY

MAGDALEN RD

GARRATT LANE

Earlsfield

RIVER WANDLE

PENWITH RD

MERTON RD

DURNSFORD RD

REVELSTOKE RD

WIMBLEDON PARK RD

Wimbledon Park

WIMBLEDON PARK RD

QUEENSMERE RD

TIBBET'S CORNER

FINISH

KINGSTON RD

WIMBLEDON PARKSIDE

To 'RICHMOND and the RIVER'

N
W — E
S

TRANSPORT ~ Start
≢ WANDSWORTH COMMON
🚍 BUSES ~ 19, 49, 189, 219

TRANSPORT ~ Finish
🚍 BUSES 77A, 93, 170
718 Green Line

©SCKIY 1991

7. OF HUSTINGS AND HUGUENOTS

FROM WANDSWORTH COMMON TO WIMBLEDON COMMON

In devising a continuous walking route encircling London and nearly a hundred miles long, there have been many problems to contend with. And the biggest and most intractable has been that of finding a way through central South London. The Thames-side route is too far to the north, the leafier spaces of Merton too far to the south, and the string of urban commons between them are separated from each other by too many miles of dull and traffic dominated streets. This section, the South London link, is undoubtedly the weakest part of *The Green London Way*. It plots a route between the Wandsworth and Wimbledon commons along 4½ miles of what is largely road walking. The walker who sets out to complete the passage, will have to look for compensations in the area's rich historical associations.

Two themes link the section, one geographical, the other historical. From Wandsworth to Wimbledon we are in effect undertaking a traverse of the Wandle valley. On either side, the commons survive on Thames terrace gravels which made their soils too poor for cultivation. Between the commons, the gentle slopes of the valley cut down through the London clay to a rich layer of alluvial soil which coats the valley bottom. The value of this soil for horticulture was soon overtaken by the value of the River Wandle and its banks for trades dependent on water and on water power. In particular the Wandle became a centre for Huguenot immigrants who arrived here with their special skills, built their mills and played a central part in the industrial development of Wandsworth.

The two commons also mark the extent of the one-time estate of the Spencers. The Wandsworth Borough has been particularly proud of this family connection with the present Princess of Wales, but in fact the family's impact upon the area has been almost entirely destructive. The story of the Spencers in Wandsworth and Wimbledon is a story of constant encroachments on common land, encroachments which in the case of Wandsworth Common have led to one of the most dissected pieces of open space in London. It was only as a result of long struggles against successive Earls Spencer that Wandsworth Common, Wimbledon Common, and Wimbledon Park have been preserved at all. But these struggles also give rise to their own stories and chief among them is the amazing account of the 'Garratt elections'; huge and ribald celebrations that took place around elections of a mock 'mayor' for an insignificant hamlet and which became in turn a sort of long-running farce on the state of national politics. The persevering walker who pounds these pavements will find this, with many other stories, has been buried beneath them

---

This chapter covers a single walk of 4½ miles from Wandsworth Common Station to Tibbet's Corner, Wimbledon Common.

WALK 10: Balham to Tibbet's Corner

Getting Started

From Wandsworth Common Station:
   Turn right on leaving station.
From Walk 9: There is a a ½ mile linking section from Balham Station.
   From Balham Station Road cross Balham High Road into Chestnut Grove and turn immediately left into Boundaries Road.
   Take the first right into Balham Park Road.
   Where the road bends left take the footpath on the right onto Wandsworth Common. Follow alongside the railway to Wandsworth Common Station.

Wandsworth Common and the Scope

ROUTE:
- From the station follow alongside the railway to reach the main road. Cross the road and follow the tarmac path which continues alongside the railway across the common.
- On reaching the lakes cross the bridge between them and carry on, turning left at the junction with the tarmac path.
- Leave the path where it curves right alongside the backs of houses and instead keep straight ahead along an avenue of trees.
- On reaching the main road go straight across to follow the path opposite. Follow this to the first junction, by a lamp-post.
- Turn right and carry on to reach Lyford Road. Carry on ahead up Lyford Road and turn left onto Loxley Road.
- At the end of Loxley Road turn right onto Ellerton Road.
- Cross Magdalen Road at the end, to enter Wandsworth Cemetery.

LOOKING AT WILDLIFE: Wandsworth Common has over 50 species of tree among which the sweet smelling balsam poplar is well worth finding. The ponds have a variety of common wildfowl with some less usual species sometimes turning up in winter. The Scope is an area of semi-natural grassland dominated by purple moor grass. Among the interesting plants to be found here, strawberry clover is of particular interest.

The 175 acre Wandsworth Common has suffered more from encroachment and is more cut up by roads and railways than any other of the metropolitan commons of London. This poor, emaciated, ill-used open space is now in no less than ten separate sections. From the 18th century onwards Wandsworth and Wimbledon Commons and all the area between them were in the hands of the Spencer family, and the Spencers, according to Robert Hunter writing in the *English Illustrated Magazine* in 1886, appear to have regarded the common 'as a means of being generous at other people's expense'. Henry Warwick Cole writing in *Fraser's Magazine* in May of the same year, is just as scathing:

> Wandsworth Common which was once from its great beauty a very jewel of the metropolis, has fared cruelly under the Spencer family. It now comprises about 150 acres only; but the present lord and his predecessor have sold, within the last 13 years, upwards of 140 acres for sums which have realised £15,336 ... The consequences of the want of spirit displayed by the commoners of Wandsworth have been most calamitous. Not only has half the common been illegally enclosed but the remaining half has been subject to the vilest treatment. The green turf has been stripped off its surface, the trees have been injured or destroyed, enormous quantities of gravel have been extracted without regard to any considerations but the convenience of those who dig it and large pits have been formed, filled to the depth of several feet with water from which one morning there was pulled out the body of a drowned man, who had vainly sought health and recreation there and had lost his life in the attempt. Mr Rose ... gave his personal assistance in fishing for the dead body, but found that the personal excitement it gave him before breakfast was, after all, only a poor competitor for the former amenities of the place.

Between 1794 and 1866 there were 53 enclosures carried out on the Common, varying in size from a quarter of an acre to 96 acres. Some were illegal but all of them were approved by the successive Earls Spencer. In the 1850s the situation was compounded by the railway companies, with the London and South Western and the London and Brighton Railways both driving across the common, major routes which splintered it into fragments.

Finally, in 1870, Henry Peek, an active campaigner in the protection of commons, got together a committee to save what was left. The situation at Wandsworth between the commoners, the local community and the landowners was only settled after agreement had been reached in a long-running dispute over the larger Wimbledon Common (see p.123). But in 1871 the Wandsworth Common Act was passed and the common assigned to Conservators elected by the Parish ratepayers. In a settlement very similar to that reached in Wimbledon, Earl Spencer received an annuity of £250, calculated as his average earnings from the sale of gravel from the common. By 1887 the Parish ratepayers were fed up with bearing the cost locally and Wandsworth Common, more of a nuisance than a place of recreation according to Cecil, passed under the management of the Metropolitan Board Of Works.

Despite this sad history, the common still has a few interesting attributes. The local authorities, for example, have planted a wide variety of trees: alder, aspen, swamp cypress, Turkey oak, red oak, balsam poplar, elm, silver maple, manna ash, scarlet hawthorn and many more. There are also the lakes, remnants of the era of gravel digging. They have reed-beds and bracken covered islands with rhododendrons, crack willow, giant hogweed and some storm-beaten birches – and a population of brown rats which can be seen running in their purposeful way here and there along the banks. There is the usual collection of town park water birds: mallard and feral duck and an assortment of odd shaped hybrids, with coot, moorhen, black-headed gulls and the ubiquitous Canada geese. It is when these are supplemented by winter visitors such as pochard or even barnacle or white-fronted geese that the ponds become particularly interesting.

But both the exotic tree species and the rather tame park-type pond are clearly the usual municipal additions attempting to revive an otherwise desecrated space. They lack the vigour, diversity, excitement and restorative power of genuine wildness. And there is just one corner of Wandsworth Common where this can still be found. It is tucked away in the south west corner, where our route lies and where, in 1852, the Reverend John Craig built an 85 foot long telescope. It was slung from towers 64 foot high and rested on a support running on a circular railway. It was a very imperfect instrument, but was the largest telescope ever built up to its time, and it gave its name to this part of the common – 'the Scope'.

The Scope today is an area of semi-natural grassland almost unique in inner London. It supports twenty species of grass, including large tussocks of the purple-moor grass so reminiscent of soggy Pennine walks. This flourishes in the damper areas and, with hairy sedge, surrounds the little pond dug here by the British Trust for Conservation Volunteers in 1980. It is an attractive place at any time of year, even in winter when the moor-grass tussocks turn from green to pale yellow, the last bristly leaves of comfrey stand alongside the browning flower spires of weld, polypore fungi project from the bare birch trees and robins sing that characteristic, thin and melancholic trill.

Earlsfield and the Mayors of Garratt

ROUTE:

• In Wandsworth Cemetery take any route leading to the left and down to the exit at the far end.

• Turn right onto Magdalen Road then right again onto the main road at the end.

• Follow the main road (Garratt Lane) under the railway bridge and take the second turning left into Penwith Road.

FACILITIES: Toilets on corner of Magdalen Road and Garratt Lane. Pubs and cafés on Garratt Lane.

The hamlet of Garratt, once described as 'an insignificant dirt village in the parish of Wandsworth' became, in the 18th century, the scene of one of the strangest, and most popular street celebrations in London – the fantastical elections of a completely fictitious mayor.

Although several different versions are given of the origins of these proceedings, it seems most probable that they stem from one of the earlier attempts of Wandsworth commoners to protect their rights. In the early 1700s a group of them formed a society and their chairperson became known, with mock dignity, as the 'Mayor of Garratt'. The elections for this post became, in time, a burlesque of national politics, and were held to coincide with General Elections.

The first recorded elections were in 1747 and by the 1760s the event was attended by up to 100,000 people whose carriages, carts and horses were said to have blocked every road around Wandsworth for over a mile. The candidates were generally working-class London characters, whose chief requirement, according to Colonel Sexby, was 'an unlimited capacity for talking' preferably combined 'with some physical deformity or peculiarity'. On election day they would gather in fantastic costume, each with their own retinue, and process in decorated carts and carriages – often provided or even driven by the aristocracy – from Wandsworth to Garrrat Green. Here it was that 'Squire Blow-me-down', 'Lord Twankum', 'Sir Trincalo Boreas', 'Admiral Sir Christopher Dashwood', and many other characters over the years, took 'The Oath of Qualification for the ancient Borough of Garrat, according, and as it stands on the old record, handed down to us by the grand Volgee, by order of the great Chin Kaw Chipo, first Emperor of the Moon. Anno Mundi 68.' After this, to much heckling, ribald comment or raucous support, the candidates made their election speeches. Finally the succesful candidate was chosen by popular acclaim and the crowds got down to the serious business of drinking the local pubs dry.

Like the Horn Fair, the Middlesex elections and many other good English festivities, the elections were a scene of bawdy and almost riotous behaviour. The candidates' speeches were a mix of sexual innuendo and political satire. Some of the speeches were written by leading political and theatrical figures of the day, including Samuel Foote, David Garrick and John Wilkes. And from the 1760s the Garrat election became particularly associated with radical politics.

One of the most succesful of the Garrat mayors was 'Sir Jeffrey Dunstan', a strong supporter of John Wilkes, who was returned to 'office' three times and was described as 'the most popular candidate that ever appeared on the Garrat hustings'. Dunstan was a foundling who took his name from the parish where he had been abandoned as a baby. He was only four foot high, with a large head and knock knees, a vagrant wig-seller by trade and a man of outspoken wit. According to Hone's 1826 *Everyday Book*,

He was no respecter of persons and was so severe in his jokes on the corruptions and compromises of power that this street-jester was prosecuted for using what were then called seditious expressions; and, as a caricature of the times, which ought never to be forgotten, he was in 1793 tried, convicted and imprisoned.

Dunstan died in 1797, after a bout of heavy drinking. One year before this the Garrat elections had been finally suppressed by an establishment which the French revolution had made increasingly nervous of the 'mob' and all its manifestations. Despite several attempts to revive it since, the Garrat Elections have joined the Charlton Horn Fair as one of the great, anarchic expressions of exuberance which have disappeared from the streets of London.

Garrat too has disappeared, swallowed up in the expansion of urban Wandsworth. Its name survives in Garratt Lane and in Garratt Green, now an uninspiring grass triangle on nearby Burntwood Road. The area has had its very name appropriated by the Victorian developers. The last Lord of this, the Manor of All Farthing, covered the surrounding fields with housing in the late 19th century, and proceeded to rename the area after his wife, Earl. Hence Earlsfield – a name with about as much historical or social significance as Hillview, Sunnyside or The Cedars.

The only open space now left on this part of the walk is the 34 trim and not particularly appealing acres of Wandsworth Cemetery. This, with its two Gothic chapels, was laid out in 1878. The site also boasts eight war memorials and the remains of two air raid shelters – presumably intended to prevent those who tended the dead from joining them.

Across the Valley of the Wandle

ROUTE:
- Follow Penwith Road, taking the second turning on the left into Acuba Road.
- Take the first right into Ravensbury Road and follow it to the main road (Merton Road).
- Cross Merton Road and follow Revelstoke Road straight ahead to the entrance to Wimbledon Park.

LOOKING AT WILDLIFE: Fool's watercress (*apium nodiflorum*) can be seen growing on the concrete encasement of the River Wandle on either side of the bridge.

From Wandsworth Common we have been dropping down from the Boyn Hill terraces of the River Thames, across the buried surfaces of London clay and into the alluvium filled valley of another of the Thames tributaries – the River Wandle. The river rises near Croydon and runs about 10 miles to join the Thames in the heart of Wandsworth – the Borough that still bears its name.

The river where anglers once fished for brown marble trout is now, like most of London's rivers, a sadly reduced affair, concretised and canalised and hidden away from public view as though it were some sort of inconvenience. This same river however has played a central part in the industrial development of Wandsworth and of London as a whole, and, before its head-waters were tapped, served as many as 68 different mills. As long ago as 1376 the fullers (cloth bleachers) were in dispute with the hurrers (hat makers) over rights to the river, a dispute which ended in court action and with the fullers establishing a virtual monopoly. All this changed with the arrival of the Huguenots.

In 1685 the French King, Louis XIV, revoked the Edict of Nantes under which the nation's protestants had been given a measure of toleration. This led to an exodus of 'huguenots' to protestant European countries. Of those who came to England many settled in Wandsworth, Streatham and Tooting. They brought with them energy, determination and a knowledge of industrial processes, in particular of the harnessing of water power. The mildly alkaline waters of the Wandle were ideal for their industries: silk weaving, copper engraving, hat making, bleaching, dyeing and colouring. Ironically their customers came to include the Roman Catholic cardinals, who turned to the Huguenots for their red robes and hats. In recognition of their contribution to the Borough the presence of the Huguenots was represented on the coat of arms. Against a background of the chequers of Surrey is incorporated a pattern of small droplets – the tears of the refugees.

Today the Wandle is being rediscovered and an attempt made to establish a heritage walk along its entire length. Here, at its northern end, it is patchy in the extreme, but should the attempt be successful and the walk be improved, it will form a link for London walkers between the 180 mile Thames path and the 62 mile Vanguard Way – a continuous route from the source of the Thames to the sea at Seaford in Sussex.

The historical associations of the area do little to relieve the tedium of the streets of Earlsfield and Southfields. Revelstoke Road, Acuba Road, Ravensbury Road, Penwith Road – even the names have the nondescript nature of late Victorian development. The stolidity of the area is reinforced in the Southfields Methodist Church, on the corner of Merton Road. It is a huge mausoleum-like structure in yellow stock brick with stone ornament and a square columned tower topped with a flag pole. It is as much like a book depository as a place of worship.

Wimbledon Park to the Common

ROUTE:

- On entering Wimbledon Park turn right along the tarmac path. When the path curves to the left carry on into wooded strip ahead and follow one of the trodden paths parallel to the main path but through the trees.
- Rejoin the main path near the children's play area and continue to the gate ahead.
- Turn left along the main road (Wimbledon Park Road). At the bottom of the hill two roads leave on the right together. Take the one to the left (Bathgate Road).
- Take the first turning on the right (Queensmere Road) and follow it to the main road (Wimbledon Park Side).

- Turn right along the main road and cross at the pedestrian crossing. Just ahead several paths radiate across the common. Ignore the path sharp left and EITHER:
- Take the path ahead and to the left to reach the windmill and join the next section, OR:
- Take the large drive further to the right. Where it crosses a main horse ride turn right and follow this to Tibbet's Corner and the end of the walk.

LOOKING AT WILDLIFE: Waterfowl on the lake in Wimbledon Park including great crested grebe and cormorant. A lovely relic of oak and hornbeam woodland along the northern edge of Wimbledon Park.

With the bursting of the South Sea Bubble in 1732 one of the bankrupted directors was forced to put his estate, the Manor of Wimbledon, onto the market. It was bought by Sarah, Duchess of Marlborough, who in turn bequeathed it, in 1744, to her favourite grandson John Spencer. John had done well to ingratiate himself with the Duchess for he had a notorious reputation, was known as 'Bad Jack' and had drunk himself to death by the age of 38. But the Manor has stayed with the Spencer family ever since. The Manor House was just to the south of the present Wimbledon Park and the area of the park was part of the demesne lands – that is the lands which the lord holds in absolute right and does not have to 'share' with commoners. Bad Jack's son, also John Spencer, became the first Earl Spencer. He decided to landscape the grounds around his manor house and employed Lancelot Brown to do the job. Brown was the most famous landscape gardener of his day and earned his famous nickname, 'Capability' Brown, from his idiosyncratic use of English. 'This area,' he would say, surveying a park or estate on which he was being consulted, 'has a great capability'.

The present bland park, with its sports fields and running track, has little to remind us of what Brown's vision must have been, but the feature he has left us is the lake, incongruously sited on the highest part of the park. This was created by the damming of several streams which ran across the grounds, and enabled Brown to drain the marshy areas lower down. Interestingly, Capability Brown was not the only famous gardener to be connected with Wimbledon Park. Joseph Paxton, later to design the Crystal Palace, once worked here for a time.

The two John Spencers had been forbidden by a clause in the Duchess of Marlborough's will from taking an active part in politics. No such injunction lay upon the second Earl, George John Spencer. He began as MP for Northampton in 1780 and by 1794 had risen to be First Lord of the Admiralty, and the person instrumental in Nelson's advancement to Admiral. He was a staunch supporter of the Whigs and when his manor house burnt down in 1785, the new one he built became a social centre for the party, and for all those in society with whig leanings. The most popular events organised by him and his wife Lavinia were grand whig 'breakfasts', which in fact went on well into the afternoon. One of the practical effects of his entertaining was that the estate was almost bankrupted.

It was these financial problems which led the Spencers to sell off or let out their

Wimbledon possessions in 1834, including the demesne lands of the Wimbledon Park estate itself. Much of the park was developed for housing in the 1840s and 50s and in 1914 Wimbledon Council purchased the remaining part, intending themselves to sell it for building. Pressure from Wandsworth Council and from the public led to a change of heart and the grounds were laid out as a public park with the large lake occupying 22 of its 45 acres.

Apart from the lake, well worth a visit for its wildfowl, the park contains one other feature of natural interest. This is the narrow strip of woodland, of oak, hornbeam and scrub, which runs down its northern side. It is a visual reminder of what the whole of this area, from Wandsworth to Wimbledon, must once have looked like; and a beautiful contrast with the grassy desolation which fills the rest of the park. It is a small fragment of wild land which has escaped the 'improving' attentions of everybody from Capability Brown to Wimbledon Council and for that reason alone it deserves our attention.

From the Park itself the last stretch of walk takes us through suburban streets to Wimbledon Common. It was in Wimbledon Park Road that Mary Anne Evans lived with George Lucas, unmarried and therefore shunned by society. It was here too, in 1860, that she completed *The Mill on the Floss* published under her pen name of George Eliot. Bathgate Road is possibly named after one of the gates to the Spencer estate and takes us past the neo-Gothic, stone-clad Southlands College. And at Parkside, we reach Wimbledon Common and a welcome walk along heathland horse rides; an introduction to the section to come, a section which, by complete contrast, will cover twice as many miles without following a road at all.

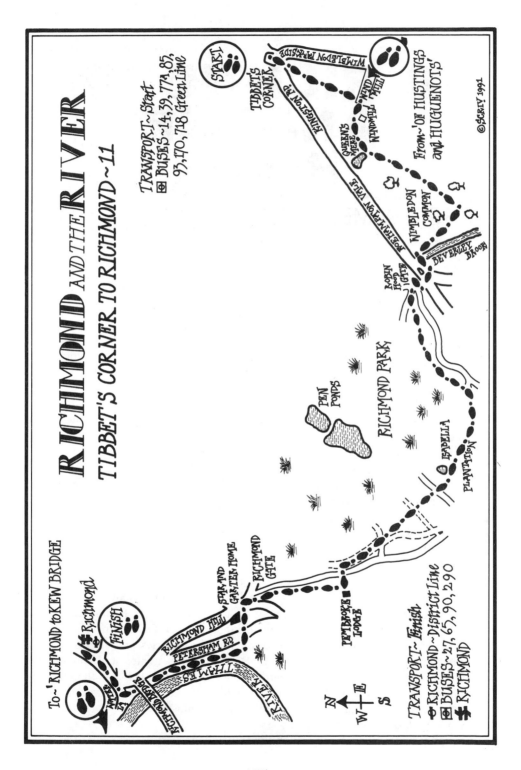

RICHMOND AND THE RIVER

TIBBET'S CORNER TO RICHMOND ~ 11

TRANSPORT ~ Start
BUSES ~ 14, 39, 77A, 85,
93, 170, 718 Green Line

TIBBET'S CORNER

START

WIMBLEDON PARKSIDE

WIND MILL

From ~ 'OF HASTINGS and HUGUENOTS'

©GERTY 1991

KINGSTON RD

MARRYAT

QUEEN'S MERE

PUTNEY VALE

WIMBLEDON COMMON

BEVERLEY BROOK

ROBIN HOOD GATE

RICHMOND PARK

PEN PONDS

ISABELLA PLANTATION

RICHMOND GATE

STAR AND GARTER HOME

PEMBROKE LODGE

RICHMOND HILL

PETERSHAM RD

RIVER THAMES

RICHMOND BRIDGE

To ~ 'RICHMOND to KEW BRIDGE

Richmond

FINISH

TRANSPORT ~ Finish
RICHMOND ~ District Line
BUSES ~ 27, 65, 90, 290
RICHMOND

N
W · E
S

−119−

8. RICHMOND AND THE RIVER

FROM WIMBLEDON COMMON TO KEW BRIDGE

Between Wimbledon Common and Kew Bridge *The Green London Way* offers the unique experience of eight miles of urban off-road walking. From the high plateau of the common and the rolling parkland of Richmond, down through the birchwood of Petersham and the sheep-grazed meadows of the riverside, along past Old Deer Park and Kew Gardens on the tow-path, this route may lead us across the occasional road, but not once do we have to follow one. There is some beautiful walking here, but more than this, when put into the context of the whole route there is a striking insight into the social layout of London.

On this Richmond section, in London's leafy south west, we are at the diametrically opposite side of London from where we began our walk down through Hackney and Newham. And these two areas are more than geographical opposites. London, like so many other cities, concentrates its rich in the west and its poor in the east. Anyone who has completed all of the London walk so far, or more dramatically perhaps, who has got on the North London line in Hackney and got off the same train in Richmond, cannot fail to be struck by the stark contrast between these two areas. It is difficult to accept that they are parts of one and the same city.

In Richmond our route follows royal parks and beautiful wooded commons; in north-east London it runs along the top of a Victorian sewer. In Richmond we pass huge villas and a riverside development in modern mock-Georgian; in north-east London the rivers are surrounded by tower blocks, factories and streets of large decaying houses in multi-occupation. In Richmond the homes look out on the commons or the river; in north-east London thousands of people live in the shadows, and amongst the fumes, of chemical plants, sugar refineries and gas works. This is strikingly apparent at a time when the leader of Westminster Council is claiming that 'the working classes no longer exist'.

The story of Richmond and the riverside has been very much the story of the aristocracy and the royalty who lived here; at Richmond Lodge, Richmond Palace, Zion House, Kew Palace or at one of a large number of other fabulous and fashionable villas. And between them they would have made the whole walk impossible had it not been for the struggles of the more humble inhabitants of Richmond. Without these people, Wimbledon Common, Richmond Park and Petersham Common would all now be lost to public access. This section of the walk illustrates the greatness of ordinary people and the ordinariness of great ones. For in this chapter Lords are defeated and Kings are beheaded and George III meets the tragic fate of a growing and incurable insanity. On the other hand, we have very ordinary people like the brewer John Lewis of Richmond who, almost single-handed, took on the courts and the King's daughter and kept Richmond Park open for our enjoyment today.

This chapter covers 8 miles from Wimbledon Common to Kew Bridge. It can be taken as two separate walks:

WALK 11: Tibbet's Corner to Richmond (5 miles).

WALK 12: Water Lane to Kew Bridge (3 miles)

WALK 11: Tibbet's Corner to Richmond

Getting Started

From Tibbet's Corner:
>   From the complex of paths in the centre of the Tibbet's Corner roundabout,
>   follow the path signposted to Wimbledon Common which leads directly onto a
>   main horse ride. Follow this all the way to the windmill.

From Walk 10:
>   Follow variation at end of Walk 10 leading to the windmill.

Wimbledon Common and the Windmill

ROUTE:
- There is a café to the right of the windmill. Follow the path running in front of the café, between this and the car park. At the end head straight on following the path into the trees and down to Queensmere.
- As you face the very tip of the pool there is a path on the left leading uphill. Follow this to a golf fairway.
- Go straight across the fairway onto a path into the trees opposite, beginning by a post. Ignore the path to the right.
- Keep straight ahead to reach a second golf fairway. The path continues directly opposite, though it is not easily visible until you have crossed the fairway.

- Follow the path for some distance until it is crossed by a gravel ride. Turn right and follow this beside the riding ring and downhill.
- Ignore cross paths and continue to eventually reach Beverley Brook. Follow the lane alongside the brook until you approach a sport's pavilion.
- Cross the footbridge on your left and head across the grass to reach and cross the footbridge over the main road.

FACILITIES: Toilets at the windmill. Café (9.30-5 daily). Windmill Museum (Sat and Sun, 2-5. Entrance fee).

LOOKING AT WILDLIFE: A rich variety of woodland and meadow birds including skylark, woodpeckers, cuckoo, warblers, spotted flycatcher, redpoll, yellowhammer, tree pipit, tree creeper and many more, with heron and a variety of wildfowl on the meres. Waterside plants at Queensmere include marsh pennywort and marsh willowherb, while a speciality on the common is the white-flowered climbing corydalis (*Corydalis claviculata*). There is a good variety of autumn fungi and the purple hairstreak butterfly can be found in the oaks around Queensmere.

At the highest point of a high plateau set in a crook of the Thames, stands a common without rival in London. Across 1412 acres of heathland, scrub, grassland and wood, Wimbledon Common and Putney Heath run into one another and jointly cover an area more than three times the size of north London's Hampstead Heath. Hudson described this common as 'wider and more refreshing to the spirit than any other in the metropolis', and it remains true today despite the intrusion of both traffic noise and golf across large tracts of its otherwise unspoilt acres.

Roughly speaking the common can be considered in two parts. The eastern section is higher, with areas of scrub and rough grassland dominating its glacial gravels. Westwards it slopes away into the vale cut by the Beverley Brook and it is here, on the London clay, that the main areas of woodland are found. Oak, beech, hornbeam, sweet chestnut, rowan and maple all grow here while right down in the vale itself and alongside the brook aspens and dogwood are found on the alluvial soils. There are even areas of sphagnum bog, a habitat otherwise rare in London.

Once these woodlands supported what was supposed to be the finest concert of nightingales in London. The nightingales have gone but a very wide range of visiting and breeding bird species remain, making this an exciting area for birdwatchers. The London Bird Report for 1985, for example, listed 21 pairs of great spotted woodpecker, 6 pairs of lesser spotted woodpecker, 10 pairs of green woodpecker, 63 pairs of blackcap and 6 pairs of goldcrest, among the many other birds nesting here. There are butterflies too and the oaks around Queensmere support a colony of the beautiful purple hairstreaks. The adults, which vary greatly in number from year to year, spend much of their time in the upper canopy of the trees. They can therefore be quite difficult to see but closer examination often reveals the caterpillars. These brownish, woodlouse-shaped creatures live inside a silk web spun around the base of a clump of leaves. They can be found in June by feeling the bases of leaf clumps until you come across one which is spongy to the touch.

Wimbledon Common and Putney Heath were originally part of the Manor of Mortlake and as such were granted by Edward the Confessor to the See of Canterbury. The ensuing centuries saw many changes of ownership, the owners including several figures of national renown: Thomas Cromwell, whose father was said to have been a butcher in Putney, but rose to become first minister to Henry VIII; Queen Henrietta Maria, wife of the ill-fated Charles I; and the Roundhead General Lambert who retired here when he felt he had been slighted by the Protector. In 1744 it was bequeathed, together with Wandsworth Common, to John Spencer (see p.117). With this began the modern story of the struggle with the Spencer family to preserve the common.

For generations past the commoners of Wimbledon had cut furze and pollarded oaks for fuel, grazed cattle, gathered wild foods, and dug for gravel, turf and loam. These rights were restricted to certain parts of the year. At Michaelmas, in September, the Parish Beadle went around with a bell to 'cry the common open' and on Lady Day, in the following April, he 'cried it shut'. For the rest of the year the Lord of the Manor had exclusive use.

There were regular disputes of course and these were regulated by the Manor Court, which met three or four times every year and consisted of all the Lord's tenants presided over by his steward. The Rolls for the Wimbledon Manor Court exist as far back as 1461, but although it survived into the days of the Spencers it had long ceased to be an effective regulatory body. Encroachments had become numerous, as had other depredations such as 'persons shooting night soil or other filth onto the common'. But in 1812 it was the Lord of the Manor himself who broke custom and rule by cutting down all the pollarded oaks and selling them off for timber. In 1864 matters came to a head when the then Earl Spencer came up with a plan to sell off 300 acres of common, using the proceeds to enclose the remaining 700 acres. There was not much the Manor Court could do. By this time it only had nine members left and by one means or another the Earl was able to secure their compliance. The proposal then went forward as a Private Bill to Parliament in 1865.

At this stage Earl Spencer found he had a second group to reckon with. The passage of years had brought the development of the urban fringes to the edges of Wimbledon Common and the new middle classes who had settled there did not hesitate to make their voices heard. In 1865 they set up a Wimbledon Common Committee, electing Henry Peek as their chair. A House of Commons committee came out against the Bill on its second reading but by this time the Wimbledon Common Committee had already taken the case to law. They initiated proceedings in Chancery concerning the dilapidated state of the common, and these dragged on untill April 1870 when Spencer decided to reach an out of court settlement. Ownership of the commons passed to a board of trustees and Spencer received an annuity equal to his average earnings from the common over the last ten years. The continued upkeep of the common was to be paid for from the proceeds of a rate levied on all properties within ¾ mile of the Common with a rateable value over £35. The system was incorporated into an Act of Parliament in 1871. The trustees purchased Earl Spencer's annuity from him in 1967 and the rest of the scheme survives to this day.

Our route across the common begins at its noisy northern apex where bridle ways and footpaths dip under the subways into the complex central roundabout of Tibbet's Corner. The iron signboard bears the figure of a pistolled highwayman but Tibbet, less romantically, was one of the gatekeepers of the Spencer's Wimbledon Park estate. From the roundabout a broad ride, known officially as Ladies Mile, leads down to one of the common's most attractive features. A black cone of slatted wood sits atop a low octagonal brick building and supports the white, revolving body of the Wimbledon Windmill. With its white sails to the front and its fantail wheel projecting outwards and upwards to the rear, it resembles a white dove perched on a black branch. It is an elegant building, beautifully restored. The 'old Surrey working woman', as John Betjeman described it, now looks positively adolescent.

In 1817 Charles March of Roehampton petitioned for the enclosure of ¼ acre of the common for the erection of a mill. This was granted 'upon this special condition that he shall erect and keep up a public Corn Mill, for the advantage and convenience of the neighbourhood'. The first miller was Thomas Dann who was required to combine his work as miller with the office of constable, by using his vantage point in the mill to keep watch for thieves and robbers – and for that other scourge of the Common, the duellist.

Wimbledon Common had been a favoured place for duelling since at least 1652 when Lord Chandos is recorded as having killed a Colonel Compton. It was here too that Castlereagh and Canning, the Duke of York and Lieutenant Colonel Lennox, and other famous names duelled out their differences and shot out their slights. On one famous occasion in 1798, William Pitt met William Tierney, MP for Southwark; the two gentlemen measured out the required twelve paces, raised their pistols and fired, but both being totally ignorant in the use of firearms, they missed. They fired again, and missed again. Perhaps it was deliberate – 'Honour' had been satisfied. But there is one other little detail of this story to interest us. The duel was fought by a little hillock on the north east side of the common. It is known to this day as Jerry's Hill, after Jerry Abershaw, a famous highwayman whose body hung here from a gibbet. It was in the shadow of his still dangling corpse that Pitt and Tierney fought out their duel. Of Jerry Abershaw we shall be hearing more on our route to Kew.

The last recorded duel on the common took place in 1840 between Lord Cardigan and Captain Tuckett, and was witnessed from his tower by Thomas Dann. Since the practice was now illegal Thomas reported the incident. Cardigan was brought to trial the following year in the House of Lords and though clearly guilty was acquitted by a jury of his own 'peers' at the end of the first day. The mill itself ended its working life in 1864 when Earl Spencer, as part of his plan to sell off this part of the common, persuaded the miller to leave so that he could take back the leasehold. The mill was taken over by the Conservators in 1871 and fell into a state of dilapidation. In 1976 it was restored and re-opened as a Windmill Museum.

Not far to the east of the windmill, Queensmere, one of the most pleasant of the Wimbledon pools, lies hidden in a wooded hollow. It is a pear shaped pool overhung with trees, the home of clumsy coot and early morning heron. In spring toads spawn here in their hundreds. In summer, sunlight filters down onto the surface of the water through the leaves of oak and beech. And in autumn, mist hangs below the trees and the large leaves of the American Red Oak put on their spectacular display of colour. The pool was created in Victorian times by the damming of a stream running into a boggy clearing in the woods. As with many other London pools and springs, it was made possible by the junction of porous gravels with the impervious clay.

Beverley Brook, the stream which has carved the valley here, and cut down through the gravels into the clay, draws its name from the beavers which existed in England even into Saxon times. It is this brook which we follow down to the main road in Kingston Vale. Running twelve miles from Sutton to join the Thames at Barn Elms, it is rather a sluggish river, its last seven miles all being less than 50 feet above sea level.

Richmond Park

ROUTE:
• Enter the park through Robin Hood Gate, at the far end of the little terrace of houses, and follow the road straight ahead. Immediately after the crossroads take the broad, rather muddy horse ride off to the left and follow it away through the trees.
• Shortly after the top of the hill there is a crossing of routes, with a car park away to your left. Turn right and follow the track to reach the gate of Isabella Plantation.
• Follow the brook all the way through the Plantation and leave by the gate behind Peg's Pond at the opposite end.
• Follow the drive straight ahead. On reaching the road go straight across and continue on the path ahead, with the small wood (Hamcross Plantation) to your left.
• The path becomes less distinct at times but continues ahead through rough grassland and bracken to reach a pond. Pass the pond and carry on ahead to join the broad, dark horse ride running parallel to the road.
• Cross the road to reach Pembroke Lodge. Facing the lodge turn right and follow paths running parallel to the road, with views over London to your left, to reach Richmond Gate.

FACILITIES:Toilets at Robin Hood Gate. Refreshment kiosk (summer months) at the car park on Broomfield Hill. Toilets at Pembroke Lodge; café (10-4 weekdays, 9-4 weekends, later in summer); information caravan (summer months only). Toilets at Richmond Gate.

LOOKING AT WILDLIFE: Large herds of red and fallow deer. Beautiful old parkland trees including oaks, wych elm, beech, sweet and horse chestnuts. A wide variety of parkland birds. Specialities include jackdaw, green woodpecker, tree sparrow, treecreeper and meadow pipit. Isabella Plantation has a collection of rhododendrons, azaleas and camelias and beautiful clumps of royal fern along the brook. It is a very good place to see and hear tits, nuthatch and warblers. There is a collection of ornamental waterfowl on Peg's Pond.

When Queen Caroline asked Horace Walpole what it would cost her to enclose the royal parks in central London, he is said to have replied, 'Your throne, madam.' Perhaps he had learnt from the folly of King Charles I and the consequences of his attempt, two hundred years earlier, to enclose the royal park at Richmond.

Shene Chase at Richmond had been a royal hunting ground since before the time of Henry VIII. Charles I hit upon the idea of enclosing it – and not just the Chase but an equally large area around it belonging to local landowners. The landowners resisted but when many of them refused to sell, the King began work anyway, building a perimeter fence which denied them access to half their own land. It was a rank injustice, and from a king whose incompetence, vanity and folly were already leading to a dangerous dissatisfaction amongst the people. The news soon spread and, as the Earl of Clarendon said, in his *History of the Rebellion*, 'It increased the murmur and noise of the people who were not concerned as well as of them who were; and it was too near London not to be the common discourse.'

Despite opposition from his own advisers, the king had completed the enclosure by 1637. This was just one in the long line of actions that, in 1649, was to cost him his head.

That original wall, 13 miles long, still encloses the 2,470 acres of Richmond Park today. Despite the fate of Charles, he was not the last of the monarchy to attempt to exclude the public. In 1747 George II appointed his youngest and favourite daughter Amelia to be Ranger of Richmond Park. Three years later she closed the park to everyone but personal friends and key-holders. The procedure for obtaining a key was made so difficult that few could achieve it. Even the Lord Chancellor, it was said, was refused a key. A public petition was ignored and a test case brought against the Deputy Ranger was dismissed. And there matters might have rested were it not for the direct action undertaken by John Lewis, a brewer of Richmond.

In 1755 Lewis waited outside the Sheen Gate until it was opened to admit a carriage. He followed it in and, claiming a public right of way, set out to walk across the park. He was intercepted by gatekeeper Martha Gray and ejected. He then brought a case, nominally against the gatekeeper but effectively against Princess Amelia herself. By one means or another the judiciary put off the case for three years but eventually, in 1758, it came to court. Lewis claimed a right of way granted to pedestrians by Charles I, a concession he had been forced into when enclosing the land in the first place. And on this the case was won. Amelia put up ladder stiles for public use but made sure that the rungs were so widely spaced that they were unuseable. Lewis went back to court to challenge this and once more won his case.

Single-handed, John Lewis had taken on the daughter of the reigning monarch and won. In 1761 Amelia lost interest in what was no longer her private garden, resigned the Rangership and retired to Gunnersbury. Nonetheless she probably fared better than Lewis himself. The personal expenses he had incurred at law were compounded when the River Thames flooded his brewery and counting house at Petersham. He died in poverty in 1792, having lived his last years supported only by a small annuity raised from the residents at Richmond at the instigation of the local parson.

The oldest inhabitants of the Park today are the deer. They have been there since before enclosure and one of the earliest of all the park records shows a payment of £100 made in 1637 to keepers Lodowick Carlile and Humfry Rogers for 'pease, tares and hay, for the red and fallow deer'. It is these two species which still graze the grass of Richmond, up to 350 red deer and 450 fallow. Their numbers fluctuate from year to year, but hopefully not as much as they did in 1886-87, when rabies reduced the population by more than a hundred.

These open, tree-dotted grasslands, with grazing herds of deer slowly moving across them, make this the picture of traditional English parkland. There are over 200,000 trees here including English elm, wych elm, beech, hornbeam, Spanish and horse chestnut. But it is the oaks which predominate, some of them pre-dating enclosure and many more of them at least 200 years old. The large, old and often hollow trees attract nesting birds including tree sparrows and green woodpeckers. According to Eric Simms, Richmond has more birds and small mammals than any other London park – including the not so welcome presence of more than 2000 grey squirrels. Among the birds, there are reckoned to be over 100 visiting species, with 52 of them nesting. The flocks of wild turkeys kept in the park in the reign of George III have now gone, but there are still treecreepers, yellowhammers, pheasant, red-legged and common partridge, little owl and much, much more. But perhaps the last word should go to the jackdaws. W.H. Hudson says he was, assured by a keeper that there were 'millions', adding that his informant was 'a very tall white-haired old man with aquiline features and dark fierce eyes and therefore must have known what he was talking about'.

Our route through the park begins at the Robin Hood Gate and proceeds up Broomfield Hill to reach the Isabella Plantation. The Plantation was originally natural woodland which was transformed in 1951 by the then Park Superintendant, George Thomson. Now a little brook winds through a woodland garden to reach Peg's Pond at the far end. It is best seen in early spring for the blossom or in late autumn for the leaf colour. The trees are underplanted with a great variety of rhododendrons, azaleas, camelias, magnolias and heathers and with such beautiful specimen shrubs as the Pocket Handkerchief Tree or *rhododendron fictolactum*, known as Nature's Weather Vane. It is good to be able to note that the gardeners have been commemorated here, in particular Wally Miller, one time Head Gardener. He has both an island named after him, Wally's Island in Peg's Pond, and his own rhododendron, the grandiosely but engagingly entitled *Rhododendron yakusimanum x glamour 'Wally Miller'*.

From the Plantation our route crosses coarse grassland close to the little White Ash Pond and passes between Sidmouth Wood and Pembroke Lodge. Sidmouth Wood is named after Lord Sidmouth, Deputy Ranger, who lived at White Lodge in the Park and died there in 1844. The various parkland plantations were originally established as pheasant cover but this one has now been enclosed as a bird sanctuary.

Pembroke Lodge was originally, and more interestingly, known as Molecatcher's Cottage. It was enlarged in 1788 by the architect Sir John Soane and renamed when Eliza, Countess of Pembroke moved in. In 1847 it was granted by Queen Victoria to her Prime Minister, Lord John Russell who died here in 1878. His grandson, Bertrand Russell, spent most of his childhood and early youth here. The lodge ceased to be a private residence at the end of the nineteenth century. It currently houses a café for the park; a recent attempt by the Department of the Environment to sell it into private ownership met strong public resistance.

Petersham and the Riverside

ROUTE:
- Leaving the park through the Richmond Gate, turn left and then follow paths directly beside and then behind the Star and Garter Home.
- From the back of the home fork left downhill.
- Cross Petersham Road and go through the gate onto the meadow.
- Ignore the path leading off left and bear right across the meadow to reach a tarmac path. Follow it right then through the gardens parallel to the river to join the tow-path. TO AVOID USING STILE TURN RIGHT ALONG PETERSHAM ROAD THEN LEFT INTO RIVERSIDE GARDENS
- Follow the tow-path beneath Richmond Bridge and past the terraces to where Water Lane comes right down to the river.

FACILITIES: Toilets in park by Petersham Meadows. Tea bars, cafés, pubs etc. along the tow-path.

LOOKING AT WILDLIFE: Some woodland bird and plant species amongst woods around Star and Garter Home. Gipsywort, hemlock water dropwort and angelica along the riverside as well as a magnificent old plane tree. Cormorant and wildfowl on the river.

The stone piers of the Richmond Gate bear the monograms of George III and Queen Charlotte and the date 1798 in Roman numerals. The gates are often said to have been designed by Capability Brown but are just as likely to have been the work of Sir John Soane, the architect of Pembroke Lodge. They lead out onto a group of impressive, yellow-brick and bow-fronted Georgian villas, an interesting contrast with the gross red-brick pile of the Star and Garter Home across the road.

The Star and Garter stands at the highest point of Richmond Hill and takes its name from an inn which previously stood here. It began in 1738 as a 'small tavern' and ended its days as a luxury hotel. It was demolished in 1924 and this home for disabled ex-servicemen built on the site. The pleasant little woods sloping down Star and Garter Hill towards the river are part of the 17 acre Petersham Common. They were saved by the Commons Preservation Society after their owner, Lord Dysart, had tried to slip an Enclosure Bill through parliament unnoticed. The ploy was uncovered by the Society and the attempt failed. The Commons Preservation Society, under its new name The Open Spaces Society, remains one of the great campaigning organisations struggling against threats to our open spaces today.

Below the hill and along the riverside we cross Petersham Meadows where sheep still graze a waterside field with a view of white villas across the river in a scene which

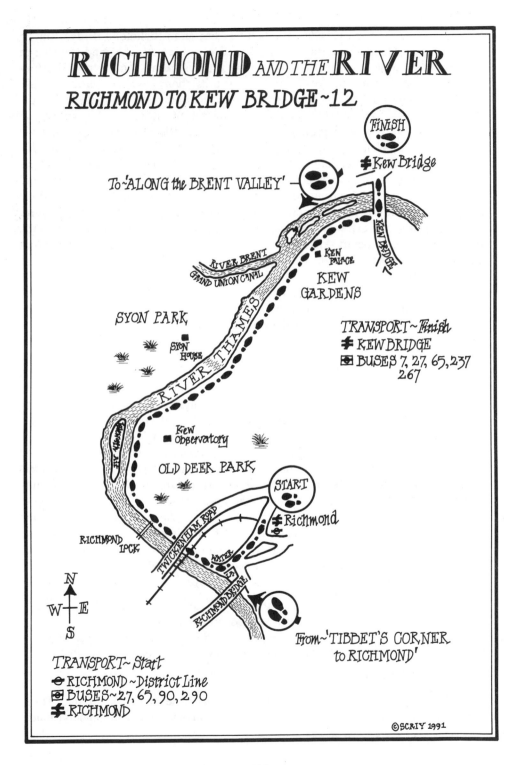

RICHMOND AND THE RIVER

RICHMOND TO KEW BRIDGE ~12

FINISH

Kew Bridge

To 'ALONG the BRENT VALLEY'

RIVER BRENT
GRAND UNION CANAL

KEW PALACE

KEW GARDENS

KEW BRIDGE

SYON PARK

SYON HOUSE

RIVER THAMES

TRANSPORT ~ *Finish*
KEW BRIDGE
BUSES 7, 27, 65, 237 267

Kew Observatory

OLD DEER PARK

START
Richmond

RICHMOND LOCK

TWICKENHAM ROAD

WEIR

RICHMOND BRIDGE

From ~ 'TIBBET'S CORNER to RICHMOND'

N
W E
S

TRANSPORT ~ *Start*
RICHMOND ~ District Line
BUSES ~ 27, 65, 90, 290
RICHMOND

© SCRIY 1991

is almost arcadian. The riverside path then leads us on to Richmond Bridge, among the best of all Thames bridges. It has distinctively pointed arches and a facing of Purbeck stone which is ageing into a variety of tones from fawn to grey. For four hundred years from the reign of Edward III onwards, there was a ferry crossing here, and it was not until 1773 that an Act of Parliament permitted the building of a bridge. Under the Act a body of 90 Commissioners was set up to oversee the project and among these were several prominent inhabitants of Richmond, including David Garrick, Horace Walpole and Capability Brown. The bridge was completed in 1777 and remained a toll bridge until 1859, passing into public ownership only as late as 1931. But by this time, according to a letter to the *Evening Standard*, it had become, 'probably the most dangerous of all the bridges which span the Thames'. Huge increases in traffic created a dangerous congestion and threatened the very structure. 'The effect of a shower,' wrote the same correspondent, 'is terrific. Not only do the heavy lumbering landcraft skid about ... but the roadway is churned into a mass of oily mud which is flung over the clothes of the pedestrians by the heavy wheels of the traffic. There is no escape.'

The problem was how to widen the bridge without destroying its beautiful proportions, the debate continuing until 1939 when part of the solution was to reface the widened span with the original Purbeck stone. Today the undersides of the arches give evidence of this succesful ploy; the lighter colour of the added section being almost the only visual clue of the work that has taken place.

No doubt the wealth and influence of many of the inhabitants of Richmond helped to secure the respectful treatment of the bridge. But the attempt to retain the character of the area has led to some strange consequences elsewhere. Immediately beyond the bridge we come to a series of formal stepped terraces, lined with gravel paths and leading up to an amazing assemblage of seemingly Georgian buildings. Most are in red brick, others in stucco. There are elegant windows and ballustrated porches and a facade of towers, domes, belvederes and decorated urns. A central arch leads up steps into Heron Square with its not unattractive but positively chilly and rather hybrid assemblage of offices and homes.

The whole complex is not Georgian at all – it is the now famous Richmond Riverside Development, with its curious mix of completely new building and new facades on old structures. It was designed by Quinlan Terry, whose work is part of the reaction to modernism espoused by Prince Charles, who is a great admirer of the development. But as 'Piloti' pointed out in *Private Eye*:

> few ever noticed that behind the neo-Georgian facades there were abominations like reinforced concrete construction, or that the gratuitous arched tops of Georgian windows exposed dropped ceilings and service ducts. For all that matters is to lard buildings with lots of details copied from Palladio and Bramante.

TO COMPLETE WALK 11: Turn right up Water Lane onto the main road. Turn left on ithe main road for buses and to reach Richmond Station (BR and underground).

WALK 12: Richmond to Kew Bridge

Getting Started

From Walk 11:
  Continue along the tow-path past Water Lane.
To start walk here:
  From Richmond Station cross the road and turn left to follow the road through
  Richmond town centre.
  After the road bends left you reach the post office. Turn right beside it down
  Water Lane.
  At Water Lane turn right along the tow-path.

Along the river to Kew

ROUTE:
* Follow the tow-path to Kew Bridge.

FACILITIES: Pubs and cafés at the Richmond end of the towpath.

LOOKING AT WILDLIFE: An interesting flora along the riverside and also in
the ditches alongside the tow-path. It includes tansy, cuckoo flower and marshland
species. Trees include large old black poplars, white poplars, alders, oaks and willows.
There are plenty of birds including linnets and other finches in the riverside trees, and
gulls, heron and cormorant on the river.

Along the riverside path the aristocratic villas of Cholmondeley Walk soon
give way to the cast-iron girders of the Richmond Railway Bridge and the
concrete monstrosity of the Twickenham Bridge, built in 1933 as part of
major road developments in West London. The bridge is a suitably ugly monument
to the motor car but would have been uglier still had Maxwell Ayrton's original
design – which included two fortress-like towers with flanking walls at each end of
the bridge – been allowed to proceed. These towers were only removed from the
design after a concerted campaign by the public, the Fine Arts Commission and the
Daily Telegraph. There is another river crossing not much further along the towpath,
this one a footbridge. It runs across the top of the Richmond Lock, the very last of
the locks as one travels downstream along the Thames. It is an interesting structure
in green and yellow painted cast iron with stone piers and alcoves.

In the second half of the nineteenth century there were numerous complaints to
the Thames Conservators concerning the increasing quantities of mud being
deposited along the river banks. This was blocking the navigation as well as creating
offensive smells and it was a particular headache, perhaps literally, to the operators
of ferries and passenger steamers. As one witness put it at an enquiry in 1873, 'you

may stand on Richmond Bridge and see the scum coming up from London and … sometimes it seems thick enough to walk upon.'

In 1871 an engineers' report stated that the abstraction of water by the metropolitan water companies was reducing the river's flow by up to 110,000,000 gallons a day, and that increasing amounts of raw sewage were being discharged into this reduced flow. The quantity of local sewage was compounded by that from the rest of the city which, after the removal of the old London Bridge, was daily washed back upstream by the tide. The engineers came out against a proposed weir on the grounds of the great amount of 'excrementitious material' that would become impounded. Their own suggestion was that a deeper channel should be dredged.

This did not satisfy the complainants. They appointed their own engineer and it was his proposal for a combined lock and weir that finally won the day. But not quite soon enough. Thames river steamers were designed to be able to float in a mere sixteen inches of water. Nonetheless on Monday 25 August 1873, every steamer between Richmond and Teddington went aground. They were forced to discharge their passengers into small boats in mid-channel and the steamers remained stuck on the bare and stinking mud from 10 am to 10 pm. 'The silvery Thames,' said the 1873 report, 'was unserviceable for traffic, whether of pleasure or commerce … it threatens to become a noisome dried-up ditch during the most enjoyable period of the summer months'. The lock and weir was completed in the next few years and the footbridge above it opened in 1894.

If the silting here was largely due to sewage, the silting further on along the river, where it gently curves northwards, is of a more natural kind. It has led to the creation of the long low island where the bend in the river coincides with the emergence, on the opposite bank, of the River Crane. In fact the island has constantly changed its shape. A map of 1635 shows four separate islands on this spot and these have gradually reduced in number over the years to the single ten-acre island remaining today. This is the Isleworth Ait, sharing the 'ait' part of its name with many of the Thames islands. This old word for island also occurs in other forms – in 'eyot' and in the word endings -ey and -ea in place names such as Bermondsey, Hackney and Swansea, evidence that at one time at least, an island existed in these places.

All along this stretch of the river we have been walking alongside the Old Deer Park, a large flat expanse of grassland disappointingly devoid of deer of any age. The main point of interest remaining is the distant prospect of the Kew Observatory, looking like a stumpy white lighthouse amidst a sea of green. The Deer Park was part of the grounds of George III's palace and it was he who ordered the building of the Observatory. Designed by William Chambers, it was completed for the express purpose of observing the transit of Venus in 1769. The two plain obelisks in the park close to the tow-path are, despite their resemblance to funerary monuments, attached to the Observatory. They were set up during the building process in order to adjust the transit instruments. Later the Observatory had its own full-time staff of astronomers and became the centre for the setting of national mean time, a responsibility which later passed to Greenwich. Today it serves as a meteorological station.

One of the porters at the Observatory in its earlier days was John Little, who was often the sole attendant on George III during his walks in the grounds. On the night of 23 June 1795 this 'quiet, gentlemanly person' left the Observatory, walked across the park and entered the house of two elderly friends to whom he was in debt. There he beat them to death with a large stone. He could have got away and left no clues as to his identity but, as he himself later said, having completed the crime he found it completely impossible to quit the building. He was arrested in the house, brought to trial and sentenced to death. In August of that year he was taken by cart from the gaol to Kennington Common, there to be hung. In the same cart, on his way to meet the same fate, was the famous highwayman, Jerry Abershaw, whose name is commemorated at Wimbledon Common, (see p.124).

As we reach the end of the Deer Park, much of it now covered by a golf course, the vista of Syon Park opens up on the opposite bank. It is dominated in the centre by Syon House and is still part of the estate of the Duke of Northumberland. The name is a corruption of Zion, for the site once held the 'Monastery of the Holy Saviour and St Brigid of Zion', founded by Henry V in 1415. The grounds owe their present appearance to the landscaping of Capability Brown who, from the evidence of *The Green London Way* alone, either had some equally capable assistants or was an extremely busy man. Among his plantings were the famous swamp cypresses which can still be seen clearly from our side of the river.

Syon House has seen several unhappy occupants, chief amongst them the unfortunate Lady Jane Grey. During the reign of young Edward VI, the Duke of Northumberland had become one of the most powerful figures in the Council of Regency which governed the country. When it became clear that Edward was dying and that Northumberland would be unable to maintain his position under Mary, the heir to the throne, he prepared a coup d'etat. He married his son to Lady Jane Grey, a granddaughter of Henry VII and here at Syon House, bestowed upon her the crown of England. But the country rallied to Mary and even Northumberland's men refused to fight for him. Jane's reign lasted exactly twelve days and this reluctant queen, the innocent victim of ambitious men, died on the block. A later Earl of Northumberland had the house restored in the 1640s by Inigo Jones. Despite this it remains a rather bland building, topped with a large lion which makes it rather reminiscent of the old Waterloo Station.

From way back along the towpath we have been catching incongruous glimpses of a Japanese pagoda. It is our first introduction to Kew Gardens and to the many stories which surround this site. Kew has particular associations with the Hanoverians, the German family imported to sit on the English throne in 1715. In the 1720s George II and Queen Caroline were living in Richmond Lodge, the grounds of which included the Old Deer Park. Their eldest son, Frederick, Prince of Wales lived in the old Kew Palace. The two estates were separated by Love Lane; but between the two halves of the family there was no love lost at all. Frederick led a scandalous life and was hated by his very rigid and strictly orthodox parents. His mother once told Lord Hervey, 'My dear first-born is the greatest ass and the greatest liar and the greatest canaille and the greatest beast in the whole world, and ... I heartily wish him out of it.' She was to have her way. Frederic died in 1751 before he could inherit the throne. 'Here lies Fred', wrote the satirists, 'Who was alive and is dead'. They then went on to berate the entire family ending with the couplet, 'Had it been the whole generation, much better for the nation'.

It was Fred's widow, Augusta, who started the Botanic Gardens, laying out nine acres of the estate, complete with two dozen exotic ornamental structures designed by William Chambers. These included an orangery, a ruined arch, the House of Confucius, the Temple of the Sun, the Temple of Aeolus, the Temple of Belladonna, the Alhambra and a Mosque. Of the buildings which still survive the pagoda is the most noticeable. It is an octagonal structure rising to ten stories and 163 feet in height. It represents the rage for chinoiserie that was just then sweeping Europe.

The eldest son of Frederic and Augusta came to the throne as George III. He inherited Richmond Lodge on the death of George II and the Kew estate on the death of his mother. The two properties were then joined and Sir Joseph Banks became the unofficial director of the grounds. Banks had sailed with Cook on 'The Endeavour' and had collected plants from many countries in the course of his extensive travels. During the reign of George III he, and the many other collectors he sent out, introduced 7,000 new species of plant to Britain. Banks himself had tried to bring back a 'noble savage' to crown his collection, 'to keep as a curiousity as well as my neighbours do lions and tigers'. His candidate for this post, perhaps mercifully, died in Batavia en route to England.

George and his queen, Charlotte, went on to have thirteen children and to outgrow the Kew Palace they were now living in. Their answer was to buy the house 'next door' and to use it as an extension – largely as a nursery for the children. It is this building, the 'Dutch House', which we see over the wall as we come towards the end of the gardens. It had been built in 1631 for a merchant of Dutch origin and is an attractive building of red brick laid in Flemish bond, which was just then becoming fashionable in English building.

From 1788 George III began to show increasing signs of madness, suffering from a condition now recognised as porphyria. In 1802 he was moved into the Dutch House. Here, he lived out the years in virtual confinement under the constant supervision and unpleasant ministrations of the two Doctors Willis. In 1811 his insanity became permanent but it was not until 1820 that his ordeal finally came to an end.

Unlike the king, and despite some difficult early years, Kew Gardens was to go from strength to strength. Today its 300 acres constitute one of the most beautiful botanic gardens in the world. But more than this they also house a famous School of Horticulture, important research laboratories, a library of more than 120,000 volumes and a herbarium, with more than 5 million specimens of plant from all over the world.

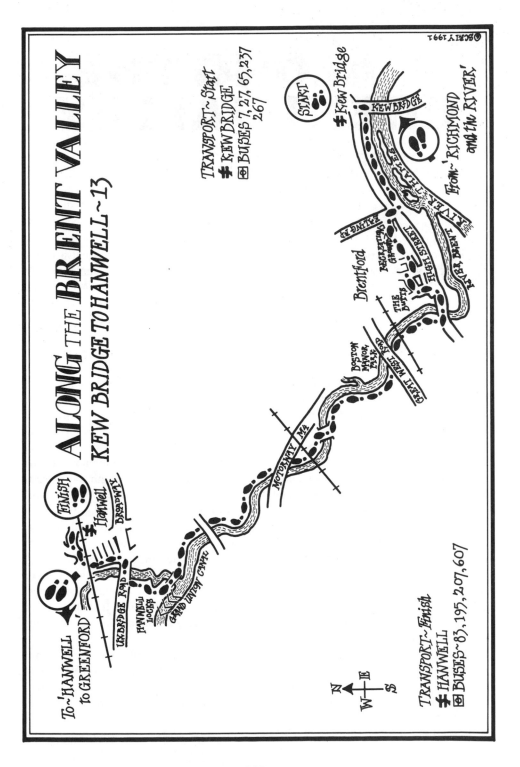

ALONG THE BRENT VALLEY
KEW BRIDGE TO HANWELL ~ 13

© GERRY 1991.

TRANSPORT ~ Start
🚆 KEW BRIDGE
🚌 BUSES 7, 27, 65, 237
267

START

🚆 Kew Bridge

From 'RICHMOND
and the RIVER'

KEW BRIDGE

RIVER THAMES

RIVER BRENT

EALING RD

HIGH STREET
RECREATION GROUND
Brentford
THE BUTTS

GREAT WEST ROAD

BOSTON MANOR PARK

MOTORWAY M4

GRAND UNION CANAL

HANWELL LOCKS

UXBRIDGE ROAD

Hanwell
BROADWAY

FINISH

🚆
To ~ 'HANWELL
to GREENFORD'

N
W — E
S

TRANSPORT ~ Finish
🚆 HANWELL
🚌 BUSES ~ 83, 195, 207, 607

9. ALONG THE BRENT VALLEY

FROM BRENTFORD TO GREENFORD

On the west side of London the River Brent and its tributaries cut a valley running down from the low hills of south Hertfordshire to a junction with the Thames opposite Kew. This is a gentler river than its east London equivalent, the Lea; a more amicable flow in a smaller valley, characterised by meadows rather than marshland. Despite urbanisation it remains a pleasant, meandering and surprisingly rural walk.

Brentford and Greenford stand at either end of our route up the valley. They both derive their names from river crossings but apart from this they have little in common. Greenford represents higher reaches of the river, with a rural history surviving into the twentieth century. Here was a small hamlet surrounded by the hayfields which once characterised much of Middlesex. Urbanisation arrived here rather later than in the southern suburbs and as a result of the motor car as much as of the railways. The building of major arterial roads between London and the west brought industry to the urban fringes, and the houses followed. The fields disappeared and the hamlet in the meadows became an amorphous and industrialised suburb, its configuration something of a mystery, even to its own inhabitants.

Brentford, on the other hand, was always an important town. The significance of its location, at the point where the Thames, the Brent and the Bath road all meet, is reflected in the fact that two major battles have been fought here. One was an engagement beween Edmund Ironside and the Danes, the other a battle of the Civil War. Brentford has a history as a lively, and often notorious, market town, later seeing the early arrival of the industrial revolution – with gas works and distilleries, soap works, docks and wharves, and the slum streets of Troy Town. It is also a town of great radical credentials, of John Wilkes, John Horn Tooke and the infamous business of the Middlesex elections.

Between 'urban' Brentford and 'rural' Greenford we have walks which take in not just a river, but the Grand Junction Canal and its narrow-boats, the Great Western's viaduct and its bats, a beautiful church disowned by its architect, and a 'lunatic' asylum which occupies one of the most progressive places in the history of British psychiatry.

This chapter covers 8 miles from Kew Bridge to Greenford Station. It can be taken as two separate walks.

WALK 13: Kew Bridge to Hanwell (4½ miles).

WALK 14: Hanwell to Greenford (3½ miles).

WALK 13: Kew Bridge to Hanwell

Getting Started

From Kew Bridge Road (station and buses):
Walk up the approach to Kew Bridge and take the steps on the right hand side leading down to The Hollows.
From Walk 12:
Cross Kew Bridge from the south bank. Take the steps on the left leading down to The Hollows.

Gas Works and Withy Beds

ROUTE:
- Follow the riverside walk until it turns right to rejoin the main road.
- Turn left on the road. Pass Victoria Steps and take the entrance to Waterside Park.
- Follow the riverside through the Park and alongside the Watermans Arts Centre.
- Beyond the Arts Centre turn right up a stepped alleyway to rejoin the main road.

FACILITIES: Pub at Kew Bridge and bar at Watermans Art Centre.

LOOKING AT WILDLIFE: There are interesting riverside and wasteland wild flowers along the riverside walk. The islands support willows and poplars. Look for heron and cormorant, wagtails, waterfowl and occasional waders at low tide.

The elegant Kew Bridge, 366 feet of Cornwall and Aberdine granite surmounted by the arms of Middlesex and Surrey, was opened on 20 May 1903. Its three arches form flattened ellipses and the piers between them, with pointed fronts like the prows of ships, penetrate eighteen foot into the London clay beneath the river bed.

The demolition of the old Kew Bridge, 'at once so picturesque and so fraught with memories' was regarded by many artistic people as 'little less than a local calamity'. according to E. Beresford Chancellor writing in 1903. The *Daily Mail*'s reporter shared the same view:

Could the old bridge tell only a little of the meetings it saw! The lovers who met and kissed there; the sweethearts who sighed and said their fond goodbyes ... The tranquil twilight time when youth and maid first understood; the silent star time, when heart spoke to heart as never before; the moonlight time, when the tender gleams of reverie played with the old man's thoughts till he brushed aside a tear; the mysterious midnight time when night's lamp had gone behind a cloud and the lily-stars looked down on grief and guilt and darkness ... Life is always cheating us; our hopes are dashed and our dreams come to nothing.

So wrote Charles Cutting on the opening of the new bridge. Like the traffic, the journalism goes much faster today.

Before 1757, when the first bridge was built, the crossing was made by ferry. The ferry service was established in 1659 by Robert Tunstall who also operated lime-kilns alongside the river. It is perhaps the kilns which gave the name of The Hollows to this first stretch of riverside we follow. Here today neat house-boats are lined along the waterside each with its own little fenced patch of privacy. There are wasteland and waterside wild flowers too; Himalayan balsam, pellitory-of-the-wall, reed canary grass and two plants which although unrelated share the characteristic of leaving a sharp peppery taste on the tongue – biting stonecrop and water pepper.

Rejoining the main road briefly we have a view of one of West London's finest landmarks. Although the main buildings of the Kew Bridge Pumping Station are ungainly and inelegant, this matters little next to the wonderfully tapering tower, 235 foot of yellow brick cut across with stone courses in red and beige. With its shallow recesses, running the height of each face, its octagonal lantern and crowning wind vein, it rates alongside Abbey Mills Pumping Station and Stoke Newington Waterworks as one of the loveliest examples of Victorian industrial architecture.

The station was built in 1837 by the Grand Junction Water Works Company as their third attempt to establish a pollution free source of drinking water for West London. The tower was added in 1867 and houses two systems of vertical pipes through which the water was pumped by Cornish beam engines to give it sufficient head before entering the mains. The beam engines survive here in what is now the Kew Bridge Engines Trust and Water Supply Museum, which is home to an extensive collection of large steam engines.

The waterworks were just part of the concentration of industry which came to the Brentford riverside. Waterside Park, opened in 1984, now occupies the site of one of the oldest gasworks in the world, covering 8 acres of land and ¼ mile of river frontage. It was established in 1824 specifically to light the turnpike road from Kensington to Hounslow. Within a few years the gasworks was taken over by the Brentford Gas Company, under the chairmanship of Felix Booth. By 1926, it had grown to serve 124,000 customers across 130 square miles of London. At this stage it was taken over again, this time by the ambitious Gas, Light and Coke Company, whose story we encountered in Beckton (see p. 34). Like the Beckton plant it closed in 1964, made redundant by the advent of North Sea gas.

Felix Booth also happened to be the owner of the breweries and malthouses next door. This even larger site covered 11 acres, including the area now occupied by the Watermans Theatre. Together the Gas Company and the Royal Brewery constituted two of the largest industrial units in early nineteenth century Britain. The main building of the Brewery was a huge granary with a double purpose. On one level it served a distillery producing a million gallons of the famous gin a year while on the floor below it stood a bullock house fattening 300 beasts at a time for the London market.

Booth's proudest year was 1829 when William IV came to the brewery to discuss the arrangements for a Polar expedition which Booth was financing. Booth contributed £17,000 to the voyage of Sir John Ross and in due course received both a baronetcy and a place in the atlas, when a newly discovered peninsular was given the name Boothia Felix in his honour. Meanwhile, opposite what was now the Royal Brewery, High Street was lined with atrocious slum dwellings occupied by poorly paid labourers from Booth's two plants. Behind these, in an area known as Troy Town, many more were packed into one of the most overcrowded slum areas in London.

Today both the slums and the works are gone. The sole survivor from the period is the low white stone church with stumpy octagonal tower, glimpsed across High Street and the park wall. Though built in the shadow of the gas works in 1867 it looks as if it belonged in fields on the edge of the Essex marshes. Next door, in an older whitewashed building is the Church School, founded in 1768 by Sarah Trimmer, as the inscription says, 'for religious instruction and industry sponsored by annual subscriptions and benefactors and the produce of the childrens work'. The church was closed in 1959 and is today one of London's more eccentric museums. Here Frank Holland, looking for a home for his collection of automatic pianos, founded the Musical Museum in 1963. Today it contains – and demonstrates – mechanical pianos of all types.

The two larger islands just off-shore from the Park are Brentford Aits, separated by a gap once known as Hog's Hole. Waterfowl paddle in the shallow water, heron stand on the tidally revealed mud and cormorant perch in the island trees. The willows and poplars form a lovely grouping of contrasting shapes but from the 1300s to the 18th century it was osier willows which were cultivated here. With the industrial and residential growth of Brentford the many market gardens here began to disappear, as did the demand for baskets which had maintained the trade in osiers for 400 years.

Lots Ait, a third and slightly higher island, can be seen alongside the Arts Centre. From 1881 to 1965 the Thames and General Lighterage Company had boat building yards along the riverside here and these were enlarged by slipways on the Ait itself in 1926. The dilapidated and slightly mysterious buildings still dominate the island. In the 1980s the Ait was purchased by the Speyhawk Company who proposed to develop it as an exclusive residential village. The proposals were rejected after a public enquiry in which the London Wildlife Trust played an important part. Part of the opposition case was the presence here of a breeding colony of rare snails. The two-lipped door snail (*Clausilia biplicata*) is rare enough to feature in the *Red Data Books* of threatened species and is found in only five other locations in Britain. One of these is just across the river, beside the Public Records Office in Kew, where it has been found to subsist on dog faeces. The only puzzle is this: if the creature can feed on dog shit, why is it not a common species throughout the capital?

Troy Town

ROUTE:

• From the top of the alleyway cross the main road (High Street) and go straight ahead up the major road opposite (Ealing Road). Take the first turning on the left (Albany Road).

• From Albany Road take the second turning on the right (Brook Road South) and then the first on the left (Grosvenor Road).

• Continue straight ahead, down Grosvenor Road, through the Recreation Ground and along St Pauls Road to reach Half Acre.

FACILITIES: Pubs on Ealing Road.

LOOKING AT WILDLIFE: Beautiful tall limes in the recreation ground.

Brentford, it is refreshing to be able to say, was unbeloved of poets. James Thomson called it 'a town of mud', John Gay a 'tedious town ... For dirty streets and white-legged chickens known'. In *Oliver Twist*, Dickens describes Brentford as 'in the prime of its muddiness', with the mire so thick that it was often up to the axle boxes of the coaches'.

For several million years the River Brent has carried down to Brentford masses of brickearth, the fertile loam which lines the lower valleys of many of the Thames tributaries. As the Thames makes its sharp curve to the south, it cuts into the brickearth creating an area which was good for market gardening but less so for transport. In any rainy spell the main road through Brentford became saturated and was churned by the passage of vehicles into a thick mud. In 1754 *Gentleman's Magazine* desribed High Street as 'the worst public road in Europe'.

But paradoxically it was transport which helped make of Brentford the prime market and manufacturing town of Middlesex. High Street carried the major road from London to Bath and at the Brent crossing, it reached its first staging post. In 1800, 83 stage coaches a day were passing through the town. In that same year the Grand Junction Canal was completed, linking the Thames through Brentford Lock with the entire canal network to Oxford and the Midlands. The 'great fruit garden north of the Thames' was turning into an industrial town with a population of labourers employed in soap and varnish factories, saw mills, flour mills, tile and pottery works, breweries and distilleries. By the middle of the century the town was afflicted with a combination of heavy traffic, malodorous factories, slum dwellings, polluted air and a polluted river. It was said that no town in the country had more poverty relative to its size. By 1873 it was described in the *Brentford Advertiser* as 'the filthiest place in England'.

From Ealing Road, through the back streets to Half Acre, we cross the site of the worst of all Brentford's slum areas, Troy Town, its name drawn from a Cornish expression describing a labyrinth of disorderly streets. It was here that Booth's workers, and many more, lived in back-to-back terraces and dilapidated weatherboard cottages – dwellings with high rents, low states of repair and no sanitation whatsoever.

The clearance of Troy Town began in 1910, but it was not until 1958 that the last of the derelict cottages was demolished. Before this, however, the wealthier inhabitants of the town had already made their own contribution to urban improvement. In 1887, to mark Queen Victoria's Jubilee, they raised a public subscription to open a recreation ground on the edge of Troy Town, complete with a domed drinking fountain and an inscribed commemorative 'needle'.

The simple square recreation ground is surprisingly atmospheric, largely due to the avenues of tall limes which bisect it and the alignment of this central avenue with the roads at either end. Look to the north from the park and you see a simple but attractive terrace of red-brick housing. Look to the south and you see an inchoate mess of post-war planning, the development with which the planners replaced Troy Town. It looks suspiciously as if the architects who designed the site never got round to visiting it.

St Pauls Road, beyond the Recreation Ground, has some attractive old church school buildings on the left, and St Pauls Church itself on the right. The church was built in 1868 to serve the growing population of the town and is a typical white ragstone Victorian church with no particular distinguishing features – except perhaps its very high steeple. It does however have one unique feature inside. In the late 1800s John Zoffany, who lived in Kew, painted a picture of 'The Last Supper' and presented it to St Anne's on Kew Green. St Anne's turned the gift down. Their objection was that the faces of the apostles had been modelled on local fishermen; a particularly surprising objection since a fair proportion of the disciples had been fishermen themselves. The painting eventually was brought to St Paul's, on the edge of old Troy Town, where it should probably have been all the time.

From the Butts to the Bells

ROUTE:
- From St Pauls Road turn right onto Half Acre and then left onto The Butts. Cross the square at the end and follow the alleyway in the far left hand corner into Market Place.
- Follow Market Place to the main road and turn right to cross the bridge over the River Brent.

FACILITIES: Pubs and cafés on Market Place and High Street.

In 1760 John Horne Tooke became incumbent of the third and oldest of Brentford's churches. He had wanted to be a lawyer but entered the church to please his father and was of that eccentric order of clergymen who believed that the social welfare of his parishioners was as important as their spiritual health. Accordingly he took up the study of medicine in order to help those members of his congregation too poor to afford a doctor. In 1767, during a visit to Paris, he met the radical politician John Wilkes. It was an encounter that was to change the course of both men's lives and to have some interesting consequences for Brentford.

Wilkes had gone to Paris in avoidance of British 'justice'. In 1762, whilst MP for Aylesbury he had started a magazine, the *North Briton*, virulently critical of the corrupt condition of British politics. His particular targets were Lord Bute, the Prime Minister, and all the Whig circle that surrounded and supported George III. In the famous issue number 45, Wilkes attacked the kings' speech at the opening of parliament, showing that in it the king had countenanced a lie by Bute. Bute resigned but Wilkes was imprisoned in the Tower for sedition. The charge could not stand: Wilkes was protected by privilege and the Lord Chief Justice was forced into the ignomony of ordering his release. Wilkes sued the government for illegal arrest – and won – and the government in response dug up another charge against him. On the basis of another contribution to the magazine, this time a poem, he was expelled from the House and charged with 'obscene libel'. A trip to Paris became expedient and he was found guilty in his absence.

During their meeting in Paris, Horne Tooke persuaded Wilkes to contest the constituency of Middlesex, which held its hustings in Brentford. On election day the roads to the town were packed with excited crowds of Wilksites. No-one was allowed to pass unless they displayed about their body the famous number 45. Cries of 'Wilkes and Liberty' rang out all over Brentford as the announcement was made that Wilkes had been elected, beating his nearest rival by a margin of six to one. Parliament immediately declared the elections void. But the Middlesex voters remained undaunted. They continued to elect Wilkes in three consecutive contests until Parliament finally allowed him to take his seat in 1774. He went on to become a Lord Mayor of London and a Chamberlain of the City, retiring from politics at the age of 73. He remained all his life a champion of press freedom.

Wilkes' influence on Tooke, even though they later fell out, was far-reaching. Tooke intensified his interest in social reform and resigned his place at St Lawrence's in 1773 to resume his legal studies. He campaigned against Enclosure Acts and in favour of parliamentary reform. In 1775 he organised a subscription for 'our beloved American fellow subjects who had preferred death to slavery' and 'were for that reason only murdered by the King's troops'. For this he was fined £200 and imprisoned for a year. He maintained a flow of radical writing throughout his life. Along with Thomas Paine he was a founding member of the Corresponding Society, the first working class political organisation in the country. In 1794 he was put on trial for treason, along with other members of the Society, but was triumphantly acquitted.

John Horne Tooke died in 1812. He had wanted to be buried in his own garden in Windmill Lane, Hanwell and to this end had inscribed his own memorial stone to 'John Horn Tooke, late proprietor and now occupier of this spot. Content and grateful'. He was buried instead in St Mary's Church, Ealing.

This section of our route brings together Tooke, Wilkes and the Middlesex elections. It also takes us through the most attractive parts of present-day Brentford. The Butts is a wobbly, dipping and irregular square, its attractiveness only marred by the tarmac with which it has been disrespectfully surfaced. The surrounding houses are almost all pre-1720, large, luxurious but unfussy dwellings with beautifully proportioned and regularly arranged windows, contrasting with the irregularly ridged red-tiled rooves. On the dipping west side of the square is a much later but equally characterful building. This is the 1904 Boatmens Institute, now a private house but originally a London City Mission serving the boat people who plied the adjacent canal. The narrow-boat families, constantly on the move, living in the cramped conditions of their tiny cabins, working longer hours for less pay as competition from the railways intensified, were some of the country's poorest workers. Here in one building they were provided by the Mission with a school, a church, and a maternity hospital.

The Butts was originally an archery range. It was also the main site for public festivals and local celebrations. When development began in the 1690s, it soon became a select residential area, and this was a source of friction, for the boisterous annual Brentford fairs, and the even more boisterous Middlesex elections, took place here or in the adjacent Market Place. The elections for Knights of the Shire, and subsequently for the MP for Middlesex, were always a very bawdy affair, even before the Wilkes years. They are described in contemporary accounts as 'riotous', 'disorderly', 'tumultuous' and 'drunken'. In 1768 for example, Sir William Proctor, one of Wilkes' opponents, included in his election expenses the sum of £1090 for drinks and food consumed by his supporters and for damage done by them to public houses.

Meanwhile Market Place had its own unfettered outpourings in the annual six-day fair. The Market itself had outgrown High Street and moved here in 1560. Traders could avoid the greater congestion and sharper competition of the City and make use of riverside meadows for storing their goods or fattening their cattle. As the Bath Road and the river were only 50 yards apart it was an ideal spot for the transfer of loads and the whole town became known as 'Market Brentford'. It was not only buying and selling which took place here. Market days also saw the sentencing of offenders to a public flogging or the pillory. When Market House was pulled down its site, appropriately enough, became the Magistrates Court. The market itself was abolished in 1933 and the Brentford Fairs died with it.

Back on High Road we pass on the left the pale body of St.Lawrence's Church, looking sad and wan behind a line of lime and horse chestnut. There has been a church here since at least the 12th century but the present building dates from the incumbency of John Horn Tooke himself. It was while the church was closed for rebuilding – in yellow stock brick with a white ragstone tower – that Tooke took the opportunity to visit Paris and hence his meeting with Wilkes.

The church was closed again in 1961, this time for good. In 1979 it was leased to the St Lawrence Brentford Trust whose aim was to convert it into a 'Brent Dock Theatre and Community Centre'. Sadly there has been little visible progress. The fading church building continues to look out across the Brent River to the Six Bells pub, named after the now silent peel of St Lawrence.

From Brentford Lock to Hanwell Locks

ROUTE:
- After crossing the bridge turn right onto the riverside.
- Follow the towpath, changing banks at one stage over a 'roving' footbridge, and continue to the Hanwell lock flight.

LOOKING AT WILDLIFE: There is an interesting flora all along the towpath including wasteland, hedgerow and waterside species. Arrow-head grows in the water of the Brentford Depot and just beyond it a large clump of Duke of Argyll's tea tree is growing on the towpath. Clitheroes Island has more than a hundred species of wild flowers including purple loosestrife, gypsywort, parsley water dropwort, water pepper, meadowsweet, giant hogweed and two species of balsam. There is a fragment of relic oakwood alongside Osterley Lock with a ground flora including red campion, common cow wheat and goldilocks. Birds to look out for include the commoner waterfowl, Canada goose, heron, grey and yellow wagtail and the kingfisher.

River Brent rises in Hertfordshire as the Dollis Brook. It is joined at Neasden by the Silk Stream and flows on as the Brent. It formed at one time the boundary between the two great kingdoms of the East and West Saxons, and Offa himself held a Council on the banks of the river in Brentford in 780. Later a new kingdom was carved out between these two and gave its name to the county of Middlesex. That too is now extinct – a county and an Anglo-Saxon people surviving only in the name of a cricket club and a postal district.

The last three miles of the Brent today have been canalised to form the lowest section of the Grand Union Canal running into Brentford Dock and the Thames. The canal, originally called the Grand Junction Canal, was launched at a meeting in Birmingham in 1792. The purpose was to build a canal from Brentford to Braunston in Northamptonshire, thus shortening the water route between London and Birmingham by 60 miles.

The section from Brentord to Uxbridge was the first part of the canal to be completed and was opened in 1794. The company charged for use of the canal according to load – half penny per ton per mile – and as we turn onto the canal from High Street we pass the Guaging Lock at the entrance to the Brentford Depot where the charges would have been reckoned. In its day the Brentford Depot was a major freight terminal, trade on the canal building up until in the early 1900s it was used by over 20,000 narrow boats a year. Thereafter begins the sad story of the waterways decline, with over half the network now lost and a great national asset largely neglected. The Depot is not on the scale of the abandoned river docks of East London, but it is still an exciting place to walk through, with a great width of water adequate for narrow boats to turn in and rows of dilapidated warehouses and boat-yards painted in a muddy violet-grey. In places these project right out over the water so that our footpath runs below them, through a dismal and resounding interior of still water under corrugated iron.

From here we follow the canal for nearly three miles to Hanwell, passing first under the railway and then under the Great West Road – the two routes which between them finally put an end to the importance of the Old Bath Road through Brentford High Street. The Great West Road was specifically built to ease this congested highway and, having been talked about for over a hundred years was finally opened in 1925. The section we pass became known as the 'Golden Mile', and was lined with large and stylish factories such as Firestone, Gillette and Pyrene. They were built in the modernist and Art Deco styles of the 1920s and 30s, criticised at the time but campaigned for as treasures today – particularly after the Firestone building was hurriedly demolished by developers in 1980 to avoid the effects of a preservation order.

Beyond Boston Manor Park, on the opposite bank, we come to Clitheroes Lock, where the natural river and the navigable cut flow round either side of Clitheroe's Island. The island is a good place to look for wildlife. It has 22 species of tree and shrub, more than a hundred of wild flowers and 29 species of bird. The apex of the island, where the canal rejoins the natural river, forms a little marsh with flag iris and reedmace and the graceful hanging heads of pendulous sedge. There are two invasive plants which crop up here – and often elsewhere along the towpath. For a tough plant Himalayan Balsam has its pink flowers hanging on remarkably slender threads. They are called Policeman's Helmets but most closely resemble something worn by the Keystone cops or an earlier generation of firemen. Giant hogweed is an even tougher plant which came to us from the Caucasus via Kew; so perhaps this canalside was one of the first places where it took hold in this country.

The survival of all this wildlife is made more remarkable by the huge, ugly and aggressive intrusion of the M4. It strides on raised piers like an insensitive giant across what would otherwise be a beautiful stretch of riverside, cutting off canal from meadow and polluting a whole area, not just visually but with its noise, a continuous, mechanical thunder. It is a constant reminder of a society which values going places above being there.

Beneath the spans of the motorway we can look back across the playing fields to the Boston Manor House in a corner of the park. The Boston – originally Bordestone – estate, dates back to at least 1157 but the present Boston House was built in 1623. It was purchased by James Clitherow, the Sheriff of Middlesex in 1670 and remained with his family for over two hundred years. Their estate extended down to include The Butts and several generations of the family are buried in St.Lawrence's Church. In 1923 however they sold up most of the land for building, and Brentford District Council bought up the house and the surrounding 34 acres for a public park. The house today belongs to a housing association, the Over 40s Association for Women Workers. One wonders whether any of them have met Lady Boston. Her husband murdered her when he discovered her *in flagrante delecto* with a lover. He tried to keep her death a secret by burying her body in the park, but today, it is said, she reappears, drifting shadow-like across the parklands to the site of a great cypress. And here, she disappears.

Fitzroy Walk and the Hanwell Asylum

ROUTE:

• At Hanwell Locks the river and the canal separate. Between the first two locks in the Hanwell flight take the path off to the right, following the river along the signposted Fitzherbert Walk.

• Follow the riverside as far as Hanwell Bridge.

FACILITIES: Pub at Hanwell Bridge. Pubs, cafés and shops in Hanwell.

LOOKING AT WILDLIFE: There are hay meadows and new hedgerows on the opposite bank at Hanwell Locks. The interesting riverside flora continues and kingfishers breed around Hanwell.

Just below Hanwell, river and canal part company. As it swings off to the west the Grand Union Canal leaves the Brent valley behind, climbing fifty-three feet through a flight of six locks. It takes a narrow boat approximately 1½ hours to negotiate this one third of a mile of waterway, a process which looses tens of thousands of gallons of water into the downstream canal. The Hanwell Locks were built between 1793 and 1796 and are today a scheduled Ancient Monument.

From the Hanwell Locks to Hanwell Bridge we follow Fitzherbert Walk, named after the founder of the Brent River and Canal Society. For most of its length this path follows the boundary of the new St Bernard's Hospital – and the old Hanwell Asylum. Built in 1830, largely by French prisoners of war, the asylum dates from a time when the 'insane' were regarded as something sub-human, when conditions were squalid and degrading, and when regimes were based on whipping, intimidation and physical restraint. But from this tradition Hanwell stands aside. From the day it opened, with 600 patients, on 16 May 1831, it was at the forefront of radical change and daring experimentation. It occupies a special place in the history of psychiatric medicine.

The first medical superintendant was William Ellis, with his wife as matron. They regarded the hospital as a community or family and held the startling view that 'there are but few ... who, if a particle of mind be left, are not to be won by affectionate attention'. Ellis was largely self-taught and was highly influenced by the doctrine of phrenology, but he also championed two great causes in psychiatric nursing; that of proper training and pay for mental nurses – who had previously played more the role of prison warders – and of gainful employment and training for patients. For this the Hanwell site was ideal. It occupied 44 acres and within them developed its own bakery, brewery and farm, where patients grew most of the hospital's supply of vegetables. By 1837, 454 of the 612 patients at Hanwell were engaged in daily work.

Sadly Ellis only lasted one more year resigning after a row with his management committee, but he was replaced by another remarkable man. Ellis had already abolished physical punishment at Hanwell. Now, within four months of taking post at the largest asylum in the country, and with no previous experience of asylum management, Dr John Connolly abolished every form of personal restraint, including straitjackets, shackles and coercion chairs. It was Connolly's belief that there was no strong and definable boundary between sanity and insanity and this led him to develop the concept of community outreach and a mental health service that would treat many of its patients in their own homes. He propounded these and other ideas in a series of lectures which became hugely popular and highly influential. He died in 1866, described by Sir James Crichton-Brown as 'a Wilberforce who devoted his life to the abolition of slavery of a particularly grievous kind'.

The Hanwell Asylum was renamed St Bernard's Hospital in 1937. In 1980 the large, new Ealing district hospital was built on what used to be the asylum's staff playing fields. Thus, in the year of its 150th anniversary, the old Hanwell Asylum became the new St Bernard's Annexe.

TO COMPLETE WALK 13: Leave the riverside at Hanwell Bridge.
- For buses turn left to the terminus beside the hospital.
- For Hanwell Station (trains to Paddington) turn right on main road and take first left (Half Acre). Follow the path at the end of Half Acre. At the end of the path turn left under the railway bridge then right into Golden Manor. Campbell Road on the right leads to the station entrance.

WALK 14: Hanwell to Greenford

Getting Started

From Walk 13:
  From Hanwell Bridge continue along the riverside towards the viaduct.
  Cross the footbridge and turn left under the viaduct.
To start walk here:
  From Hanwell Station follow Campbell Road round to the left. Turn left into Golden Manor at end.
  Go under railway bridge and turn immediately right onto the footpath.
  After about a hundred yards take the gate on the right and follow the path to reach the river. Turn right under the viaduct.

From Hanwell to Greenford Bridge

ROUTE:
- Go through the wooden gate at the other side of the viaduct and turn left to follow the riverside.
- Go through the gate into Brent Lodge Park. There are a variety of routes through the park but make towards the church steeple in the top right hand corner.
- Go through the lych gate and turn immediately left down the path to the river bridge.
- Cross the bridge and take the right fork.

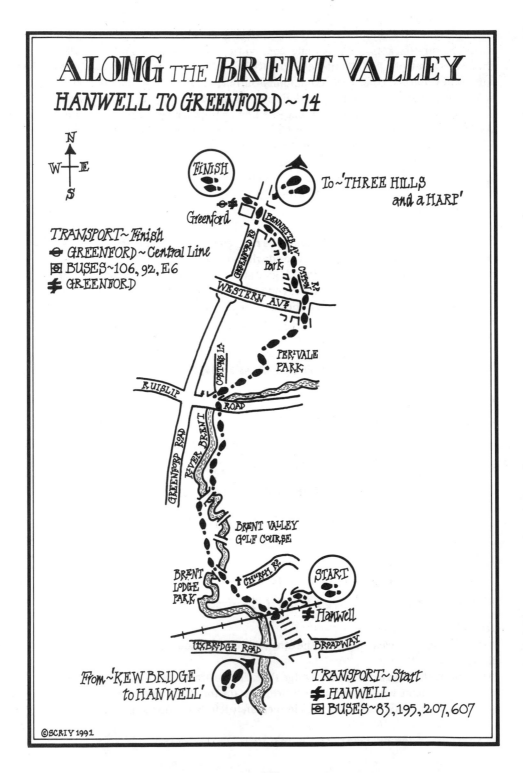

ALONG THE BRENT VALLEY
HANWELL TO GREENFORD ~ 14

N
W · E
S

FINISH
Greenford

To ~ 'THREE HILLS and a HARP'

TRANSPORT ~ Finish
GREENFORD ~ Central Line
BUSES ~ 106, 92, E6
GREENFORD

BENNETTS BAY
Park
CASTON RD

WESTERN AVE

CASTONS LA

PERIVALE PARK

RUISLIP ROAD

GREENFORD ROAD

RIVER BRENT

BRENT VALLEY GOLF COURSE

BRENT LODGE PARK

CHURCH RD

START

Hanwell

UXBRIDGE ROAD

BROADWAY

From ~ 'KEW BRIDGE to HANWELL'

TRANSPORT ~ Start
HANWELL
BUSES ~ 83, 195, 207, 607

©SCRIV 1991

- At the Y junction of gravel paths, bear left.
- Follow the path along the hedgerow line across the golf course until the point where the hedgerow and the low wooden fence make a right angled turn on your right. Take the earthen path here across to the footbridge.
- Cross the bridge and turn left to follow the river bank all the way to Ruislip Road and the Greenford Bridge.

FACILITIES: Viaduct Inn at Hanwell Bridge. Brent Lodge Park has toilets and a café (daily 10-7 summer, 10-3 winter).

LOOKING AT WILDLIFE: Heron and kingfisher are sometimes seen along the riverside. Waterside and wasteland plants include giant hogweed, angelica, pepperwort and goats rue. Brent Lodge Park has a large collection of birds and animals including cranes, rhea, monkeys, deer, parrots, wallabies etc. There is also a reptile and insect house (entrance fee). The old hedgerows on the golf course are worth examining for hedgerow shrubs, flowers and small birds including warblers.

From Hanwell Bridge to the Wharncliffe Viaduct the river flows peacefully across Brent Meadow. Here where blackthorn hedges line the riverside it is possible to relive the time described by 19th century novelist Bulwer-Lytton who walked with his sweetheart 'on the green banks that shade Brent's humble flood'. But such pleasures were not to last too long.

In 1897 the engineer E.Bailey Denton was commissioned to survey the reaches of the now polluted Brent. His report describes the upper river as 'merely an open sewer'. Between Hanwell and Ealing all the fish had long since been killed and 'even the water rats had fallen victims to the foulness of the water'. Further up 'black lumps of sewage were floating down stream and on all sides gases were building up from its bed'. The smell in general 'was such as to make my companion and myself ill'.

Denton blamed the local sewage works and the local councils proceeded to blame each other. Eventually the matter of 'the unfortunate valley of the Brent' was raised in Parliament and an Act passed to deal with the sewage problem. It is a different form of pollution which remains today: industrial effluent and road run-off water poison the river, their concentrations intensified by the amount of water drawn off at the Welsh Harp Reservoir.

The river runs through 4½ miles of Ealing, its banks and surrounding parklands forming a continuous ribbon of land which varies in width from 200 yards to half a mile. Within one mile of this strip live 160,000 people, a greater concentration than the entire population of Bournemouth or Northampton. It was to serve these people that the founder members of the Brent River and Canal Society conceived the development of a linear waterside park. The existing dereliction should be cleared away, hundreds of forest trees planted, all-weather paths established and all improvements based on the existing landscape. The organisation began its work in 1974, enrolling 600 members within its first year. By 1976 it had convinced the Ealing council of its case and thereafter the two bodies began a close co-operation which has given rise to the Brent River Park and several miles of the best in city walking. The planners of the Brent River Park showed from the beginning the sense that was so conspicuously lacking in the early days of the Lea Valley Regional Park – the awareness that a landscape is a resource of its own not just an open space for the development of 'leisure facilities'. Their philosophy was summed up by landscape architect Brian Green in an early report for the Society.

> Many landscape architects in the past have designed from a basis of being arbiters of leisure and recreation facilities. Provide the people with that which is eminently designable ... and assume that dog owners will find somewhere else to walk their pets, the courting couples will find somewhere else to be alone, the pensioner somewhere else to study the runners in the 2.30 at Newmarket ... I would prefer to leave alone entirely and land to continue to give the pleasure it already does than to design for the sake of designing.

Bulwer-Lytton would surely have approved.

The elegant eight arch span of the Wharncliffe Viaduct (named after Lord Wharncliffe who chaired the Lords Committee that passed the Great Western Railway Bill) was built in 1835 by Isombard Kingdom Brunel to carry the Great Western Railway across 300 yards of the Brent Valley. At 65 feet high it was the first of his large-scale designs to be constructed and, in stark contrast to the motorway flyover passed earlier, enhances rather than denigrates the landscape. Beneath the motorway all is dark and dead, beneath the viaduct the high brick spans let light into an attractive glade on a picturesque curve of the river where bird-song and butterflies enliven the bushes. The huge brick piers are hollow and there are plans to further enhance the wildlife by developing them as bat roosts.

Beyond the viaduct we follow the edge of Church Fields where the distant and incongruous calling of peacocks leads us into the Brent Lodge Park. Brent Lodge was once one of the largest houses in the area but was demolished in 1932. Only the stable block still stands and is today an environmental centre. The private gardens have become an exceedingly pleasant park where peacock and guinea fowl wander at will. The small zoo is one of the largest municipal collections and houses a surprisingly varied collection of birds and animals.

St Mary's, the parish church of Hanwell, stands at the top of the park. It is a large, dark and imposing building with a flint frontage and a tall tower topped with a tapering spire. It is undeniably a church of the Victorian middle classes and was erected for them by George Gilbert Scott in 1841. Scott, whose work we have met often on our route round London, designed this as one of a batch of six intended to revolutionise concepts of church architecture. He was later to turn against his own work describing all six as 'a mass of horrors'. His original church had no chancel and this was added in 1898, only to be damaged by a serious fire in 1912.

The attractive white pebble dash Rectory Cottage opposite the church was built by the Reverend George Glasse. Glasse was a man of high connections and considerable wealth who extended his domains by acquiring the adjacent Brent Lodge. Perhaps in so doing he ran beyond his means for in 1802 he was in trouble for defaulting on a sum of money belonging to a charity of which he was treasurer. And money problems lead to his death, but in a rather peculiar way. According to an account in *Gentleman's Magazine* in 1809, he took a coach from Hanwell to an inn in Bishopsgate. On alighting from the coach he somehow left behind him a large sum of money which, for some unspecified reason, he was carrying. Thereafter began frantic attempts to recover it, but to no immediate avail. A few hours later the honest driver returned, having discovered the money in his coach. He was too late. The Reverend Glasse had already taken his own life in desperation.

A little path beside the church leads us down to Boles Meadow and the Boles Bridge. Here we cross another another golf course along the line of ancient hedgerows where hawthorn, blackthorn and hazel arch right across the path and insulate us from the surrounding golf-green monotony. And then, along the last section of route before Greenford Bridge, we follow a shallow and placid river which winds its way around little gravel beaches. The sense of seclusion is increased by the high banks above the path, though these paradoxically have been created by infill tipping. Here the lilac coloured flowers of goats rue grow among a profusion of white pepperwort. Above, on a flat plateau of Ealing's landscaped garbage, and indifferent to this unsavoury history, skylark, pheasant and partridge have all bred in recent years.

Perivale Park and Greenford

ROUTE:
- Leave the riverside and turn left across the bridge.
- Turn right onto Costons Lane and after a short distance take the broad tarmac path on the right into Perivale Park.
- The path eventually curves left to reach a road entrance. Do not leave the park here but continue right along the edge of the playing fields.
- Turn left at the end to reach Western Avenue and cross this major road by the footbridge.
- Take Gayton Road, which begins almost opposite the Perivale Park exit point. At the end join the footpath which runs around the edge of school playing fields. Ignore the first exit on the right.
- At the end of the footpath join Bennetts Avenue and turn right at the end onto Greenford Road.
- After the railway bridge, Rockware Avenue crosses Greenford Road. Turn left then left again to reach Greenford Station or go straight across junction to join next section.

In one of the old mills along the course of the Brent, a 17th century miller had the misfortune to be crushed between his mill stones. Since his ghost continued to haunt the building no one else was prepared to take up residence there except an elderly miser. No doubt its frightening reputation and consequent isolation were exactly what he was looking for. But after a time, the miser too went missing. The only local person brave enough to enter the cursed mill to look for him was a young foundling by the name of Simon Coston. Coston stumbled across not only the old man's body but also his gold. Making a quick and surreptitious exit, he fled with it to Flanders. Thirty years later and now a respectably married man, Coston returned to the area of his childhood and bought himself an estate. His early trick, the first step on his ladder to material success, remained a secret until after his death.

Sadly, this local legend is almost entirely untrue. Simon Coston did live on an estate here but all we know about him was that he was rich, had six children and died in 1665. He left his name behind however, both in Costons Lane and in the little tributary of the Brent that we cross in Perivale Park, Costons Brook, which is about the only attractive feature of the park.

Perivale was the smallest of the parishes which later went to make up the Borough of Ealing, and the park is on the site of one of its largest hayfields. It was a regular venue for local sports and recreation, and, perhaps to preserve this use, Ealing Town Council purchased it from the ubiquitous Ecclestiacal Commissioners when it came up for building development in 1934. But it no longer has the charm of a hayfield. A few black crows strut across the dull flat expanse of playing field and golf course grass, while the air is ceaselessly burdened with the sound of passing trains, overhead airplanes and the deadening rumble of the Western Avenue.

Western Avenue was built in 1921 to replace the previous London to Oxford highway; its original redeeming feature – cycle tracks – has long since been removed. This major road was one of three arterial roads built in the area in the space of only ten years. Suddenly the small parish of Greenford, surrounded by pasture and arable land to the south, and woodland to the north, was one large industrial development site. Among the firms establishing themselves were Hoover, with their famous factory building, and the now disappeared Rockware Glassworks, which gave their name to Rockware Avenue. After the factories came the houses, but with no distinct pattern, centre or community. As a columnist in the *Middlesex County Times* wrote on 30 November 1935, 'I am now able to announce that we have discovered Greenford. Even the Greenford folk don't know where it is. Everybody one meets is a stranger'.

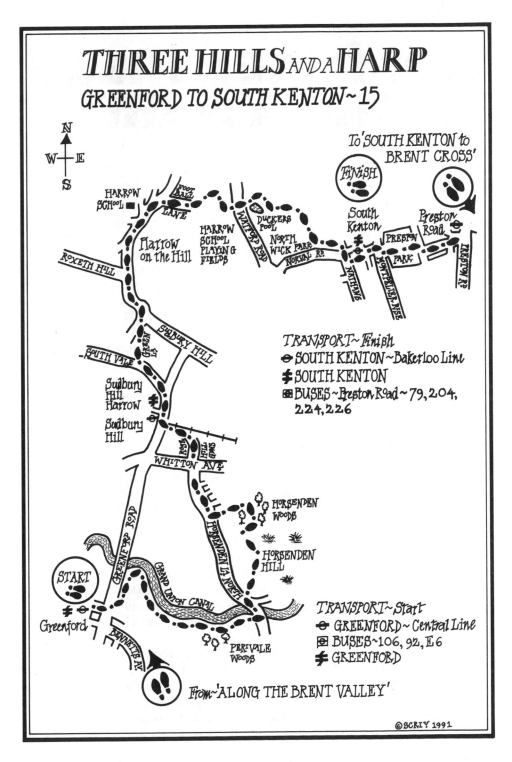

THREE HILLS AND A HARP
GREENFORD TO SOUTH KENTON ~ 15

To 'SOUTH KENTON to BRENT CROSS'

FINISH

HARROW SCHOOL
FOOTBALL
LANE
HARROW SCHOOL PLAYING FIELDS
Harrow on the Hill
WATFORD ROAD
DUCKERS POOL
NORTH WICK PARK
NORVAL RD.
South Kenton
PRESTON PARK
Preston Road
ROXETH HILL
NATHING
MONTPELIER RISE
PRESTON RD.

SUDBURY HILL
SOUTH VALE
GREEN LA.

Sudbury Hill Harrow

Sudbury Hill

VALE FARM
SHOB HILL
WHITTON AVE.

HORSENDEN WOODS
HORSENDEN HILL

GREENFORD ROAD
HILL
HORSENDEN LA. NORTH

TRANSPORT ~ Finish
- SOUTH KENTON ~ Bakerloo Line
- SOUTH KENTON
- BUSES ~ Preston Road ~ 79, 204, 224, 226

START
Greenford
BENDIOTTS AV.
GRAND UNION CANAL
PERIVALE WOODS

TRANSPORT ~ Start
- GREENFORD ~ Central Line
- BUSES ~ 106, 92, E6
- GREENFORD

From ~ 'ALONG THE BRENT VALLEY'

©SCRLY 1991

10. THREE HILLS AND A HARP

FROM GREENFORD TO BRENT CROSS

The suburbs of north west London are Middlesex become Metroland. In 1862 the Metropolitan railway company opened the first underground railway in the world, running from Paddington to Farringdon Street. It was an 'insult to common sense' said *The Times*, to suggest that people would ever accept the idea of being driven 'amid palpable darkness through the foul subsoil of London'. *The Times* was wrong and so successful was the company that by 1884 the lines had been extended out to Harrow. It was the railway company itself which dubbed the area Metroland as the hills and hayfields of Middlesex disappeared under the urban development which was now made possible.

From the midst of an otherwise undistinguished expanse of three hills rise up, like islands above the proverbial sea of housing. Each one of them preserves in its own way something of the character of the lost county of Middlesex and our route links all three before bringing us back to the valley of the Brent. Horsenden Hill, with Perivale Wood below it and Horsenden Wood on its flank, retains the most rugged air of the three and Horsenden Lane runs below it as though it were still a country backwater. Harrow-on-the-Hill stands a short distance further north, displaying the distinctive profile of twin spires arising from the clustered trees. The village itself is brooding rather than beautiful and has become over time more an extension of the school than a village in its own right. But the climb up Harrow Hill is well worth while and the visit poses some fascinating questions, not least among them that of how an altruistic charitable foundation could become one of the most privileged and patrician institutions in the world. Finally, we climb Barn Hill, now part of the Fryent Way Country Park. The park offers at one and the same time a fascinating episode from our national history, a living nature reserve, and a landscape more like old Middlesex than anything else we are likely to see.

Barn Hill survives because local authorities of the early 20th century were able to purchase and preserve land for a variety of purposes. Though the earlier struggles of commoners feature again in this chapter, a common theme is that of beautiful open spaces surviving only because of the actions of district or County Councils. Their foresight permanently altered the shape of our city, provided a network of green spaces and a vital resource for all who live here. It is a particularly relevant point today when London councils are increasingly resorting to the sale of playing fields and other open sites, in a desperate attempt to meet ever tighter government restrictions. This too will have a permanent impact upon the shape of London.

This chapter covers 10½ miles from Greenford to Brent Cross. It can be taken as two shorter walks with a linking section of ¾ mile between them.

WALK 15: Greenford to South Kenton (5 miles).

WALK 16: South Kenton to Brent Cross (4¾ miles).

WALK 15: Greenford to South Kenton

Getting Started

From Greenford Station:
    Turn left onto Oldfield Lane under the railway bridge. Turn right onto Rockware Avenue then left onto Greenford Road.
From Walk 14:
    Continue along Greenford Road across Rockware Avenue.

Over Horsenden Hill

ROUTE:
- Past Rockware Avenue look for the footpath beginning to your right.
- On reaching the canal turn right and follow the towpath as far as the first road bridge. Join the road and cross the bridge.
- Follow the lane, ignoring the farm entrance track, and turn right at the paths beside the Horsenden Hill signboard.
- Ignore the main tarmac path and take the central trodden path to the right, running uphill through a copse. Cross the next junction and carry on uphill. The path is marked by low wooden trail posts.
- On reaching the small grassy plateau just below the summit, scramble up any route to the top of the hill and the concrete triangulation post.
- Cross the summit plateau to the left to reach the gravel path with trail posts, descending to a car park.
- Bear right through the car park and on entering Horsenden Wood turn left immediately. Walk downhill to reach the tarmac path at the bottom.
- Turn left on the path to reach Horsenden Lane North beside the Ballot Box pub.

FACILITIES: Pubs and cafés at Greenford Station. Ballot Box pub on Horsenden Lane North.

LOOKING AT WILDLIFE: There is abundant wildlife throughout this stretch of the walk; waterside species along the canal, relics of ancient oak woodland at Perivale and Horsenden Woods and meadow species on the slopes of Horsenden Hill. Specialities to look out for include the spectacular early summer display of bluebells in Perivale Wood, dyers greenweed on Horsenden Hill, and the large yellow meadow ants nests on the hillsides.

In 1805 the canal builders completed the long main line of the Grand Junction Canal, carrying trade from the manufacturing towns of the Midlands down towards the Thames at Brentford. Even before the main canal was finished however, work had taken place on a branch that would link this main line directly into the Paddington Basin and Central London. The 'Paddington arm', winding its way around the base of Horsenden Hill, immediately became a busy trade route, carrying not only numerous cargoes but also several passenger services, including the six hour packet boat journey from Paddington to Uxbridge. Thomas Homer was one of the operators on this route and it was he who dreamt up the idea of a further addition to the canal network: from Paddington it would run all the way around the city to join the Thames and the new docks at Limehouse. Thomas Homer's scheme was adopted by the Regents Canal Company and Homer himself rose to become its Treasurer. His success was short-lived. In 1815, before the new canal was even completed, an anonymous letter revealed that he had been embezzling company funds. He fled to Belgium, then to Scotland, where he was overtaken and brought back to London. Homer's career ended with a much longer boat trip when the poor man was sentenced to seven years' transportation.

Middlesex was a traditional hay growing region and by the 1840s a single parish, such as at Greenford, was producing over a 1000 tons a year. Much of this was carried into London on the narrow boats, whence they returned with loads of 'mack', a fertiliser for the hay fields comprised of domestic rubbish, butcher's offal and manure. Though no longer treated with mack, the fields on the far side of the canal are today part of the Horsenden Hill Open Space and for sound conservation reasons are being returned to traditional methods of management. Hay making has come back to this corner of Middlesex on the banks of the Paddington canal.

Another fragment of the earlier landscape survives on the towpath side of the canal, where it passes alongside the length of the Perivale Wood. This remnant of the Great Forest of Middlesex is a rich oak and hazel woodland, and one of the most important nature reserves in London. It survived the felling of the rest of the forest because of the efforts of the Selbourne Society, founded in 1885 to celebrate the work of Reverend Gilbert White, whose detailed observations of his parish in Hampshire were published in the classic *Natural History of Selbourne*. In 1920, the bicentenary of Gilbert White's birth, the Brent Valley branch of the Selbourne Society completed the purchase of these 27 acres of woodland. Just as the wood here is all that remains of the greater forest so the Brent Branch is all that remains of a once national society. It continues to manage this site which in 1957 was declared a Site of Special Scientific Interest. So far recorded here are 22 different types of butterfly, 350 species of wild flower and fern, 17 of mammal and 115 species of bird.

The reserve is most famous for its spectacular spring display of bluebells and it is only on special days at this time of year that it is open to the general public.

Above the canal, Horsenden Hill rises to 276 feet, the heart a 236 acre open space preserved for conservation and wildlife by the London Borough of Ealing. The hill draws its name from the Old English horsa's dun, or horse's down. Stories linking it with the saxon chief Horsa are fanciful but it has been in occupation for over 7,000 years and traces of an Iron Age fort can still be seen near the summit.

Our route up the hill follows the flank of Home Mead. The meadow is rich in wild flowers, particularly in high summer, and this is the place to look for dyers greenweed, a speciality of Horsenden. This yellow flowered and slightly shrubby member of the pea family is unusual in London but appears to be thriving here. Both its English name and its scientific name, *genista tinctoria* give a clue to its traditional usage. A yellow dye extracted from the plant was mixed with the blue from woad to produce a standard green dye. In Gloucestershire at one time women known as 'wood-waxers' were paid 1s 6d a hundredweight for collecting the plant from the wild, where it was torn up by the roots. Today it is too uncommon to be picked by anybody.

The ten acre Horsenden Wood on the far flank of the hill is another remnant of the Middlesex forest. Primarily of oak and hornbeam, it lacks the rich ground flora of the Perivale Wood. The trees were managed for coppice until 1810 when a local farmer began to clear it for crops. If he had not gone nearly bankrupt in the process, this piece of woodland would have disappeared along with all the others.

Between the Hills

ROUTE:
• Turn right on Horsenden Lane and follow the road to the junction with the main road (Whitton Avenue East). Go straight across and along Rosehill Gardens.
• Turn left along the path that follows the edge of the open space and the railway line, to reach Greenford Road.
• Turn right through Sudbury and immediately after the second station (Sudbury Hill and Harrow), turn left onto South Vale.
• Where South Vale curves round to the left take the public bridleway (Green Lanes) straight ahead, signposted to Sudbury Hill.
• On rejoining Sudbury Hill turn left and walk uphill. At the top of the hill fork right to follow London Road into Harrow-on-the-Hill.

FACILITIES: Cafés, pubs and restaurants in Sudbury.

LOOKING AT WILDLIFE: Mature oak trees and relic hedgerows on Rosehill Gardens Open Space. Alongside Green Lanes there are clumps of winter heliotrope and several species of fungi.

Ancient tracks and modern railways both follow the trough of lower ground between the Horsenden and Harrow Hills. The path leading us on to Horsenden Lane was originally one of the ancient forest trackways, while the path through Rosehill Gardens follows the tube lines which played such an important part in the later development of the area. Even here there are reminders of much earlier times in the mature but isolated oaks which have survived the felling of the forest all around them, and in the hedgerow relics of earlier field boundaries.

The tube line here is not the Metropolitan but the Piccadilly, which was extended to Sudbury Hill in 1931. The station was built by Charles Holden, in what was then regarded as a new architectural style. It is, says Pevsner, 'an outstanding example of how satisfactory, purely by careful detailing and good proportions, such unpretentious buildings can be.'

The name of Sudbury is first recorded in 1273 and refers to the burgh or dwellings to the south, presumably of the Harrow hill. Green Lanes is, as its name suggests, another of the ancient trackways and is shown clearly on Rocque's map of 1745. Now it is a pleasant backwater between playing fields and back gardens, then it was part of the main north-south route from Harrow to London.

The higher we get up the hill, the larger and lovelier and more prosperous the properties become. Julian House, Kennet House, and other villas surviving from before suburbanisation, display a range of styles with bays and beam-ends, cottage extensions, mock-tudor timbering and stained-glass windows. We are walking here over what was Roxeth Common until an Act of 1803 permitted enclosure of all the wastes and commons of Harrow. This Act was opposed by an association of the smaller proprietors in the area, over a hundred of whom got together to put forward a petition, but their entreaties were ignored and the enclosure was completed in 1817, at the beginning of what was to be one of the greatest periods of hardship and depression in English agricultural history. In accordance with the Biblical precept, 'him that hath, to him shall be given', the largest shares went to the largest landowners. Lord Northwick, to whom we shall return later, added 71 acres to his existing 1,187 in the area and Harrow School took over an additional 8. While local farmers were going bankrupt, these were turned into cricket pitches for the schoolboys.

Over Harrow-on-the-Hill ...

ROUTE:
- Follow London Road onto High Street and through Harrow-on-the-Hill.
- Continue onto Peterborough Road. As it begins to descend, look for Football Lane, signposted as a public footpath, on the right.

FACILITIES: Pubs, cafés and restaurants in Harrow-on-the-Hill.

The 130 metre Harrow-on-the-Hill rises from the Harrow weald, visible for miles around as a tree-clad mound topped with two steeples and flanked by open fields. It is a welcome sight, like land appearing above the choppy waves of ridge after ridge of suburban rooftop. Its height helped save it from development and also provided a strange footnote to its history. The end of the world has always been at hand and 16th century astrologers gave the official date as 1 February 1524, when a great flood would destroy all London. This led the local rector, Cuthbert Tunstall, to build himself a fortress atop the hill in which to sit out the deluge. It was demolished earlier this century.

Harrow School has played its part in preserving the hill from suburban development, but at the same time its own growth has destroyed the village. Harrow School has no distinctive campus and has simply multiplied over the centuries like the amoeba, engulfing bit by bit the existing village. 'The school,' says Pevsner, 'has sucked so much of the life blood out of the town that we can now only with difficulty reconstruct the pre-school or even pre-Victorian appearance of Harrow-on-the-Hill.' As the school spread other residents and their local shops were driven away. Mostly they went down to the bottom of the hill to form the new settlement of Greenhills and now, as Dennis Bridgeman wrote in 1978, 'Harrow-on-the Hill stands to the majority of Harrow residents as Kanchanjunga does to the natives of Darjeeling – they don't go up it.'

The story of the School begins in 1572 when local landowner John Lyon obtained a charter from Elizabeth I, 'for the perpetual education, training and instruction of boys and youths of said parish (of Harrow)'. The first buildings were completed in 1615 and the original classroom, known as the fourth form room, still exists. The charter sets a number of very strict conditions for the conduct of school life but on the question of discipline is remarkably enlightened for its day. 'The schoolmaster', says Lyons, 'shall use no kind of correction save only with a rod moderately'.

It is clear from the charter that the school is expressly established for the education of local children and Lyon's' bequest also pays for the teaching of 30 poor children from the parish. Yet from this beginning the school was to become one of the most privileged and patrician establishments in the world. According to Don Walter in his *Book of Harrow-on-the Hill*, there are three main reasons for this amazing transformation. In his original school statutes, Lyon allows for the schoolmaster to take in as many additional paying students as could properly be taught and housed. Since he also allowed the schoolmaster to set whatever fees he liked for these students, it is not surprising that they soon became the main focus of attention. Within a short period of time the 'Foreigners' were outnumbering the 'Foundationers'.

Lyons also stipulated that from the second form on, Latin should be the language of all the students – in the playground as well as the classroom. The Roxeth farmer and the Harrow butcher may not have thought this an entirely relevant education for their sons.

The rival Eton school meanwhile had developed a strong High Tory and High Church allegiance and this provided the final factor. Harrow became the natural alternative for nobility of the Whig persuasion. In 1810 local people appealed to the

Court of Chancery that the Foundation was for local use and ought to be adapted to meet local needs, but they were unsuccessful, and by 1867 the *Harrow Gazette* was complaining that 'aristocratic invaders like the vandals of old have by sheer force of numbers taken possession and overrun the Hill and excluded the aborigines from their cherished and time-honoured school.'

Our route over the hill follows London Road, passing West Acre on the left. It is a daunting red brick construction with rows and rows of symmetrical windows and a forest of chimneys. It is one of the school boarding houses and looks like something out of *Tom Browns' Schooldays*. Local history does not seem to record what started the fire which gutted it in 1908, simply that it was rebuilt that same year. The Harrow-on-the-Hill Fire Brigade at that time was still dependent on horse power and the keeper of the Kings Head Hotel, just a little further along the road, was paid an annual retainer to have horses ready for the Brigade's use. With this they guaranteed to be able to turn out their equipment in just 1½ minutes. It was little help in the case of West Acre.

The Hotel itself stands on one side of the tiny triangular green where a faded inn-sign bears the portrait of Henry VIII. The Park, further along the High Street on the right, was built in 1803 as a second home for Lord Northwick, one of the main beneficiaries of the enclosures of the same year. In 1831 this too became a school boarding house. Beyond it we come to the central school buildings, which stand around the junction of Church Hill and High Street. On the left, at the beginning of Church Hill, is the building known as Old Schools. Though set about with later additions this was the original school building and contains the unchanged Fourth Form Room, focus in its time for two 'school rebellions'. The fiercer of these broke out in 1805 when the post of headmaster became vacant. The serving Assistant Master, Reverend Mark Drury, was passed over by the school governors in favour of an outsider, Dr George Butler. The school favoured Drury and the hostilities which broke out were headed by the schoolboy Byron. For perhaps the only time, the mottoes of 'Liberty' and 'Revolution' were hung in the Fourth Form Room, while outside the main road was blockaded and all communication between Harrow and London stopped for several days. According to one account, a trail of gunpowder was laid into the Head Master's House. Nonetheless it was Butler, not Drury, who got the job.

The School War Memorial and the Master's Room stand at the apex of Church Hill and High Street while on the opposite side of High Street are two buildings which do more than any other to justify Pevsner's description of Harrow School's 'hearty and confident gloom'. Both buildings were the work of George Gilbert Scott. The school chapel was built in the 1850s when the school outgrew the use of the Parish church. Though its spire has helped create the profile of the hill, it was in fact a later addition, put up in 1865 in memory of Billy Oxenham, pupil and master at Harrow for 50 years – an odd thought since Billy himself had always opposed the idea of a steeple.

The Vaughan Library next to it was built in 1861-63 and was opened by Prime Minister Lord Palmerston. This too was an odd choice. During the mid-century debate raged intensely around the respective merits of classical and gothic styles of architecture. Palmerston was a passionate classicist and his dislike of Scott's work was public knowledge. He had previously and personally turned down Scott's design for the Foreign Office, a design which Scott recycled at St Pancras Station. It must have been galling for Palmerston to turn out for the Harrow opening, and after the ceremony he left abruptly, declining to stay for the customary meal.

Finally, as we follow High Street into Peterborough Road, we walk beneath the shadow of Speech Room, built by William Burges in 1874-77. Its situation here, on the slope of the hill, necessitated deep excavations and the shifting of huge amounts of rock and soil. With its small cupola and a balcony supported on a massive stone bracket, it is in a style labelled 'Venetian Gothic'. It was very unpopular when first built, and not surprisingly, for the effect is severe and foreboding. Today its impact has been softened beyond measure by a vigorous growth of ivy, a striking example of nature excelling, or at least improving, Art.

The Ducker Pool and Northwick Park

ROUTE:
- From Peterborough Road turn right onto Football Lane. At the bottom of the lane turn left onto the cinder track signposted to Watford Lane.
- Follow the track for a short distance, then turn right alongside an old wooden fence and a line of oak trees between pitches.
- At the far side of the pitch turn left over the grass between the rugby pitches and the hedgerow and continue ahead to reach the style onto the main road.
- Cross the main road and pick up the Ducker footpath immediately opposite.
- The path reaches the hospital perimeter and curves right onto a pitch and putt course. Keep straight ahead along the perimeter fence.
- At the end of the fence, cross the brook and turn right along the tarmac path. On reaching the park entrance, stay within the park, turning left over the grass along the backs of houses.
- Before the rail embankment turn right onto Nathans Road then take the subway on the left under the railway.

FACILITIES: Pub at South Kenton.

LOOKING AT WILDLIFE: The playing fields are chiefly interesting for the hedgerows and for the scattering of stags-horn oaks. These support some interesting bird species, including whitethroat, linnet, stock dove and tree sparrow. Redwing and fieldfare, and sometimes snipe and redshank, visit the fields in winter and there are occasional passage migrants. The hedgerows on the Northwick Park golf course are also interesting. Plants to look out here for include the native bluebell and stone parsley.

The 360 acres of open space which now flank the eastern slopes of Harrow-on-the-Hill were once damp meadowlands of the thick London clay, producing both a rich hay crop and an abundance of wild flowers. Here was found the beautiful and now rare snake's-head fritillary, with its strange chequer-pattern head. Part of the site, over to the east, remains the Harrow School Farm, producing enough dairy produce to supply the school and local restauranteurs, but the rest has been drained and levelled for rugby pitches and golf courses. The wild flowers are gone, but some of the hedgerows survive, with blackthorn, hawthorn, field maple, elm, ash and wild roses, often with nesting whitethroat and linnet. Above them here and there rises the tall and stark form of a stags head oak, sheltering stock doves and tree sparrows, and the nests of kestrels, tawny owls and perhaps even a pair of sparrowhawks.

In wet winters the area resumes something of its original form when water floods the playing fields with broad shallow puddles. Then the fieldfare and mistle thrush, the crow and rook, are joined by the redshank and snipe that once waded and fed amongst the wet winter grasses. The small stream which drains the fields runs alongside our route towards Watford Road and here is the last place where a few of the interesting wild flowers remain; meadow sweet and water mint, yellow flag and gipsy-wort and other plants typical of the rural stream-side.

Beyond the main road this little stream fills the Ducker Pool, which was once the Harrow School bathing pool, but is now semi-derelict. Newts instead of schoolboys swim in the water, while bats roost in the mature trees round about. Until recently these trees were also home to one of London's last rookeries. As the city spread outwards London's rooks had further and further to fly to reach feeding grounds and one by one the rookeries were abandoned. Here in Harrow eleven nests remained up to 1987 but these and the trees suffered badly in the great October storm. Only three pairs returned the following year and no young were reported. It may be that the Harrow rooks will eventually recolonise the Ducker Pool trees, but their future remains uncertain. Skirting the walled Ducker Pool, the footpath runs through a pleasant mixed woodland that was planted in 1907, before reaching the golf course and Northwick Park.

'How nature have exalted Harrow-on-the-Hill,' wrote John Norden in 1593:

> from whence in the time of harvest, a man may behold the fields round about, so sweetly to address themselves to the siccle and sith, with such comfortable abundance of all kinds of graine, that the husbandman which waiteth for the fruits of his labour, cannot but clap his hands for joy, to see the vale so to laugh and sing.

But the prospect from the hill was a very different one by the beginning of the 19th century.

When the 1803 Act of Enclosure was put into effect in 1817, Lord Northwick, already the largest landowner in the district, increased his holding substantially. Northwick, as we have seen, had built himself a house in Harrow, but despite this he remained an absentee landlord, living at his country mansion in Worcestershire, and administering his Harrow estates through a bailiff. The effect of the enclosures compounded what was already an atrocious situation for agricultural labourers who were paid wages below subsistence levels. Now they had also lost their common lands, through which they had supplemented their incomes by grazing their own cow or collecting fuel.

After the Napoleonic wars a depression set in, with grain prices plumetting and sheep remaining unsold in the markets. In 1828 heavy rain left the wheat mildewed and the sheep unhealthy, and destroyed seven-eighths of the Middlesex hay crop. The labourers would no longer accept their pitiable wages and began to riot. On farm after farm haystacks were set ablaze, and the declared culprit was always the same 'Captain Swing', a mysterious Robin Hood-style hero who appeared all over the country wreaking vengeance on landowners. Indeed he wrote a letter to Lord Northwick threatening retaliation for the wrong he had inflicted on labouring men.

The tenant farmers also suffered in the depression. The situation on the Northwick estate became so bad that the bailiff Quilton, not usually loathe to enforce his master's commands, was forced to ask for rent reductions for the tenants. Northwick was unbending. Either the farmers payed up or the farmers were out – and so was Quilton. In Roxeth, Farmer Samuel Greenhill hung himself in despair. In the south east the terrible conditions led to rioting throughout the area. The government's response was repression – 450 men were transported and 9 were sentenced to death. Today we have the ultimate irony – a public park named after a man who oppressed his tenants, on the land which he obtained by stealing the people's commons.

TO COMPLETE WALK 15: The walk ends at South Kenton BR and tube stations.

WALK 16: South Kenton to Brent Cross

Getting Started

From Walk 15: There is a linking section between South Kenton and Preston Road
    From South Kenton Station turn right onto Windermere Avenue.
    Take the first left onto Allonby Gardens and at the end find the footpath that leads through to the next road (Montpelier Rise).
    Turn right her then immediately left into Preston Park. Head straight across the park to reach College Road.
    Turn right on College Road and take the first left into Glendale Gardens.
    At the end of the road turn left into Longfield Avenue, then right into Grasmere Avenue, to reach Preston Road.
    Turn left up Preston Road to reach the station.
To Start Walk Here:
    Begin at Preston Road Station.

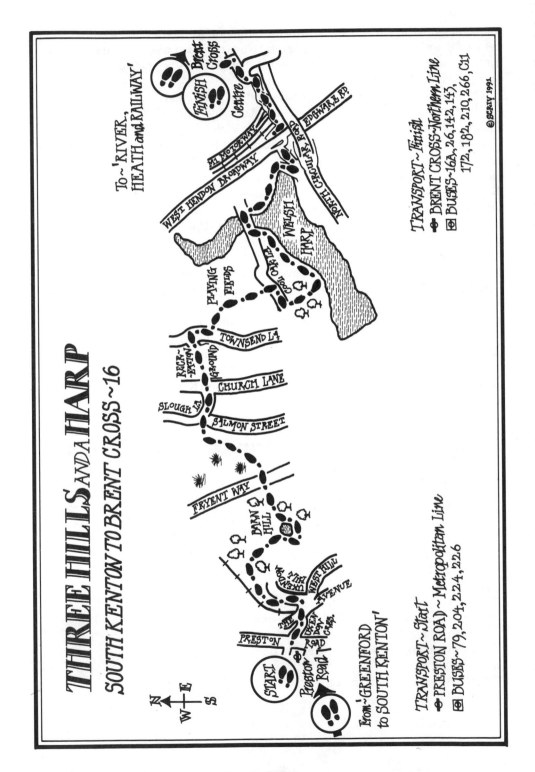

THREE HILLS AND A HARP

SOUTH KENTON TO BRENT CROSS ~16

From 'GREENFORD
to SOUTH KENTON'

To 'RIVER,
HEATH and RAILWAY'

START

PRESTON
Road

GRENDON GDNS.
TREE
WEST HILL
AVENUE
GRENDON HILL

DAM HILL

FRYENT WAY

SALMON STREET

CHURCH LANE

TOWNSEND L4

RECREATION GROUND

SLOUGH LA

PLAYING FIELDS

Cool Oak La

WELSH HARP

WEST HENDON BROADWAY

M1 MOTORWAY

EDGWARE RD.

NORTH CIRCULAR RD.

Brent Cross
Centre

FINISH

TRANSPORT ~ Start
◆ PRESTON ROAD ~ Metropolitan Line
⊞ BUSES ~ 79, 204, 224, 226

TRANSPORT ~ Finish
◆ BRENT CROSS ~ Northern Line
⊞ BUSES ~ 16A, 26, 142, 143,
172, 182, 210, 266, C11

© SERLY 1992

Uxendon Farm and the Babington Plot

ROUTE:
- From the station turn left onto Preston Road and then almost immediately right onto Uxendon Crescent.
- Turn right under the railway bridge at the end and then keep to the left to reach Uxendon Hill.

FACILITIES: Cafés on Preston Road.

When the Wealdstone Brook, now a concrete encrusted and litter-choked channel, was still a living and soft-banked stream, it ran through the dense Forest of Middlesex, linking the isolated settlements that had grown up along its length. Of these settlements, Coena's homestead was eventually to become Kenton, while the Priest's farm survives in the name of Preston. Slightly south of them both, the Wixans, a Saxon tribe who also gave their name to Uxbridge, founded a settlement which survived for centuries as Uxendon Farm. It remains today only in street names; Uxendon Crescent and Uxendon Hill stand on either side of the modern channel of the Brook. Yet Uxendon in its time played a small but dramatic part in one of the most compelling stories in our national history.

By 1585, Mary Queen of Scots had been in luxurious imprisonment in England for seventeen years. As a focus for the Catholic opposition she was a potential threat to Queen Elizabeth, who for year after year was unable to decide whether to release her or to put her to death. Execution was the course favoured by Elizabeth's Chief Secretary, Lord Walsingham, who knew that for years Mary had been involved in secret and smuggled correspondence with foreign powers and enemies of the state. He decided to secure evidence against Mary and in December 1585 she was moved to a tighter and more secure confinement at Chartley in south Derbyshire. There she began to smuggle letters in and out of the castle using beer barrels. She did not know that the system had been set up for her by Walsingham and that every word she wrote or received was first intercepted, read and copied. It was in the course of this correspondence that she became involved in the Babington plot.

Anthony Babington was a young Catholic noble, still only 25 years old when he was elected to lead the group pledged to Elizabeth's overthrow. The conspirators would assassinate the Queen and release Mary, thus signalling a general rising of the English catholics supported by an invasion from Spain. It was a crude, unrealistic and insubstantial plot. But Mary went along with it, and smuggled out a note on 17 July 1586, giving her support.

It was everything that Walsingham needed, and more. In August he moved against the conspirators. Babington got wind of developments and fled. He made for the thickest part of St John's Wood, where he hid himself for a time, cutting off his hair and staining his skin with walnut juice. It is at this stage that Uxendon Farm enters the story. It was in the hands of the Bellamy family and Jerome Bellamy, was a recent convert to Catholicism. Regarding it therefore as a safe house, Babington left the wood and headed towards Harrow. Despite the danger, Bellamy took him in. But no doubt Walsingham's spies already knew everything. They arrived at Uxendon Farm late in August, searched it, and took Babington away. With him they took Bellamy.

On 20 September, Anthony Babington was tied to a hurdle and dragged across London. At St Giles' Fields he was hung, drawn and quartered in an execution so prolonged and barbarous that Elizabeth ordered that the rest of the conspirators should be merely hung. A few days later Jerome Bellamy was executed alongside them. On 4 February 1587, Mary Stuart herself went to her death at Fotheringay.

Over Barn Hill

ROUTE:
- Follow Uxendon Hill. Where it begins to curve to the right look for an unmade track on the left which runs between houses onto an open space.
- Turn right to follow the path across the meadow, parallel to the tube line.
- Continue ahead across the meadow where it broadens out until reaching a cross path which originates from the footbridge on your left. Turn right on this path heading towards the woodland.
- Keep straight ahead through the woodland heading for the top of the hill and the pond.
- Walk to the right around the pond to reach the triangulation point. Follow the broad drive to your left, down to a line of pencil-shaped Lombardy poplars.
- Passing the poplars turn left along the far side of the hedgerow to pick up a mown path. Take the left fork to reach another cross-path, where an avenue of poplars leads off to your left. Turn right here.
- Cross the main road (Fryent Way) and pick out the gap in the verge and the footpath which runs across the meadow directly alongside an old hedgerow.
- After about 150 yards take the left fork heading diagonally across the fields. Pass an isolated young oak and fork right immediately afterwards.
- Follow the path, between gaps in hedgerows, and keeping to the right, until reaching and following a paddock fence.
- Turn right alongside stables to leave the meadows through a car park and onto the road.
- Cross the road and follow Slough Lane opposite. Go straight across the main road (Church Lane) at the end and into the recreation ground.
- Go straight across the recreation ground to find the exit, just to the right of garages, which leads onto Elthorne Way. Walk straight ahead to join Townsend Lane opposite another open space.

LOOKING AT WILDLIFE: The woodland of Barn Hill is rich in both birds and butterflies. Look in the glades for interesting plant species such as betony, devil's bit scabious and the adder's tongue fern. In the meadow areas there is an abundance of both vetch and grass species. Other plants to look out for include greater burnet, salsify, pepper saxifrage, sneezewort, stone parsley and the rare narrow-leaved bitter vetch. The ancient hedgerow relics also support a great diversity of wildlife.

It was not until the 1930s that Uxendon Farm followed its erstwhile owner into extinction. It was then that railway lines, orderly streets and neat ranks of semi-detached housing began to cover its fields and pastures. One corner of the former farmlands survives, Barn Hill, now part of the wider expanses of the Fryent Way Country Park. The 252 acres of the park include regenerating woodland, traditional meadow and no less than 15 ponds, many of them old farm ponds of the sort that have almost disappeared from our countryside. It is home to 70 species of bird, 22 of butterfly and 5 of dragonfly, and it exists because of the purchasing policies of local authorities in the 1920s and 30s, policies that government constraints have made impossible today.

From the open meadows beside the Jubilee rail line, lush with grasses and aglow with buttercups, we climb through some of the 50 acres of woodland that flank the hill. Here there are oak, ash and hornbeam, with scrub between, and the healthy sign of young saplings regenerating the woodland. Speckled wood butterflies fly along the path edges and from the trees comes the repetetive two-note song of the chiff-chaff.

At the top of the hill we come suddenly upon a clearing around a pond. A few anglers sit amongst reeds and yellow flag iris, in a studied silence broken only by the calling of song thrushes from surrounding trees – it looks like a scene from an 18th century painting, and perhaps it is as deliberately composed. It was probably the work of landscape architect Humphrey Repton, who was employed here in 1792-93 by Richard Page, the owner of the large Wembley Park estate which once spread from here as far south as the present Wembley Stadium.

It is the stadium which dominates the view from the top of the hill. With its twin, domed entrance towers, it looks like something from the British raj in New Delhi. Perhaps this is deliberate, for the stadium was built in 1922-23 to house the British Empire Exhibition. It was completed just in time to host the 1923 FA Cup Final, when Bolton beat West Ham. As a suitably grand gesture for the last days of empire, it was to be the largest stadium in the world, housing 120,000 spectators. It was flanked with a Palace of Industry and a Palace of Art, both of which, in the spirit of our times, have now been turned into warehouses. In 1933 the Wembley Arena and the Empire Pool were added and in 1948 the whole complex became the site of the 14th Olympic Games, where Fanny Blankers-Koen of the Netherlands took four gold medals and became the first woman to hold the Victrix Ludorum. But the complex also holds a significant, if less well known, place in the history of ornithology. In 1926 a pair of black redstarts nested in the Palace of Industry, the first recorded breeding of these birds in London. Pairs continued to breed here until the war, thus playing a part in the fascinating story of the colonisation of a major urban centre by a previously rare British bird.

From the top of the hill we descend through open woods and meadows to reach the Fryent Way, the busy main road that cuts through the centre of the country park like an ever-open wound. The area to the east of the road has large expanses of meadow and constitutes a view almost unique in London; that of flower-rich fields surrounded by suburban housing. It represents, according to the London Ecology Unit, 'a microcosm of the lost countryside of Middlesex'. This area was purchased by the County Council in 1938 and then leased to a local farmer, who turned it to arable use thus destroying much of the hedgerow in the process. Since its reversion to pasture, and to traditional forms of management, the wild flowers have made a remarkable recovery, spreading inwards from the unploughed field margins. As well as the great variety of vetches – common vetch, meadow vetchling, smooth tare, hairy tare and many more – there are several unusual species, such as stone parsley with its petrol-scented foliage, and narrow-leaved bitter cress, previously believed to be extinct in Middlesex.

The surviving hedgerows have been the subject of intensive study by Conservation Officer Lesley Williams. His work reveals that the line of the hedges is much the same as that shown in maps of 1597, while some of them can be dated as far back as the 1300s. It is one of the happiest consequences of the purchase of land by the then Wembley and Middlesex Councils that they preserved in being corners of our countryside with 700 years of continuous history.

Welsh Harp and West Hendon

ROUTE:

• From Elthorne Way turn right along Townsend Lane. Shortly, take the faint path on the left that cuts diagonally across the field to the gap in the hedgerow, just before the sports ground.

• Beyond the hedgerow turn right and follow first the hedge and then the backs of houses till joining Cool Oak Lane.

• Turn right along the lane. Where the road bends to the right take the short drive on the left which soon leads onto a footpath.

• Follow the tarmac path ahead, but where it curves to the right, take the earth path straight ahead into the woodland. The line of the path becomes indistinct but keep directly ahead till emerging from the copse onto a path leading to the waterside.

• Turn left and follow paths leading close to the water's edge until you eventually return to the road. Turn right and cross the bridge.

• Find the path on the right. It begins behind the crash barrier on the far side of the car park.

• Follow the edge of the lake. *THE PATH HERE CAN BE MUDDY AT TIMES, ESPECIALLY IN WINTER.* Reach the weir and cross the river.

• Turn left beyond the river to reach Priestley Way. Turn left along the road.

• At the end of the road you will see a flyover ahead. Cross below the flyover and turn right on the opposite side.

• Follow the footway round beneath a railway bridge and beyond it take the curving slope onto a footbridge, then straight on over the field-like traffic island ahead.

• Of the two footbridges in front of you take the one on the left, leading over to the car park. Carry straight on ahead from the end of the ramp and take the slip road which curves round to the left.

- Carry on straight ahead to cross the River Brent and turn right along Prince Charles Drive to reach the Brent Cross Shopping Centre and the bus terminus.

FACILITIES: Toilets and cafés at Brent Cross.

LOOKING AT WILDLIFE: Brent Reservoir is famous for its water birds, in particular breeding colonies of common terns and great crested grebes, and regular wintering smew. Other species inhabit the reed beds including reed warblers, water rail and, occasionally, bittern. There is also a very good range of wild flower species. The waste areas near the Brent Cross road systems are enlivened by a surprising range of wild flowers including opium poppy, flixweed, yellow melilot and a variety of wild mustards.

In 1835 the Brent River was dammed at its confluence with the Silk Stream in order to provide a source of water for the nearby Grand Union Canal. The result was a large artificial lake, submerging the old boundary of Hendon, Kingsbury and Willesden and known officially as the Brent Reservoir. More commonly, and more attractively, it is called the Welsh Harp. This would be an accurate allusion to the shape of the reservoir but the name derives instead from an old alehouse which once stood on the Edgeware Road. The presence of a lake at the back of the pub worked wonders for its popularity and from 1860 to 1910 the Welsh Harp was the place to be. It was a venue for concerts, horse races, boxing matches, pigeon and duck shooting and ice skating, and it figures in at least four different Victorian music hall songs.

The Welsh Harp remains an important centre for recreation, though today the birds are watched rather than shot and it is sailors rather than skaters who take to the water. Though sailing and bird-watching are not always compatible the reservoir has managed to accommodate them both, and the area today boasts 145 species of bird. It hosts the best documented bird life in Britain. In winter the duck population includes gadwall, teal, and smew, while in summer tufted duck, pochard, Canada geese and shovellor all breed here. But most famous among them is the great crested grebe, which has here probably the largest breeding colony in the country.

In 1860 this beautiful and fascinating bird had been hunted almost to extinction. Its soft white breast plumage had become fashionable in the trimmings of clothes and hats, leading to a wholesale massacre. In reaction to this, a small group of women formed themselves in 1889 into 'The Fur, Fin and Feather Folk' and pledged 'to refrain from wearing the feathers of any birds not killed for the purpose of food'. Both the grebes and the Feather Folk rapidly increased in numbers. By the end of its first year the group had a membership of over 5,000 and in 1904 it was remodelled as the Royal Society for the Protection of Birds. In this way the plight of the great crested grebe was to lead to the establishment of what is now the largest conservation society in Great Britain.

Our route around the waterside takes us to the eastern end of the reservoir and a rich area of reedbeds. In the 1960s, road building and the construction of the Brent Cross shopping centre pushed silt and slurry into the River Brent which then built up a shallow estuary at the point where it flows into the reservoir. This was soon colonised by reeds, providing an excellent habitat for birds. It may be the only good thing to have come out of Brent Cross. Small crustacea and insects feed on the silt beds and provide food for the diving ducks, while large numbers of small fish are food for the grebes. Here too, several rafts have been moored to encourage the nesting of common tern. Along this stretch we cross muddy ground, sometimes flooded in winter, through a secluded area of thick undergrowth and overhanging trees. It brings us out to the Brent itself and a messy, littered weir.

From the wooded tip of the lake, busy with birds and the rustling of poplar leaves in the breeze, we come out to end our walk in one of the worst horrors of west London. It is wasteland and warehouses, fly-tipping and flyovers, the ceaseless aggressive noise of countless cars. There in the centre of it all, suitably sandwiched between three major trunk roads, is a mega-store complex where the air is conditioned, the light is artificial and even the sun is out of bounds. It is Brent Cross, consumerism made concrete. The designers billed it as 'the housewife's dream'. To anyone who loves their city it is a nightmare from which one is desperate to awake.

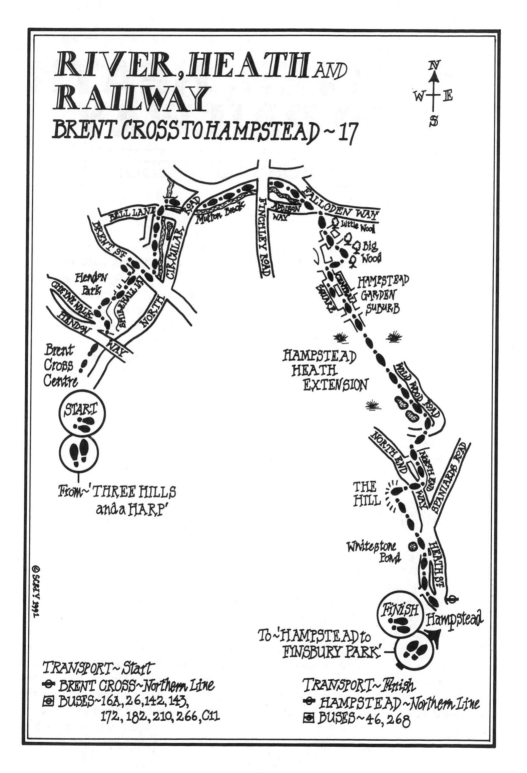

RIVER, HEATH AND RAILWAY
BRENT CROSS TO HAMPSTEAD ~ 17

START

From ~ 'THREE HILLS and a HARP'

FINISH

Hampstead

To ~ 'HAMPSTEAD to FINSBURY PARK'

TRANSPORT ~ Start
- BRENT CROSS ~ Northern Line
- BUSES ~ 16A, 26, 142, 143, 172, 182, 210, 266, C11

TRANSPORT ~ Finish
- HAMPSTEAD ~ Northern Line
- BUSES ~ 46, 268

11. RIVER, HEATH AND RAILWAY

FROM BRENT CROSS TO FINSBURY PARK

Hendon, Hampstead and Haringey are three very different parts of North London linked in this chapter by riverside and railway walks. From Hendon to Hampstead much of our route is along the upper reaches of the River Brent and its tributary the Mutton Brook, which drains the northern slopes of Hampstead Heath. Hampstead, most famous and most fashionable of London suburbs, is the focal point of this chapter. Beyond it we cross the heath to reach the Highgate woodlands and the Parkland Walk, a semi-rural ribbon formed from an abandoned railway and one of the most attractive sections of *The Green London Way*.

This route demonstrates the importance of green corridors in an urban area, and of the rich diversity of wildlife habitat they can provide. In this section of the walk these corridors link a number of outstanding open spaces, but also some interesting urban areas which serve as illustrations of different aspects of London's development. We begin at Brent Cross, that hideous shopping bunker that helped pave the way for similar 'out-of-town' shopping developments across the country. These developments come from a school of town planning which holds that civilisation stems from the motor car, and which has wreaked havoc upon our cities. The broad tree-lined streets of Hampstead Garden Suburb, by contrast, seem relatively car free. Here is town planning of a very different order; a worthy experiment in social engineering which nonetheless failed in its intention to bring all social classes together. The Garden Suburb is a totally planned environment and its undeniably beautiful homes set around a Central Square have almost the air of a museum piece, of something preserved behind glass.

Hampstead proper has a very different atmosphere with all the vigour that comes from a largely unplanned growth. Its explosive period of development came with the opening of its first medicinal wells in the early 18th century. Since then it seems to repeat a strange cycle consisting of select fashionability followed by popular growth resulting in decline. This is happening in Hampstead again today. Finally, the Parkland Walk runs through the once-select southern suburbs of Haringey; through Crouch End, Stapleton Hall and Stroud Green. These developed with the growth of the City, and with the steam boom and building boom which went hand in hand, covering the fields with the roomy villas of the Victorian professional classes.

Urban developments and green spaces – from the Brent bunker to the sandy slopes of the heath – are all integral parts of the walks in this chapter. Together they represent something of the complex tapestry of London and of different models for its development. In this respect they also present us with a challenge to consider the future of London, and to decide the kind of city in which we would like to live.

This chapter covers 12 miles from Brent Cross to Finsbury Park. It can be taken as two shorter walks:

WALK 17: Brent Cross to Hampstead (5½ miles).

WALK 18: Hampstead to Finsbury Park (6½ miles).

WALK 17: Brent Cross to Hampstead

Getting Started

From Brent Cross underground station:
From the booking hall take the tube exit to the left and turn left along Heathfield Gardens to reach the North Circular Road.
NB This exit to the station is closed on Sundays. Leave by main exit and turn left and left again to reach Heathfield Gardens.
Turn left on North Circular Road and cross the footbridge. Turn right from the footbridge and follow signs alongside the River Brent and under several flyovers. The signposted route turns right alongside a small meadow. At the T junction ahead turn left to reach the shopping centre or keep straight ahead to join main route.
From buses:
From bus terminal in front of the shopping centre cross the road (Prince Charles Drive) and turn left.
Take the tarmac path on the right just before the road enters a subway. Turn left at the T junction of paths ahead.
From Walk 16:
Continue straight ahead along Prince Charles Drive, passing the shopping centre to take the tarmac path on the right just before the road enters a subway. Turn left at the T junction of paths ahead.

Brent Cross

ROUTE:
- Follow the path ahead then turn right to take the pedestrian subway.
- Cross the first road ahead and immediately beyond it turn left into Renters Avenue.
Follow it to find a path on the right over a footbridge into Hendon Park.
- Go straight ahead across the park to pick up Shirehall Lane on the far side. Turn

left along the road and at the far end take the little path on the left between numbers 4 and 8.

• Turn right in front of The Load of Hay and join the main road (Brent Street).

FACILITIES: Toilets and cafés at Brent Cross Shopping Centre. Load of Hay pub on Brent Street.

At Brent Cross consumerism meets the motor car. Here, in the middle of a monstrous matrix of major road junctions is one of Britain's first purpose-built 'out-of-town' shopping complexes. The idea came from America, home of the car culture, in the 1950s. The preference of English town planners had previously been for the regeneration of existing town centres, but in 1959 the Hammerson Group began looking for a development site in London. With the help of the London Borough of Barnet they identified 52 strategically placed acres of semi-dereliction, the site of old chemical works and a disused greyhound stadium. Work began in 1972 and four years and £30 million later, the Brent Cross Shopping Centre was opened to a fanfare of publicity.

It is a great two-storey bunker of a building, 610 foot long. Inside 82 shops line marbled malls which converge on a domed fountain court. It is an environment completely insulated from the outside world with piped music, pumped air and a complete absence of natural light. It has thereby managed to create an almost contradictory combination of sterility and shabbiness.

The location was carefully chosen to put it within easy driving distance of a potential 1,250,000 customers and, to attract them, it has been provided with 5,217 car parking spaces. This emphasis on the motor car does more than maximise the market; it also has a role in determining what sort of shoppers come here. As a 1982 GLC report commented, 'Brent Cross caters for the car-mobile sections of the community but at the same time lies outside the choice framework of the not inconsiderable proportion who do not enjoy motorised personal mobility.' This of course coincides with the retailers' interests by culling the more prosperous consumers.

From Brent Cross to Brent Street we pass a few reminders of the area's rural past. Renters Avenue is named after Renters Farm, which existed here from at least the 14th century. Across the railway footbridge, Hendon Park would have been part of the farm and was known as Step Fields until it was turned into parkland in 1903. The parish of Hendon which covered this area was one of the largest in Middlesex and just on its fringes stood the hamlet of Brent Street. Among the genteel villas for which it was renowned was Shire Hall, giving its name to Shirehall Lane. The Hall was demolished in 1920 but at the end of the street there still exists a small but attractive group of 18th and early 19th century houses, one of them with its old Sun Insurance fire mark. Between two of these houses a little passage leads us to the Load of Hay pub, decorated with barge-boardings and patterned rain-water pipes. It is the latest in a line of inns bearing the name and recalls the days when Brent Street was a drove road and cattle and sheep were herded down here towards the end of their long journeys into the London markets.

Brent Park and Mutton Brook

ROUTE:
- Turn right down Brent Street and just before the junction with the North Circular Road, take the path on the left leading through Brent Park.
- Follow the path through the park and on reaching Decoy Pond cross the little bridge and follow round to the left, between pond and river.
- On leaving the park turn left towards Mutton Bridge and take the path on the right alongside the river.
- Cross the little footbridge and turn right alongside the tributary stream (Mutton Brook). Follow the path under the subway and onto Brookside Walk.
- Continue ahead crossing Finchley Road to the gate on the opposite side. Take the path which crosses the brook and continue ahead following the other bank as far as possible. At its end the path joins the road (Addison Way) on the right.

LOOKING AT WILDLIFE: Woodland flora in Brent Park includes cow parsley, red campion, wild garlic and Jack-by-the-hedge. There is a pendant silver lime tree on the riverside path beyond Mutton Bridge. Mutton Brook has stands of giant knotweed, a rather different plant from the more familiar Japanese knotweed.

From Brent Street we follow linear parks along the upper reaches of the River Brent and its tributary, the Mutton Brook. Brent Park is a long, wooded dell: shady, rather seedy and with an air of down-at-heel gentility. Close to the park entrance a little, litter-strewn weir spans the river and standing on either side are circular and sadly dilapidated towers. They are remnants of the old villas of Brent Street and of the villa gardens which have given their atmosphere to the park today. But there are older associations too. The Manor of Hendon belonged originally to the Abbots of Westminster who some time between 1319 and 1326 built themselves a Manor House here. To serve their kitchens they dammed the Brent to form fish ponds and in later years these were turned into a duck decoy which survives as the quiet, tree-shaded pond half-way along the length of Brent Park.

Duck decoys were an elaborate method of trapping wildfowl for food. Artificial funnel-shaped channels were dug from an existing water course, gradually narrowing into 'pipes' covered with osier and reed and ending in a net. The wild birds would be attracted by tame duck, or driven by specially trained little dogs known as pipers; once inside the narrowing channel the birds would fly onwards until trapped. The construction of an effective decoy was a considerable skill and only 200 of them are known from the whole of the British Isles, the majority in the Norfolk Broads. The existence of Decoy Pond in Brent Park is therefore something of an archaeological rarity.

At the end of Brent Park, the attractively balustraded Mutton Bridge carries Bell Lane over the river, and a short distance beyond here the Brent splits into two. The larger stream is the Dollis Brook which flows down from Hertfordshire, while our path follows the Mutton Brook which drains from the northern slopes of Hampstead Heath. Brookside Walk occupies 25 acres of what used to be Fox Hole Wood and was acquired by Barnet Council in 1930. Though most of the woodland is gone it could still be an attractive waterside walk through undulating meadows fringed with hedgerows, were it not for two features. One is the constant drone of traffic from the nearby North Circular Road, the other is the state of the water.

In March 1990 local residents, who had long been alarmed at the state of the Mutton Brook, paid for an independent analysis of its water. The resulting report concluded that it was highly polluted and constituted a health hazard, particularly to children. Barnet Council, who were presented with the report claimed to have spent over £50,000 looking for the source of the problem without being able to isolate its cause. The 'solution' instead has been to line the walk with warning signs, thus giving the Brookside Walk the distinction of a being a green strip running between a highly polluting road and a highly polluted river.

Hampstead Garden Suburb

ROUTE:
- Turn left along Addison Way. Look for the small opening between houses on the right that leads into Little Wood.
- Keep straight ahead through the wood to join Denman Drive South on the far side. Follow the Drive ahead to reach the path into Big Wood.
- Follow the path ahead through Big Wood and at the first crosspaths turn right. Follow the path up to the T junction and turn right again to reach the road (Temple Fortune Hill).
- Turn left at the crossroads ahead into Erskine Hill and walk down here to reach the Free Church at one end of Central Square.
- Follow the road round to the right and take the steps onto the pedestrian route across the square and under the ornamental lantern. At the end of the square follow the road to the left around the far side of St Jude's.
- Take the first right into Heathgate. Follow it across Mead Way to reach the steps leading onto Hampstead Heath Extension.

LOOKING AT WILDLIFE: Big and Little Woods are relict oak woodland. Plants worth looking for include the wild service tree, wild bluebell and lily-of-the-valley. There are a variety of woodland birds including jays, tits and warblers. Between the two woods, white comfrey grows on Denham Drive.

On Christmas Eve 1884, the Whitechapel settlement of Toynbee Hall first opened its doors. Founded by Canon Samuel Barnett its aim was to bring relief to the East End poor and in particular to offer them the advantages of a liberal education. Early 'settlers' here included William Beveridge, R.H. Tawney and Clement Attlee and the work of the Hall was to give rise to both the Worker's Educational Association and the Whitechapel Art Gallery. The Youth Hostels Association had its first office here and it was here too that the idea for the Hampstead Garden Suburb was born.

It was part of settlement thinking that the working classes would benefit by mixing with those of a more privileged background who, through education and example, would attempt to share their advantages. For Henrietta Barnett, the Canon's wife, this did not go far enough. Her dream was to create a place where people of all walks of life could live alongside each other, in quality housing and in pleasant surrounds. When the Eton College estate put onto the market its property near Golders Green, she decided that her moment had come.

Wyldes Farm had been owned by the college since 1449. It was situated to the north of Hampstead and the expected extension of the Northern line meant that it would soon be within easy commuting distance of Central London. Henrietta bought the estate in 1905 and two years later work began on the Hampstead Garden Suburb. The planners for the scheme were Raymond Unwin and Barry Parker, who had been involved in the first Garden City experiment at Letchworth. The guiding principles were laid down by Mrs Barnett and the committee she had established. There were directives on the density of housing, the materials to be used, the width of the streets and the planting of trees. The roads were to be on a variety of lines – neither all straight nor all winding – and to respect the existing contours. The focal point, to be placed at the highest part of the suburb, was the Central Square. In keeping with Mrs Barnett's vision and values, it was to contain two churches and an Educational Institute, to be designed by Edward Lutyens.

The most intriguing question concerning the Garden Suburb is how something intended as a social leveller can have become so exclusively the territory of the upper middle classes. To walk through the tree-lined avenues today is to feel like a trespasser within a private and very inward-looking domain. 'Sanctuary!', wrote Philip Davies in the *Evening Standard* in February 1991. 'That's why I live here.' Much of the explanation lies in the original design. The plans included housing for a variety of income brackets but the different groups were segregated from the start. Smaller flats for artisans were concentrated in the north of the suburb; middle class homes were located in the west; and the choicest, richest villas were sited in the south and overlooking the heath. Soon, rising rents and house prices were to force out the manual workers altogether. Moreover the plans for the suburb had deliberately relegated all shops, pubs, cafés and cinemas to the unreformed fringes, and public transport was almost non-existent. For all but the wealthy and the totally mobile, it was an impossible place to live. In the history of English town planning, Hampstead Garden Suburb was of enormous importance, its influence spreading across the country and out to Holland, Germany and America. But as a social experiment it has failed.

Our route across the suburb takes us through two remnants of the ancient Middlesex oak forest which the planners wisely incorporated into their designs. Completely surrounded by housing, the two woods are quiet, private places. Little Wood has an oak canopy underset with hornbeam and field maple. The 18 acre Big Wood has few hornbeam but a greater variety of other shrubs and trees including hawthorn, hazel, crab apple and the wild service tree. In both woods, chiff-chaff, willow warbler and blackcap can be heard in early summer when the wild bluebells are blooming across the woodland floor. The London Borough of Barnet has reintroduced hazel coppicing to Big Wood and this practice should eventually encourage both plant and bird diversity.

From Big Wood, Erskine Hill leads us into Lutyen's Central Square. Here the Free Church and the Anglican Church stand at opposite ends of the neat lawns. With their dark red brick and their huge roofs swooping down almost to the ground, they seem to be turned in on themselves, brooding perhaps about the quietness of the square. The Free Church is domed and has a rather Byzantine feel, while the Anglican Church – named St Jude's after Canon Barnett's parish in Whitechapel – has a fine steeple arising from an open tower and is a landmark for many miles around. The Institute separating the two is a determinedly formal building in what might be called a National Provincial Bank style.

From the south side of the square, Heathgate leads us along an attractive paved piazza onto the Heath. The solid line of houses along the edge of the Hampstead Heath Extension is known, revealingly, as the Great Wall. It stands like a defensive barrier to protect the suburb against the rest of the world with its confusing diversity and its perplexing and perpetual change.

North Hampstead and The Hill

ROUTE:
- From the end of Heathgate walk across the grass, ahead and to the left, to reach the bridge over a little brook by a gap in the line of trees.
- Head straight across the next field towards the pavilion.
- Turn left on the broad track in front of the pavilion and follow it as it curves round to the right.
- Continue on this main track, passing ponds to the right. Eventually the track curves to the right at the top end of the Extension, parallel to a road, and reaches a crosspath. On the right a path leads off to a stone fountain, while on the left 5 steps lead up to the road beside a bench.
- Turn left and cross the road. Continue straight ahead between two wooden posts and immediately bear right. After a short distance the path runs along backs of houses then curves round left to join North End Avenue.
- Go straight ahead at the cross-roads. The road reverts to track and continues along an avenue of trees, curving right at the top of the slope to join the main road (North End Way).
- Cross the road and turn right then immediately left onto Inverforth Close following

signs to The Hill Garden. Take the signposted footpath off to the right leading to the gate into The Hill.

• Go through the park gate and turn right. Follow the path ahead as it loops around the bottom of the park, eventually reaching the bottom of a long and imposing flight of steps. Climb steps to top of loggia with views across London.

• Continue along the pillared arcade and shortly, take the first gate on the right back onto the Heath.

NB The rest of the arcade walk is being restored and it should later be possible to follow the full length and join the Heath further along.

• From the gate follow the path which runs ahead and to the left and make your way down the steep bank to join the track which runs alongside the wall of the gardens. Turn right, and then left at the T junction ahead.

• Follow this path across West Heath. Keep straight ahead, ignoring crosspaths, till emerging at the summit of the heath close to the flagstaff.

• Walk ahead between the two small fenced areas to reach the complex of roads by Whitestone Pond. Walk ahead between the pond and the radio mast towards the traffic lights but turn right down a road closed to cars just before the main road junction (Hampstead Grove).

• Follow Hampstead Grove straight ahead, passing Fenton House, and carry on down Holly Hill to emerge onto Heath Street opposite the tube station.

LOOKING AT WILDLIFE: The grassland of the Heath Extension supports sorrel and stitchwort, with foxgloves along the hedgerows. The ponds have a particularly rich flora with common reed and bulrush and a variety of other flowering plants including ragged robin. Sandy Heath and West Heath are good places to look for redpoll and siskin on birch trees in winter. Rabbits can be seen grazing in The Hill at dusk.

In the hundred years since the first 220 acres of Hampstead Heath passed into public ownership, this beautiful urban open space has expanded to occupy 800 acres. This the result of a positive policy of acquisition, which is almost impossible under local authority financing today. It has added to the Heath not just extent, but also diversity, and has given it some of its most characterful corners: The Hill, Pitt's Garden, Wildwood and many more. Among these later additions is the prosaically named Hampstead Heath Extension, the gift of Henrietta Barnett and part of her original Wyldes Farm purchase. It forms a protruding tongue of land running up through the neat housing of Golders Green to end at the Great Wall, and bears the unmistakeable imprint of an earlier agricultural landscape. The open expanses of the fields are made more interesting by hedgerow boundaries, remnants of woodland and by the string of little ponds along the brook. Growing here are white water lilies, blue forget-me-nots, yellow spearworts, and the greater willow-herb with its blossom a soft pink and cream. Here too is the lovely ragged robin, with its red and tattered-looking flowers, a typical plant of damp meadows but unusual in London.

From the Extension we cross a corner of Sandy Heath and follow a pleasant tree-lined avenue before curving through a corner of heath known as Pitts Garden. It was to a house on this site that William Pitt the Elder moved in 1767 after a serious mental collapse which forced him to resign as Prime Minister. Here at Hampstead he locked himself in a room, communicating with no-one and receiving his meals through a hatch in the wall. In 1778, having emerged from his retirement, Pitt was in the House of Lords, delivering an impassioned harangue against the war with America. At the end of the speech he fainted in his seat and was carried back home to die. The large house was demolished after bomb damage in World War Two and its garden was added to the Heath in 1954.

From Pitt's Garden we cross North End Road to reach The Hill, one of the most beautiful and most secluded parks in London. In 1776 the actress Mrs Lessingham caused a riot by building herself Heath Lodge on the common land of Hampstead. In 1906 this house was bought by the soap magnate William Lever who already owned the adjacent property known as The Hill. Lever demolished Heath Lodge and linked the two gardens with a system of elevated walkways, stone terraces and gazebos. The two gardens were separated only by a public right of way which Lever spanned with an ornamental arch. He wanted to go even further and eliminate the footpath but in this he was strongly opposed by the Hampstead Heath Protection Society and the matter was still in dispute when he died in 1925.

The site is now divided again. The old house and its immediate grounds belong to the Manor House Hospital while on the other side of the footpath The Hill Garden was purchased for the public in 1963. Here a well-managed and shrub-lined formal garden forms a wonderful contrast with the wildness of the West Heath beyond. Rabbit-grazed lawns slope steeply upwards to a formal pond and, above it, the raised walkways and pergolas give a wonderful view out over London. The terraces have deteriorated badly over the years but are now being restored by the Corporation of London. They form one of the most romantic settings along *The Green London Way*.

Across West Heath we reach the summit of Hampstead Heath, marked by the flagstaff beside Whitestone Pond. The Victorians adapted an earlier dew pond here and fitted it with ramps, so that a thirsty horse which had pulled a heavy carriage up the hill could walk straight in at one end and out at the other. At 443 feet above sea level this is the highest point in Central London. ''Tis so near Heaven,' said Daniel Defoe in his 1724 *Tour through the Whole Island of Great Britain*, 'that I dare not say it can be a proper Situation for any but a race of mountaineers, whose lungs had been used to a rarify'd air'. The adjacent housing development, 'The Summit', has attempted to capitalise on this setting but instead has created something that looks like a modern Alcatraz, complete with perimeter wall and guard towers.

The covered reservoir at the top end of Hampstead Grove was built in 1856 and is now the site of the Hampstead Scientific Society's Observatory. This was previously the Hampstead village green and the parliamentary elections for Middlesex were held here until they moved to Brentford in 1700 (see p.142). It was in this same year that Admiral's House was built, just a short distance off Hampstead Grove to the right. In 1791 it was occupied by a naval officer called Fountain North who amended the flat roof to look like the quarter-deck of a ship. He is said to have moved several cannons here and to have fired them off on celebratory occasions. For walkers of *The Green London Way* it is of interest as the one-time home of the architect George

Gilbert Scott whose work has featured repeatedly on our route around London.

Further down Hampstead Grove is Fenton House, built in 1693 and therefore probably the oldest surviving house in Hampstead. It was built by Joshua Gee, a silk trader, but gets its name from Philip Fenton, a Riga merchant who purchased it in 1793. Fenton played a leading part in 1829 in the opposition to the Lord of the Manor's plans to build on the Heath. In 1952 the house was bequeathed to the National Trust and today houses a collection of early keyboard musical instruments. From Fenton House, Hampstead Grove descends into Holly Hill and makes its narrow way down past the Holly Bush Inn and a row of artisan's cottages, to reach the very heart of the village. At the cross-roads of Hampstead High Street and Heath Street stands the Hampstead Underground Station and the end of our walk. In Hampstead even the tube station has to be remarkable: at 220 feet it has the deepest tunnel in the whole of London.

WALK 18: HAMPSTEAD TO FINSBURY PARK

Getting Started

The walk begins from Hampstead Underground Station and continues directly from Walk 17.

Hampstead Village

ROUTE:
● Turn left out of the station and down Hampstead High Street. After a short distance take Flask Walk on the left.
● Follow Flask Walk as it broadens into a road and then continue ahead into Well Walk. Follow Well Walk to its end opposite the heath.

FACILITIES: Cafés, restaurants and pubs throughout Hampstead. Burgh House has a good café in the basement.

More words have been written about Hampstead than about any other part of London. It is probably also true that more words have been written in Hampstead than in any other part of London. According to a local joke, Hampstead book shops put on special promotions for books 'Not Written By Local Author'. Hampstead is extremely beautiful, atrociously rich and highly fashionable, but this has not always been the case. Until the end of the 17th century it was a small village surrounded by wild heathland and inhabited by pig farmers and washerwomen. Then came the development of its chalybeate wells and the fortunes of the village became, largely, the fortunes of its medicinal spa.

In 1698 the Honourable Susannah Noel, acting on behalf of her 13 year old son, the Earl of Gainsborough, Lord of the Manor of Hampstead, granted 6 acres of land

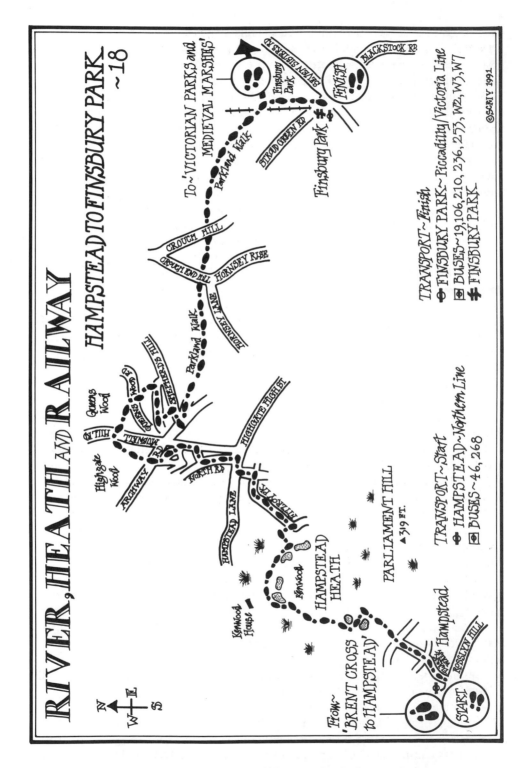

RIVER, HEATH AND RAILWAY

HAMPSTEAD TO FINSBURY PARK ~18

©SARIY 1991

N
W—E
S

To ~ 'VICTORIAN PARKS and MEDIEVAL MARSHES'

Parkland Walk

Finsbury Park

Finsbury Park

SEVEN SISTERS RD

STROUD GREEN RD

FINISH

BLACKSTOCK RD

CROUCH HILL

CROUCH END HILL

HORNSEY RISE

HORNSEY LANE

Parkland Walk

Queens Wood

QUEENS WOOD RD

SHEPHERD'S HILL

Highgate Wood

HIGHGATE HIGH ST

ARCHWAY

HILL RD

MUSWELL HILL RD

NORTH RD

HAMPSTEAD LANE

PARLIAMENT HILL
▲319 FT.

HAMPSTEAD HEATH

Kenwood

Kenwood House

Hampstead

ROSSLYN HILL

From ~ 'BRENT CROSS to HAMPSTEAD'

START

TRANSPORT ~ Start
⊖ HAMPSTEAD ~ Northern Line
🚌 BUSES ~ 46, 268

TRANSPORT ~ Finish
⊖ FINSBURY PARK ~ Piccadilly/Victoria Line
🚌 BUSES ~ 19, 106, 210, 236, 253, W2, W3, W7
🚆 FINSBURY PARK

on the edge of the heath for the benefit of the poor. The land contained springs which were high in iron content and had an unpleasant, bitter taste that qualified them as a cure for almost anything. A charitable Wells Trust was established to exploit the springs and began to bottle the water for sale to the apothecaries of London. Then, in 1701, the Trust appointed John Duffield to manage the site. Duffield was an entrepreneur with ambitious intentions, and he built the famous 'Long Room' where visitors could take the waters and then recuperate to music, dancing, cards or other entertainments. The growth of Hampstead as a fashionable spa had begun. By the 1720 it had risen, wrote Daniel Defoe, 'from a Country Village to a City'.

This growth had unforeseen results. With an increasing range of attractions, including a race-course, bowling greens, tea houses and alehouses, and with its closeness to London, Hampstead began to attract more and more day trippers. It was no longer select and, according to some, it had become downright disreputable. The rich and fashionable ceased to arrive, the wells were closed and John Duffield went bankrupt. In the 1730s the spa was relaunched, with a brand new Long Room, but history repeated itself and after a period of success this too fell into disfavour and decline. Perhaps this whole cycle is repeating itself. Having developed as the fashionable home of the liberal literati, Hampstead is again becoming a victim of its own popularity. The Sunday streets are packed with trippers, boutiques have burgeoned, and restaurants have opened shoulder to shoulder. The smell of cooking permeates the whole of Hampstead and its South End has become more like Southend.

The history of the Hampstead wells can be retraced in the course of our walk. Flask Walk draws its name from the days when water was bottled at the Flask Tavern and sold for 3d a bottle. The Walk today opens up into a very pleasant lane with a narrow green and with houses in a wide variety of styles. At the end of the Walk are the 1888 buildings of the Wells and Campden Baths and Wash Houses, one of the charitable products of the Wells Trust, now converted into a private house. At the junction with Well Walk, Burgh House can be seen off to the left, a tidy Queen Anne building erected in 1703 and occupied at one time by the physician to the wells. The house was purchased by the Hampstead Borough Council in 1946 and opened as a community centre but the fabric was so badly neglected that by 1963 Camden Council was considering demolishing it. Saved by a public campaign the building is now administered by its own Trust and run as a museum and exhibition centre.

Wells House, the Council estate in front of Burgh House, occupies the site of the second Long Room which was demolished after bomb damage in World War Two. The flats were designed to harmonise with Burgh House and for this they won a RIBA Bronze Medal. The first Long Room stood on the site of Gainsborough Gardens just off Well Walk and it is here that we come across the original chalybeate spring with its memorial to Susannah Noel:

Drink traveller and with strength renewed
Let a kind thought be given
To her who has thy thirst subdued
Then render thanks to heaven.

Underneath this is the more recent addition, 'Unfit for drinking'.

Across the Heath

ROUTE:

- From Well Walk cross the main road and follow the broad tarmac path straight ahead alongside The Pryors.
- The path becomes a pleasant avenue of limes and reaches a second crosspaths beside a commemorative stone to the 1987 storm. Turn left here.
- Follow the path across The Viaduct and bear right after this to reach Bird Bridge. Cross the bridge and carry on straight ahead to reach the gate into Ken Wood.
- Fork left inside the wood and continue ahead between wooden fences. Ignore a first small turning on the left to reach a major fork. Bear left here.
- The path ends at a T junction before the lake. Turn left and cross the bridge and follow the path between the meadow and the pond to eventually reach a gate out of Kenwood and onto another meadow (Cohen's Fields).
- Turn right along the tarmac path leading down past the spring and alongside Stock Pond.
- At the end of Stock Pond turn left and of the two worn paths in front of you take the one on the right. On reaching the allotments turn right to reach the lane.

FACILITES: Café and toilets in the Coach House block at Kenwood House.

LOOKING AT WILDLIFE: Hampstead Heath is a very good venue for bird watching and supports a large number of species. On our route water rail can sometimes be seen in winter from The Viaduct and tits and nuthatches can be watched at close quarters at Bird Bridge and in Kenwood. Stock dove, kestrel and woodpeckers also breed in the woods. There is a varied flora on the heath but it has to be looked for in areas less trodden by visitors. There is a rich collection of fungi in autumn. Bats can often be seen above Stock Pond on summer evenings.

If Hampstead is the most written about place in London, then the heath has the most documented flora. It seems impossible to be a plant in Hampstead and not be listed. As long ago as the 16th century London's apothecaries were coming here to gather herbs for their medicines, among them John Gerard, who walked here regularly from his home in Holborn. Gerard's famous *Herbal* was published in 1597 and is still available today.

Early in the next century, botanist Thomas Johnson explored the heath, recording all the plants he found and producing the first known local Flora in Britain. Floras of Hampstead have been compiled from that day to this and reading them illustrates some of the depradations the heath has suffered: progressive loss of habitats to building, digging, in-filling, sand-pits, brick works, and the sheer pressure of tens of thousands of visitors a year. Though the heath has grown to encompass a much larger area it has lost its original character as an acid heathland, rich in heathers. The last remnants of this once extensive plant were thought to have been destroyed by the tipping of blitz rubble after World War Two until a single surviving plant was discovered in the 1980s. The Hampstead Heath Conservation Team, which protects the plant in a 'secret' location, is now trying to recreate an additional area of heather heathland.

Of all the threats to the heath over the past few hundred years none has been as persistent or as damaging as the wilful obstinacy of a single person, Sir Thomas Maryon Wilson, who became Lord of the Manor of Hampstead in 1821. His estates also included the Manor of Charlton and in this connection we have already met the family in chapter 4. In 1826 Parliament approved a new turnpike, the Finchley Road, which crossed the heath and thereby increased its value for development, and in 1829 Maryon Wilson introduced a Bill to Parliament which would give him the power to lease off plots to builders. With this, a forty year battle had begun.

Maryon Wilson's Bill was greeted by a storm of public opposition and was withdrawn before its second reading. But Wilson was a stubborn and uncompromising man, made furious by any attempt to restrict what he saw as his absolute right of ownership. Over the following years he was to introduce no less than fifteen different parliamentary bills in pursuit of his aim to profit from the heath. His last Bill was narrowly defeated in 1866, but nevertheless he began to build, provocatively choosing the summit of the heath as the site of his estate office. He was challenged by Samuel Gurney Hoare, a wealthy local Quaker who had led much of the public struggle against him. Assisted by Octavia Hill and the Commons Preservation Society Hoare began legal proceedings against Wilson, who, embittered and embattled to the last, died before the case could come to court.

The new Lord of the Manor was his brother Sir John Maryon Wilson, who took a very different attitude and sold his rights to the Heath to the Metropolitan Board of Works. The purchase was ratified by Parliament and in 1871 Hampstead Heath became a public open space. Since then a succession of purchases has added Parliament Hill, Kenwood, Golders Hill Park and numerous other smaller parcels of land. Today the whole complex is run by the Corporation of the City of London, which successfully bid for control of the Heath on the abolition of the GLC.

From Well Walk our route follows Sandy Lane and an atmospheric avenue of lime trees planted by the LCC in 1905. At a crossing beside a stone commemorating the replanting of the avenue after the great storm of October 1987, we turn left onto a path which marks a remnant of one of Thomas Maryon Wilson's many attempts at building. In 1844 he planned the grand estate of East Park and began work on a road which would run through the middle of the development. A swampy valley was dammed to form an ornamental pond and the road taken across the top of this on a viaduct. But Wilson forgot to allow for the softness of the underlying soils and the foundations of the viaduct repeatedly collapsed. By the time the viaduct was finished he had run out of funds to continue with the scheme and the isolated bridge became known as Wilson's Folly.

Kenwood, with its house, gardens and woodlands, constitutes its own separate sanctuary within the confines of the Heath. The mature woodlands, unfortunately underplanted with rhododendrons, provide a sense of seclusion hard to come by on other parts of the busy heath. The broad paths wind beneath a canopy of oak, sweet chestnut and holly and are maze-like in their complexity. Here and there are tree stumps used as regular bird feeding stations, where tits, and even nuthatches, have become so tame that they will take food from the hand. And from the woods the formal lawns slope up from ornamental ponds towards a perfectly sited mansion.

Kenwood House was built in 1616 but was extensively remodelled in 1724 under the ownership of William Murray, first Earl of Mansfield. Mansfield was a judge, a liberal man for his day, who had reversed the conviction of John Wilkes for seditious libel (see p.142). He played a mayor role in the reform of English commercial law and developed the modern concept of copyright; he was also a staunch opponent of slavery. Mansfield had the Kenwood grounds landscaped and then called in the famous Robert Adam to remodel the house. Adam created a cool, white and perfectly proportioned mansion – perhaps too cool a building. The adjacent servant's quarters and coach house block, with their more interesting shapes and purple-brown brick, make it seem almost bland.

In 1914 the 6th Earl of Mansfield attempted to sell off the Kenwood estate for building. The Kenwood Preservation Appeal raised money to purchase as much of the land as it could, but by 1925 had run out of funds. The LCC intervened to buy the rest of the grounds and that same year businessman Edward Cecil Guinness, first Earl of Iveagh, bought the house. He had it refurbished to contain his collection of paintings, including works by Rembrandt, Vermeer, Gainsborough, Van Dyck and Turner. When he died, only two years later, the house with all its contents was bequeathed to the public.

Highgate

ROUTE:
- Follow the lane then turn left along Fitzroy Park. At the end turn left into The Grove and right along the main road (Hampstead Lane) to reach Highgate.
- Turn left at the major junction into North Road. Continue past Castle Yard to reach the entrance to Park Walk beside the Old Wrestlers Inn on the right.
- At the end of Park Walk turn left into Southwood Lane. Take the first left into The Park, then immediately right into Bloomfield Road.
- At the end of Bloomfield Road turn right into Bishops Road to reach the main road (Archway Road). Cross the road and turn left to reach Archway Gate into Highgate Wood.

FACILITES: Pubs and cafés on North Road.

From Fitzroy Park on the edge of Cohen's Fields we are in Highgate. Highgate and Hampstead constitute the twin peaks of North London, with Highgate just 16 feet, and a few degrees on the social scale, lower than Hampstead. Fitzroy Park, on the southerly slopes of the Hampstead-Highgate ridge, was built on the site of Sherricks Hole Farm. Today it has a number of millionnaire mansions and if this is not apparent in the architecture of the buildings it can be seen at least in the security devices which surround them. Highfields Grove in particular resembles an open prison, and its red-brick blocks, protected by perimeter fence and automatic gates, contrast unfavourably with the slightly shabby and much more characterful 'Elms' on the other side of the lane.

From Fitzroy Park a short section of The Grove, regarded as Highgate's most elegant street, leads us up to Hampstead Lane and the Gate House pub. The area was once part of the Hornsey estate of the Bishops of London and Highgate probably began its life as a small community around the gate to Bishop's Park. Later there was a toll gate here and it is from this that the pub gets its name. It was first licensed in the 14th century and provided the last stop-over for drovers on their way to Smithfield. It is haunted by Mother Marnes who was murdered, along with her cat, for the money she was supposed to have hidden in the house. Her black-robed figure put in several well-reported appearances in the 1960s but is said never to manifest itself if children or animals are in the building.

From the Gate House, High Street curves off to the right and down through the heart of Highgate. Our route however is off to the left along North Road. On the far side of the road are the buildings of Highgate School, in unmistakeable public school style. The school was founded in 1565 as a foundation for the poor of the parish, as well as a fee-paying school, but its main buildings date from the 19th century. Wrought-iron gates lead onto a drive at the end of which stairs rise on either side of an entrance topped with a wall-mounted sundial. The adjacent chapel is in a warm red brick pierced by a rose window. Above rises a slender spire and a clock tower topped with a pyramidal roof. T.S. Eliot was a master here for a while and Gerard Manley Hopkins was a pupil, as was John Betjeman who recalls being tormented for his foreign-sounding name.

Another poet is commemorated in a plaque on the opposite side of the road. Byron Cottage was occupied not by the poet of that name but by A.E. Housman, most famous for his volume *A Shropshire Lad*. The heavy traffic along North Road has detracted from the the lovely terrace of which this is a part. Here, behind long leafy front gardens, are cottages in soft, worn brick or in wooden Essex weather-boarding, jostling with homes in a grander Palladian style. Further down, at 92 North Road, a plaque records a stay that Dickens made in 1832, though Dickens seems to have stayed at an inordinate number of houses in North London. Just beyond this is the entrance to Park Walk which we follow along the southern boundary of what was, from 1885 to 1940, the House of Mercy. This was a High Church reformatory for prostitutes where, within the confines of a high surrounding wall, the women practised needlework or embroidered trousseaus for the bountiful ladies of Highgate.

The Woods and the Parkland Walk

ROUTE:
- From the gate follow the path, going straight ahead at the first junction and straight across the crosspaths immediately afterwards.
- Keep straight ahead for some time to reach a second crosspaths by a bench and turn right and then left to reach a gate.
- Cross the main road (Muswell Hill Road) and take the gate into Queen's Wood.
- Keep ahead on the path to take the second turning on the right. Continue straight ahead, ignoring path down to the paddling pool on the right, and carry on till reaching the backs of houses.
- Turn right to follow the path which runs alongside the fences to reach Queens Wood Road. Cross Queens Wood Road and follow the path straight ahead. Join the broader tarmac path then go uphill between houses onto Priory Gardens.
- Turn right along Priory Gardens and take the path uphill between houses (next to no.65) on the left.
- Turn right on Shepherd's Hill and left at the major road junction immediately ahead.
- Take the first left (Holmesdale Road) and join the Parkland Walk on your left through a wooden gate.
- Turn right and follow the Parkland Walk for several miles. Where it comes to an end turn left onto the footbridge over the railway.
- EITHER: keep straight ahead into Finsbury Park to join Walk One
OR: turn right down the Parkland Walk Extension to reach Finsbury Park Station.

FACILITIES: Café in Highgate Woods (summer months only). Café in Finsbury Park (March to October). Cafés and pubs near Finsbury Park Station.

LOOKING AT WILDLIFE: Highgate and Queen's Wood have a good selection of woodland bird species including nuthatch, treecreeper, blackcap and greater and lesser spotted woodpeckers. Bats can often be seen towards dusk in Highgate Woods on the edges of the meadow area. Queen's Wood has a good ground flora which includes spring woodland species and common cow-wheat in summer. The Parkland Walk has a rich variety of habitats and consequently supports a rich variety of wildlife of all sorts. The Extension section has some interesting autumn fungi.

The woodlands of Highgate, and the Parkland Walk beyond them, are a fitting finale for *The Green London Way*; more than three miles of good walking through a rich variety of wildlife habitats and with only the shortest of road stretches between them. Highgate Wood and Queen's Wood are both remnants of the Great Forest of Middlesex and the presence of plants such as wild service tree and the native wild bluebell testify to their status as relics of ancient woodland. Highgate Wood, previously known by the much more interesting name of Brew House Wood, was saved for the public when the Ecclesiastical Commissioners presented it to the City Corporation in 1886. The Commissioners hung on, however, to an adjacent portion of woodland which they intended to sell as a series of plots to the builders then developing the North London suburbs. A spirited public campaign managed to raise a quarter of the asking price and the local authorities then contributed the rest. The wood was opened to the public in 1898 and in commemoration of Queen Victoria's Jubilee the name Queen's Wood replaced its earlier name of Church Bottom Wood. It is administered today by the London Borough of Haringey.

Concern about the municipal treatment of our open spaces is not a recent phenomenon. Writing in 1898, W.H. Hudson called Church Bottom Wood, 'the wildest and most picturesque spot in North London' and went on to express his earnest hope that:

> the landscape gardener will not be called in to prepare this place for the reception of the public – the improver on nature whose conventional mind is only concerned with a fine show of fashionable blooms, whose highest standard is the pretty, cloying artificiality of Kew Gardens.

Of the two woods it was the Highgate Wood which fared worse, leading Housman to complain that once it had been tidied up it no longer blocked the view of the washing hanging out on Archway Road. Like Queen's Wood it is traditional oak and hornbeam coppice but it has been parkified with too many intersecting tarmac paths, with benches, a children's playground and a nine acre cricket pitch. Ecologically it also suffers from insufficient natural regeneration and a population of uniformly ageing trees. The cessation of coppicing has led to a denser canopy and this, together with the heavy trampling of the soil, has restricted new growth. Nonetheless it is still a richly atmospheric mature woodland and at least 63 different species of bird have been recorded. It is also a home for foxes, wood mice, field voles, two species of bat, frogs, toads and, surprisingly, a small population of slow-worms.

On the other side of the busy Muswell Hill Road, Queen's Wood has a far more natural atmosphere and ranks as one of the finest areas of woodland in Central London. Its steeper slopes have given it a more open canopy and it is much less visited than Highgate Wood. Here there is a rich understorey and the woods are best seen in spring when the white blooms of wood sorrel overhang the edges of the little brook and the dark and rather sinister leaves of the cuckoo pint begin to unfurl. Great drifts of lesser celandine and wood anemone come into flower under catkin-draped oak trees where the squirrels have built their dreys.

A short linking route leads us to the Highgate end of the Parkland Walk and the last few miles of our walk. This linear stretch of open space was originally a railway, part of the route from Finsbury Park to Edgware opened in 1867. It carried extensive passenger traffic and had its own spur line to serve Alexandra Palace, the 'People's Palace' just to the north. However, demand for the line declined: the last passenger train ran in 1954 and the last freight train ten years later. For a time the line found a use as part of the underground network and was used for the transfer of Northern Line rolling stock from Drayton Park to Highgate but by 1970 had become completely redundant. The tracks were removed and this long strip of land, fast being recolonised by shrub and tree, passed into the ownership of the Haringey Council.

The Council's first thought was to build houses along as many stretches of the route as possible. Public opposition to this eventually led to an enquiry and the protesters won the day. The Council was later to embrace the conservation cause with enthusiasm, establishing the Parkland Walk with a Field Studies Centre in one of the old station houses and a staff of conservation wardens. But this was not the last threat to this lovely urban walkway. Early in 1990 over a thousand people gathered at Haringey Town Hall to support the 'Save the Parkland Walk Campaign' in its struggle against Department of Transport proposals to run a six lane arterial road along the walk, with the additional demolition of at least three hundred flanking houses. These proposals too were defeated and for the time being the Parkland Walk remains a much loved and much used treasure for this part of London.

The Parkland Walk encompasses a wide range of habitats including grassland, woodland, cuttings and embankments, stands of bracken and copses of birch. It supports a third of all the British species of butterfly and over 50 species of bird. Conservationists have counted at least 240 species of flowering plant, with the wild clematis or traveller's joy being of special interest. The clematis is a plant of lighter and preferably limey soils and is therefore not common on the heavy London clay. But here the free-draining railway embankments have provided it with a suitable habitat and it scrambles over shrubs along the route, its white 'beards' looking in winter like a coating of hoar frost against the dark bark of the trees.

In early mornings fox cubs come and tumble together along the broad gravel path and blackcaps sing their dawn song from the oak trees. At dusk tawny owls hunt here and Naterer's bats hawk for insects along the line of the route. Yet this Walk, with its varying atmospheres and diversity of natural habitats, was described by the government appointed consultants as though it were an untidy wasteland. Their view reflected the official assumption that an open space, unlike a motorway or a shopping development, is a space without value. The survival of the Parkland Walk, and of so many other open spaces along *The Green London Way*, is a tribute to all those who, with a different sense of value, have fought to make London a place worth living in.

Index